The Origins of the Cold War

PROBLEMS IN AMERICAN CIVILIZATION

The Origins
of the Cold War

Fourth Edition

Edited and with an introduction by

Robert J. McMahon
University of Florida

Thomas G. Paterson
University of Connecticut

Houghton Mifflin Company Boston New York

*For Thomas Graham Paterson, Jr., Thomas W.
McMahon, and Michael P. McMahon*

Editor in Chief: Jean Woy
Assistant Editor: Leah Strauss
Associate Project Editor: Rebecca Bennett
Associate Production/Design Coordinator: Jodi O'Rourke
Associate Manufacturing Coordinator: Andrea Wagner
Marketing Manager: Sandra McGuire

Cover design: Sarah Melhado
Cover image: U.S. Army Photo. Courtesy of the Harry S Truman
Library.

Printed in the U.S.A.

Library of Congress Catalog Card Number: 98-72061

ISBN: 0-395-90430-7

2 3 4 5 6 7 8 9—QF—02 01 00 99

The Editors

Robert J. McMahon

Born in Bayside, New York, Robert J. McMahon is professor of history at the University of Florida. He was educated at Fairfield University (B.A., 1971) and the University of Connecticut (Ph.D., 1977). Bob has written *Colonialism and Cold War: The United States and the Struggle for Indonesian Independence, 1945–49* (1981); *The Cold War on the Periphery: The United States, India, and Pakistan* (1994); and *The Limits of Empire: The United States and Southeast Asia Since World War II* (1998). He has edited *Major Problems in the History of the Vietnam War* (1995) and co-edited several volumes in the U.S. State Department's documentary series, *Foreign Relations of the United States*. His essays have appeared in numerous books and in the *Journal of American History, Political Science Quarterly, Pacific Historical Review, International History Review,* and *Diplomatic History.*

Thomas G. Paterson

Born in Oregon City, Oregon, and graduated from the University of New Hampshire (B.A., 1963) and the University of California, Berkeley (Ph.D., 1968), Thomas G. Paterson is professor emeritus of history at the University of Connecticut. He has written *Soviet-American Confrontation* (1973), *Meeting the Communist Threat* (1988), *On Every Front* (1992), *Contesting Castro* (1994), *American Foreign Relations* (with J. Garry Clifford and Kenneth J. Hagan, 1994), *American Ascendant* (with Clifford, 1995), and *A People and a Nation* (with Mary Beth Norton et al., 1998). Tom has also edited *Kennedy's Quest for Victory* (1989), *Explaining the History of American Foreign Relations* (with Michael J. Hogan, 1991), *Imperial Surge* (with Stephen G. Rabe, 1992), and *Major Problems in American Foreign Relations* (with Dennis Merrill, 1994). With Bruce Jentleson he was senior editor for the four-volume *Encyclopedia of U.S. Foreign Relations* (1997). He has served on the editorial boards of the *Journal of American History* and *Diplomatic History.* He has been president of the Society for Historians of American Foreign Relations and has directed National Endowment for the Humanities Summer Seminars for College Teachers. His most recent award was a fellowship from the Guggenheim Foundation. He has lectured in Canada, China, Columbia, Cuba, New Zealand, Puerto Rico, Russia, and Venezuela.

Contents

I. Explanations

II. The Origins of the Cold War in Europe

III. The Cold War in Asia

Preface

Since the publication of the third edition of this book, rich and important scholarly work concerning the origins of the Cold War has been published. That new work, together with the fresh perspectives afforded by the dramatic changes in world politics since the early 1990s, has prompted this new edition. We seek to make the most recent scholarship accessible to students and instructors.

A majority of the essays in this book are new. The introduction explains the evolution of interpretations from the 1940s to the present. Part I offers broad explanations for the onset of the Cold War. Part II explores specific policies, events, and issues, focusing primarily on Europe. Finally, Part III studies the extension of the Soviet-American confrontation to Asia. The introductory notes place each selection in broad context and identify key themes. The maps and chronology include important names and dates mentioned in the essays. The extensive, updated bibliography—organized by topic—identifies additional readings in this fascinating field.

We thank the authors and publishers of the works reprinted in this volume for their cooperation. *The Origins of the Cold War* was improved by the constructive suggestions of Nick Cullather, Indiana University; Walter Hixson, University of Akron; David Painter, Georgetown University; and Michael Schaller, University of Arizona.

We are also grateful to everyone at Houghton Mifflin who has contributed to this book. In particular, we thank Jean Woy, Leah Strauss, Ruth Carwile, Peggy Roll, and Rebecca Bennett for the enthusiasm and high standards that they brought to this project.

R. J. M.

T. G. P.

Introduction

The Second World War alliance of the United States, the Soviet Union, and Great Britain crumbled quickly in 1945 after the defeat of Germany and Japan. Soon a different kind of war—the Cold War—troubled international relations. The United States and the Soviet Union, the primary adversaries in this new contest for world power, entered a bitter, decades-long competition for spheres of influence, economic and strategic advantage, nuclear-weapons supremacy, control of international organizations, and ideological superiority.

The two competitors never sent their troops into battle directly against one another but instead engaged in an intense, expensive armaments race, armed and aided their allies and client states, intervened in civil wars by supporting different factions, built rival alliance systems, sponsored exclusionist foreign economic programs, and initiated noisy propaganda campaigns—all of which divided much of the world into rival blocs or empires (popularized too simply as "the West" and "the East"). If the Soviets came to fear "capitalist encirclement," Americans complained against an "international communist conspiracy." Each side, in mirror image, saw the other as aggressive and intransigent. The Cold War contest became the dominant feature of international relations. From the start, however, many newly independent nations in the southern half of the globe—eventually called the Third World—preferred not to choose sides. They became the objects of keen superpower attention as they created another pole of power in the already volatile international system.

In the late 1980s and early 1990s, as stunning political changes were sweeping the Soviet Union and Eastern Europe in the aftermath of Soviet Premier Mikhail S. Gorbachev's new policies of *glasnost* and *perestroika*, many people began exulting that the United States had won the Cold War. With the collapse of the Soviet Union itself in 1991, and the widespread discrediting of communist ideology that accompanied its demise, some commentators in the United States assumed an air of triumph. They attributed their nation's seeming victory in its near half-century struggle with the Soviet Union to the inherent superiority of American values and institutions. Other observers remained more skeptical. They pointed to the huge military arsenals that remained in the United States and Russia, each of which maintained enough nuclear weapons to destroy people and property in awesome numbers. Other analysts pointed to America's daunting domestic problems to argue that the Cold War had no winners. These questions of Cold War demise and Cold War victory cannot be answered without knowing what the Cold War was and how and why it began. This book, then, presents a picture of the past essential to our grappling with the present and future.

For those contemporaries who knew their history, the escalating Soviet-American friction after the Second World War was not unexpected. Indeed, prolonged antagonism had marked the Soviet-American relationship since the Russian or Bolshevik Revolution of 1917. Virulent anticommunism had long coursed through domestic American politics, much as a deep suspicion of capitalist nations like the United States had typified Soviet leadership. The Bolshevik government that took power in 1917 espoused a Marxist anticapitalist ideology, championed world revolution, repudiated czarist debts (much owed to Americans), and confiscated American-owned property. President Woodrow Wilson's goal of a liberal, capitalist international order seemed threatened by what he called the "poison of Bolshevism." In 1918 many Americans found another reason to dislike Moscow's new regime when Soviet leaders withdrew their weary nation from the First World War by accepting a harsh peace from Germany. Wilson worked to topple or at least to contain the Soviets by refusing to recognize the new government, aiding anti-Bolshevik forces, restricting trade, sending thousands of American troops into Soviet Russia, and excluding the upstart nation from the postwar peace conference in Paris. At home, the Wilson administration further demonstrated its vigorous anticommunism by suppressing radicals in the Red Scare of 1919–1920. From the birth of the Soviet experiment, then, Soviet-American relations suffered deep fissures.

In the 1920s, Soviet-American antagonism continued, albeit less intensely, as the Republican administrations extended Wilson's nonrecognition policy. Still, in 1921–1924 the American Relief Administration shipped food and medicine to famine-stricken Russia. American businesses like General Electric and Ford Motor began to enter the Soviet marketplace. By 1928 one-quarter of all foreign investment in the Union of Soviet Socialist Republics (USSR) was American, and American agricultural and industrial equipment became familiar fixtures there.

When President Franklin D. Roosevelt took office in 1933, he reasoned that the nonrecognition policy had failed and that improved relations would stimulate trade (helping to pull America out of the Great Depression) and deter Japanese expansion in Asia. He subsequently struck several agreements with the Soviets, including United States recognition. The first American embassy in the Soviet Union opened in 1934. But relations remained strained. Official and public opinion in the United States registered sharp disapproval of Joseph Stalin's bloody purges, collectivization of agriculture, and brutal efforts to modernize the Soviet economy. Americans, moreover, feared that the Soviets were fomenting revolution through the Comintern.

Especially upsetting to the United States was the 1939 Nazi-Soviet pact, which stamped the Soviet Union as one of the aggressors (indeed, it soon seized part of Poland and attacked Finland) responsible for the outbreak of the Second World War. Americans rejected the Soviet argument that Great Britain and the United States, by practicing appeasement toward Adolf Hitler's Germany, had left the Soviet Union little choice but to make peace with Berlin in order to buy time to prepare for an expected German attack. Following that German attack of June 1941, Roosevelt ordered Lend-Lease aid to the beleaguered Soviets (by war's end the assistance would total $11 billion), calculating that they could hold down scores of German divisions in the east and hence ease German pressure against Britain in the west.

After the United States itself entered the Second World War in December 1941, it formed a Grand Alliance with the Soviet Union and Great Britain. Always tension-ridden, this coalition of convenience for national survival was held together by the common objective of defeating the Axis. The Allies differed frequently over the timing for the opening of a second or western front. Numerous American promises, followed by delays, angered Moscow. Roosevelt, Stalin, and Winston S. Churchill—the Big Three—met at several wartime conferences to devise military strategy and to map plans for the postwar era. At Teheran (1943) they agreed to open the second front in early 1944 (it finally came in June in

France); at Bretton Woods (1944) they founded the World Bank; and at Dumbarton Oaks (1944) they planned the United Nations Organization, granting only the United States, the Soviet Union, and three other nations veto power in the Security Council.

In February 1945, as the Red Army was fighting through Eastern Europe into Germany, the three leaders met again at the Yalta Conference. In a series of trade-offs, which included a coalition government in Soviet-dominated Poland, the division of Germany into zones, and Soviet agreement to negotiate a treaty with United States ally Jiang Jieshi (Chiang Kai-shek) in China, the Big Three seemed to have reached accord on major postwar issues. Hopes for continued Soviet-American cooperation were soon dashed, however, as the Allies jockeyed for international influence at the war's close. The Potsdam Conference of July 1945, after the defeat of Germany and just before the collapse of Japan, saw as much disagreement as agreement. Nor did the Soviets' fulfillment in August of their Yalta pledge to enter the war against Japan improve relations, because it came after the American atomic bombing of Hiroshima, a point when United States leaders no longer desired Soviet participation.

Disputes broke out with alarming frequency on a wide range of issues in the early postwar years. The American destruction of two Japanese cities by atomic bombs posed a significant diplomatic question: Would international control follow, or would the United States retain its atomic monopoly in order to gain negotiating advantage on postwar issues? How and by whom the economies of war-ravaged nations would be reconstructed also divided the victors. Eastern Europe became a diplomatic battleground as Soviet influence solidified in the region. So did Iran, where American influence had grown to challenge Soviet influence in a nation bordering the Soviet Union. Unstable politics and economic distress rocked Western Europe, where left and right faced off. The French, British, Americans, and Soviets squabbled over how to extract reparations from a hobbled Germany and over whether Germany's economy should be revived. The division of Germany became permanent as the occupying powers created separate economic and political institutions in their zones. In the new United Nations and World Bank, Americans quickly established domination, prompting the Soviets to use their veto in the first and to turn down membership in the second. In Asia, resurgent nationalist feelings, colonial conflicts that pitted European imperialists against native independence movements, a full-scale civil war in China, the American-directed occupation and ultimate restoration of Japan, and widespread economic dislocation produced further instability in world politics. Turmoil also shook the Middle East, sparked by the Arab-Israeli dispute and lingering resentments against European imperialism and fueled by American-Soviet competition for access to rich oil reserves and for strategic sites. The Truman Doctrine (1947), Rio Pact (1947), Marshall Plan (1948), and North Atlantic Treaty Organization (1949) stood as hallmarks of the American containment doctrine designed to thwart, if not roll back, Soviet power and influence. For their part, the Soviets knitted together into an empire several Eastern European states, first in the Molotov Plan (economic) and then through the Warsaw Pact (military). As well, a war of hyperbolic words echoed through diplomatic chambers. Each side characterized the other as the world's bully; each side blamed the other for the deterioration of the Grand Alliance and the beginning of the Cold War.

This book is devoted to explaining the origins of the Cold War. Do not expect a comforting unanimity of opinion or a satisfying synthesis. Even within the two major schools of thought—the traditional and the revisionist—disagreement abounds, although historians have narrowed some of their interpretive differences over time. Much of the debate still centers on one question: Whose fault was the Cold War? Scholars are moving beyond that simple query to examine shared responsibility for the Cold War, the contributing role of nations other than the United States and the Soviet Union, and the nature of the conflict-ridden international system. But the question of blame remains at the forefront of the debate.

Until the 1960s the traditional or orthodox interpretation of the origins of the Cold War prevailed. This point of view held that the Soviets, with unlimited ambitions for expansion, an uncompromising ideology, and a paranoid dictator bent on world domination and the elimination of democracy and capitalism, wrecked the postwar peace. Moscow caused the Cold War, pure and simple. This view goes on to explain that the United States, lacking self-interest and committed to democracy and high ideals, rejected a spheres-of-influence approach in favor of an open world, passed up opportunities to grab power after the war, and sought continued friendly relations with the Soviet Union. As the Cold War emerged, traditionalists have argued, negotiations with the Soviets and their communist allies elsewhere, as in China, proved useless. Forced by communist hostility and aggression to take defensive measures, the Harry S Truman administration declared the ultimately successful containment doctrine and blunted communist aggression. The Soviets acted; the Americans reacted. Moscow exploited; Washington saved. Not only did policymakers like President Truman explain events this way; until the 1960s most historians did as well.

In the early 1960s three important changes coincided to invite a very different interpretation—the revisionist—of the origins of the Cold War. First, in the late 1950s the decline of McCarthyism, a virulent version of the Cold War anticommunism, calmed the repressive atmosphere whipped up by the Wisconsin senator and by the Truman and Dwight D. Eisenhower administrations. That atmosphere had stymied discussion of alternative interpretations, for the Cold War consensus treated dissent as something close to disloyalty. Indeed, unorthodox opinion sometimes earned a scholar a trip to the intimidating hearings of the House Un-American Activities Committee. With the decline of McCarthyism came more questioning of traditional assumptions, as when William Appleman Williams published his provocative book *The Tragedy of American Diplomacy* (1959), which depicted the United States not as an innocent simply reacting to overseas events but rather as a self-conscious, expansionist nation with imperial drives.

The second source for revisionism was the Vietnam War. By the mid-1960s that tragic conflict had stimulated debate not only on the origins and conduct of the war but on the Cold War assumptions that compelled American intervention in Vietnam and around the globe. What was the precise nature of the threat posed by communism? Who exactly was the enemy? Was the containment doctrine too vaguely defined and indiscriminately applied? How did Americans get started in their Cold War globalism? Were the foreign-policy assumptions judged by many to be wrong-headed in the 1960s also wrong-headed in the 1940s? To question the Vietnam War was to question American ideas and behavior in the early Cold War.

The third factor that inspired doubts about the Cold War consensus was the declassification and opening to scholars in the 1960s and later of documents from the early Cold War period—National Security Council reports, presidential memoranda, briefing papers, telegrams from embassies, diaries, and more. Historians could now test their questions against the rich documentary record; they would no longer have to rely upon the often inaccurate and self-serving memoirs of policymakers. The once-secret papers, examined at a time of questioning permitted by the decline of McCarthyism and stimulated by the Vietnam War, revealed a picture of the 1940s that did not resemble that sketched by the traditionalists.

Although revisionists, like traditionalists, have not always agreed among themselves, the basic outline of their interpretation became clear by the late 1960s and early 1970s. Revisionists have held that the traditional interpretation is too one-sided, blaming all trouble on the Soviets and ignoring the United States' own responsibility for conflict. The United States was not simply reacting to Soviet machinations; rather, it was acting on its own needs and ideas in a way that made American behavior alarm not just the Soviets but some of America's allies as well. The United States, argue the revisionists, was not an innocent defender of democracy but a self-consciously expansionist power in search of prosperity and security. Americans were determined to mold a postwar world that corresponded to their own needs. They projected their predominant power again and again, and they too often abandoned diplomacy in favor of confrontation. Nor should analysts apply a double standard, say the revisionists, because the United States was itself building spheres of influence. And if "free elections" were good for Eastern Europe, as Americans insisted, why were they not also good for Latin America, where the United States nurtured dictators like Anastasio Somoza of Nicaragua and Rafael Trujillo of the Dominican Republic?

Revisionists have written too that Americans exaggerated the Soviet/communist threat, imagining an adversary possessing more power and ambition than the postwar Soviet Union had. The Soviets actually suffered serious weaknesses in their economy and military, and they were often driven not by an unbridled thirst for empire or ideological fervor but by concern for security after suffering at least

20 million dead in the Second World War. The postwar American refusal to acknowledge Soviet security fears helped bring down the
"iron curtain" in Eastern Europe. Finally, a rigid way of thinking—
globalist containment—blinded Americans so much that they over-
looked the indigenous sources of conflict (religious, political, and
ethnic, for example) and failed to grasp the complexities of world
politics.

The revisionist-orthodox debate was exciting and important
because it focused on the fundamental question of what kind of people Americans were. Were they exceptional, selfless, anti-imperialist,
acting on high principle in the face of ugly challenges to democracy?
Or were they something else, perhaps not that much different from
other great nations through history—seeking hegemony at the expense of others? Or were they a mix, because nothing can be so simply defined?

In the 1970s, 1980s, and 1990s historians, traditionalists and
revisionists alike, groped for elusive synthesis. Some scholars began
to speak of post-revisionism, a term broad in meaning and difficult
to define because it seemed to lack a core point of view recognizably
different from either of its predecessors. To critics, post-revisionism
was essentially traditionalism: first, because it placed primary responsibility for the Cold War upon the Soviets, and, second, because it
interpreted United States empire-building as defensive, a result of
invitation by recipients of American foreign aid seeking security and
recovery rather than of American design. To proponents of post-
revisionism, however, the term meant a blending of the two schools
of thought—an acceptance of the traditionalist proposition that
Soviet expansion had precipitated the Cold War and of the revisionist proposition that the United States too had become an empire
builder.

Besides the problem of responsibility, other core questions run
through the literature on the origins of the Cold War. First, what
driving forces propelled American and Soviet foreign policy: ideology? economic needs? security? power? Second, why did Americans
come to see the Soviet Union as such an unparalleled menace to
United States interests and survival: because of Soviet military power?
Moscow's manhandling of neighbors? communism's ideological appeal? the economic crisis in Europe and around the world? American
misperception and exaggeration? Third, did the Cold War emerge

because the two great powers simply misunderstood each other, or rather because they actually understood one another quite well—that is, they squabbled because their interests and their power stood starkly at odds? Finally, why and how did the Cold War, largely originating in Europe, spread to the Third World and become a global phenomenon?

History is seldom tidy or ordered with hard, fast formulae. The diversity of opinion on the origins of the Cold War reflects the vast complexity of the 1940s events themselves. That there is no soothing, simple answer or that there is no synthesis or consensus seems inevitable. One person's truth will always be someone else's half-truth or misinterpretation. Oversimplification for the sake of synthesis, moreover, is dangerous, especially when historians do not yet have access to all of the documents—even though long-closed archives in Russia, Eastern Europe, China, and elsewhere are finally beginning to open. Major interpretive quarrels among scholars will likely remain the norm. This condition should not be cause for alarm. Rather, it is an opportunity to be grasped: to enlarge our knowledge, to refine our definitions, to respect diversity, to understand complexity, and, yes, even to narrow our differences of opinion. In this spirit of discovery, we have selected essays for this book that reflect the most recent scholarship.

Acronyms and Abbreviations

Acronyms and abbreviations in Cold War history include:

ANZUS	Australia–New Zealand–United States alliance
Benelux	Belgium–The Netherlands–Luxembourg
CCP	Chinese Communist Party
Cominform	Communist Information Bureau
Comintern	Third Communist International
ECA	Economic Cooperation Administration
ECE	Economic Commission for Europe
ERP	European Recovery Program
FDR	Franklin D. Roosevelt
GNP	Gross National Product
GARIOA	Government and Relief in Occupied Areas
JCS	Joint Chiefs of Staff
LT	Long telegram
NATO	North Atlantic Treaty Organization
NEP	New Economic Policy
NSC	National Security Council
OAS	Organization of American States
OSS	Office of Strategic Services
OEEC	Organization for European Economic Cooperation
PLA	Chinese People's Liberation Army
PPS	Policy Planning Staff of the U.S. Department of State
PRC	Peoples' Republic of China
SAC	Strategic Air Command
SEA	Southeast Asia
SWNCC	State-War-Navy Coordinating Committee
UK	United Kingdom
UN	United Nations Organization
UNRRA	United Nations Relief and Rehabilitation Administration
USSR	Union of Soviet Socialist Republics
V-E	Victory Day in Europe
V-J	Victory Day in Japan

Chronology

1944 *June*: Cross-channel invasion opening second front. *July*: Bretton Woods Conference. *August–October*: Dumbarton Oaks Conference. *October*: Churchill-Stalin sphere-of-influence agreement at Moscow; Litvinov-Snow conversation. *November*: Roosevelt elected to fourth term with Truman as vice-president. *December*: Battle of the Bulge.

1945 *January*: USSR requested loan. *February 4–11*: Yalta Conference. *February*: Cease fire in Greek civil war. *April*: Litvinov-Sulzberger interview; Roosevelt's death; Truman-Molotov argument. *May*: German surrender; cessation of Lend-Lease to Russia; Hopkins mission to Moscow. *June*: UN Charter signed at San Francisco. *July*: Byrnes became secretary of state; U.S. recognition of Communist government in Poland. *July 17– August 2*: Potsdam Conference. *August 6*: Atomic bomb on Hiroshima. *August 8*: USSR declaration of war against Japan. *August 9*: Atomic bomb on Nagasaki. *August*: USSR requested loan; independent Republic of Indonesia proclaimed. *September 11–October 2*: London Foreign Ministers meeting. *September*: independent Democratic Republic of Vietnam proclaimed. *October 27*: Truman's Navy Day speech. *November*: Communists defeated in Hungarian national elections. *December 16–26*: Moscow Foreign Ministers meeting.

1946 *January*: UN Atomic Energy Commission formed; Iran charged Soviet Union with interference in its internal affairs; Soviets charged Britain with interference in Greek affairs. *February*: Stalin election speech. *March*: U.S. found "lost" Russian loan request; Churchill's Fulton speech. *April*: Soviet troops left Iran. *April– October*: Paris Peace Conference meetings. *May*: Greek civil war began again; Clay halted German reparations to USSR. *June*: Baruch Plan; Litvinov-Hottelet interview; Bikini atomic tests began. *July*: Philippines became independent. *August*: USSR sought base from Turkey; U.S.

charged Poland with failure to create democracy. *September*: Wallace speech and firing from Cabinet; Clifford report on U.S.-USSR relations. *November*: Republicans captured Congressional elections; U.S.-China treaty. *November 4–December 12*: New York Foreign Ministers meeting. *December*: Anglo-American fusion of German zones.

1947 *January*: Marshall became secretary of state. *February*: British notes on Greece and Turkey. *March*: Communists began subversion of Hungarian government; Truman Doctrine. *March 10–April 24*: Moscow Foreign Ministers meeting. *May*: Aid to Greece-Turkey bill signed by Truman. *June*: Marshall Plan speech at Harvard. *July*: USSR rejected Marshall Plan at Paris; publication of Kennan's "X" article on containment. *August*: India and Pakistan became independent; Rio Pact in Latin America; Polish-Russian trade agreement. *October*: USSR created Cominform. *November 25–December*: London Foreign Ministers meeting. *December*: Brussels Conference on European defense; Interim Aid to Europe bill signed; Greek regime outlawed EAM and Communist Party.

1948 *February*: Brussels Treaty signed; coup in Czechoslovakia. *March*: Senate passed Marshall Plan; USSR walked out of Allied Control Council in Germany charging destruction by other three powers; House passed Marshall Plan. *April*: Truman signed European Recovery Act of $5.3 billion; Committee of European Economic Cooperation formed; OAS established; U.S. recognized new nation of Israel. *June*: Currency reform announced in western zones of Germany; Berlin blockade by USSR; Yugoslavia expelled from Cominform. *November*: Truman elected president.

1949 *January*: Truman suggested idea of Point Four program; USSR set up Council of Economic Assistance (Comecon); Acheson became secretary of state. *April*: NATO organized. *May*: West German federal constitution approved; Berlin blockade lifted. *July*: Truman signed NATO Treaty. *August*: U.S. White Paper on China; Soviets test first atomic bomb. *September*: Federal Republic of Germany established (West). *October*: People's Republic of China proclaimed; Greek civil war ended. *December*: Indonesia became independent; Jiang's government completed evacuation from mainland to Formosa; NSC 48/1 called for containment of Communism in Asia.

1950 *January*: Acheson's "defensive perimeter" speech; Truman authorized hydrogen bomb development. *January–August*: USSR boycotted UN Security Council. *February*: U.S. recognized Bao Dai regime in Vietnam; McCarthy opened attacks on alleged subversives in government; Sino-Soviet Friendship Treaty. *April*: NSC 68. *June*: Outbreak of Korean War.

I

Explanations

Joyce and Gabriel Kolko

AMERICAN CAPITALIST EXPANSION

In his *The Politics of War* (1968) and *The Limits of Power* (1972) (the latter work coauthored with Joyce Kolko), Gabriel Kolko argues that America's postwar goal of preserving world capitalism—and expanding the American hold on it—produced conflict not only with the Soviet Union but also with the political left. In an early, radical version of the revisionist perspective, Kolko claims that postwar tension grew not from external pressures on the United States but from the internal needs of American capitalism, which required overseas business expansion. Flushed with power but fearing economic depression, American leaders used foreign aid as a major tool to seek trade, the reformation of the world economy, and American prosperity. According to Kolko, American officials mistakenly saw the Left and the Soviets as intricately linked, and hence they blamed the Cold War on Moscow rather than on Washington's own drive to save capitalism.

A radical scholar recognized for his sustained criticism of United States interventionism, Gabriel Kolko has also written *The Roots of American Foreign Policy* (1969); *Anatomy of a War* (1986), a study of the Vietnam War; *Confronting the Third World* (1988), *and Century of War* (1994). He teaches at York University in Canada. Joyce Kolko is the author of *America and the Crisis of World Capitalism* (1974).

World War II was a prelude to the profound and irreversible crisis in world affairs and the structure of societies which is the hallmark of our times.

The war had come to an end, but no respite allowed the wounds of the long era of violence to heal completely. Two vast epics of bloodletting within thirty years' time had inflicted seemingly irreparable damage to traditional societies everywhere. From the moment World War II ended, civil war, uprisings, and the specter of them replaced the conflict between the Axis and Allies in many nations, and implacable hostility superseded tense relations between the Soviet Union and the other members of what had scarcely been more than a temporary alliance of convenience born wholly out of necessity. After global conflagration came not peace, but sustained violence in numerous areas of the world—violence that was to intensify with the inevitable, broadening process of social transformation and decolonization that became the dominant experience of the postwar epoch.

For the individual in vast regions of the world, the war's outcome left hunger, pain, and chaos. Politically, conflict and rivalry wracked nations, and civil war spread in Greece and in Asia. Outside of the Western Hemisphere, ruin and the urge toward reconstruction were the defining imperatives in all the areas that war had touched. Affecting the very fabric of world civilization, the postwar strife threatened to undermine the United States' reasons for having fought two great wars and its specific aims in the postwar world.

Surrounded by this vast upheaval, the United States found itself immeasurably enriched and, without rival, the strongest nation on the globe. It emerged from the war self-conscious of its new strength and confident of its ability to direct world reconstruction along lines compatible with its goals. And these objectives, carefully formulated during the war, were deceptively simple: Essentially, the United States' aim was to restructure the world so that American business could trade, operate, and profit without restrictions everywhere. On this there was absolute unanimity among the American leaders, and it was around this core that they elaborated their policies and programs. They could not consider or foresee all the dimensions of what was essential to the attainment of their objective, but certain assumptions were implicit, and these in turn defined the boundaries of future policy options. American business could operate only in a world composed of politically reliable and stable capitalist nations, and with free access to essential raw materials. Such a universal order precluded the Left from power and necessitated conservative, and ultimately subservient, political control throughout the globe. This essential aim also required limitations on independence and development in the Third World that might conflict with the interests of American capitalism.

The United States therefore ended the war with a comprehensive and remarkably precise vision of an ideal world economic order, but with only a hazy definition of the political prerequisites for such a system. With these objectives before it, Washington confronted the major challenges to their fulfillment. Preeminent among these were the prewar system of world capitalism and its accumulation of trade and investment restrictions and autarchic economic nationalism that World War I and the subsequent depression had created. Traditional nationalism, consequently, was an obstacle to America's attainment of its goals, and this shaped the United States' relations to Britain and its huge economic alliance, the sterling bloc. Washington's dealings with Britain throughout the war had been profoundly troubled because of London's reticence in collaborating with American plans for restructuring world trade. To the English such a program looked very much like expansion in the name of an internationalism that ill concealed the more tangible advancement of American power along quite conventional lines. This rivalry among nominal allies was to become a basic theme of the postwar experience as well, because in attempting to attain the leading role for itself in the international economy the English had to consider whether the United States might also recast Britain's once-dominant role in major areas of the earth.

It was this same effort to foster a reformed world economy that compelled the United States to turn its attention, with unprecedented energy and expense, to the future of the European continent and Germany's special position in it. The failure of Germany and Japan to collaborate economically with the world throughout the interwar period was, in Washington's opinion, the source of most of the misfortunes that had befallen mankind. And however weak Europe might be at the moment, the United States had to consider how its reemergence—with or without Germany— might potentially affect the United States' contemplated role on the Continent should Europe once again assume an independent role. Allied with Russia, or even a resurgent Germany, Western Europe could become the critical, perhaps decisive, factor in international economic and political power. And it was an unshakable premise of America's policy that world capitalism [would] become a unified system that would cease being divided into autonomous rivals.

Its desire and need for global economic reform, integration, and expansion almost immediately required the United States to confront the infinitely more complex issue of the political preconditions for establishing an ideal world order. This meant relating not only to the forces of nationalism and conservatism that had so aggressively undermined America's goals until 1945 but more especially to the ascendant movements of change we may loosely associate with the Left—forces that posed a fundamental threat to America's future in the world. The war had brought to fruition all the crises in the civil war within societies that World War I had unleashed, a conflict that interwar fascism and reaction had forcibly, but only temporarily, suppressed. The intensity of these national, social and class conflicts was to increase with time, spreading to Asia and the Third World even as the United States was now compelled to consider how best to cope with the immediate threat of the radicalized European workers. The manner in which America balanced its desire for the reformation of European capitalism against its need to preserve it immediately as a system in any form, in order to later attempt to integrate it, is a key chapter in postwar history involving all of Europe and Japan. For the sake of its own future in the world, Washington had to resolve whether it wished to aid in the restoration of the traditional ruling classes of Germany and Japan—the very elements who had conducted wars against America in the past. . . .

In much of Asia and Europe a resurgent and formidable Left was a major effect of World War II, just as the Soviet Union was the main outcome of World War I. Each war had generated vast upheavals and a period of flux, and the United States' own goals and interests had colored its responses to them. Washington neither feared nor suspected that the world was irrevocably in transition, decentralized, unpredictable, and beyond the control of any nation—and especially its own mastery. But, in the short run, American leaders had to consider whether the Left had the will and capacity to act and take power—and how to respond in the event it did. At the same time they had to confront the question of the future of the USSR, a prospect that the deepening wartime diplomatic crisis between Russia and the West had left enshrouded in dark pessimism. The Left and Russia usually appeared as synonymous in America's litany, as Washington often assigned the Kremlin powers in the world that must have surprised the quite circumspect rulers of that war-devastated country. For the USSR's very existence was a reminder of the profound weakening of European capitalism and the traditional order after World War I, and potentially a catalyst for undermining capitalism in the future. But was Russia, given America's self-assigned destiny, *the* critical problem for the United States to confront in the postwar era? To place this question in perspective, one has only to ask, given its articulation of its larger goals, what the United States' policy would have been regarding innumerable problems and areas had the Bolshevik Revolution never occurred. As it was, during the war the Russians repeatedly showed their conservatism in their inhibiting advice to the various Communist parties and their refusal to move freely into the power vacuum capitalism's weakness had created everywhere. And what were the possibilities of negotiations and conventional diplomacy in resolving the outstanding issues with the Soviet Union, such as Eastern Europe, the future of Germany, and Russia's future role in the world, especially given America's definitions of the causes of the world's problems as well as its own interests? In light of American needs and perspectives, and the nature of the postwar upheaval and the forces of our age, were expansion and conflict inevitable? Washington never dissociated the USSR from the Left, not only because bolshevism is but one twentieth-century expression of a much larger revolutionary trend but also because it was often politically convenient for America's leaders to fix the blame for capitalism's failures on the cautious men in the Kremlin. . . .

The United States' ultimate objective at the end of World War II was both to sustain and to reform world capitalism. The tension between doing both eventually prevented America from accomplishing either in a shape fully satisfactory to itself. The task confronting Washington was to dissolve the impact not merely of World War II on the structure of the world economy but of the depression of 1929 and World War I as well—to reverse, in brief, most of the consequences of twentieth-century history. "The main prize of the victory of the United Nations," the State Department summed up the United States' vision in November 1945, "is a limited and temporary power to establish the kind of world we want to live in." That was the prodigious task before it. . . .

The deeply etched memory of the decade-long depression of 1929 hung over all American plans for the postwar era. The war had ended that crisis in American society, but the question remained whether peace would restore it. The historical analyst is perpetually challenged and confounded by the danger that the effects of a policy may only rarely reveal its true motives, and specific interests and causal elements may distort its visible roots. But at the end of World War II the leadership of the United States determined on a policy intended to prevent the return of an economic and social crisis in American society—a policy that explicitly demanded that they resolve America's dilemma in the world arena.

The official and unofficial wartime debate on the postwar economic challenge was immense in scope and alone sufficient for a book. Yet the facts—and goals—were clear in the minds of nearly all commentators: the depression had damaged profoundly the United States' position in the world economy, lowering by almost half its share of a far smaller world trade, and the problem in the postwar era was to restore and then extend this share, to maintain the high wartime profits that had followed the parched 1930s, and to utilize a labor force temporarily absorbed in the military services and war plants. By June 1945 the capital assets in American manufacturing had increased 65 percent, largely from federal sources, over the 1939 level. Stated simply, for Washington's planners the question was how to use this vast plant after the end of hostilities. In the farm sector, the return of surplus gluts, largely due to the depression's impact on the world economy, seemed probable if no action were taken to prevent it. Apart from the vague measures and assumptions that Congress wrote into the Full Employment Bill of [1946], steps focused mainly on mitigating the extent and hardships of mass unemployment which the Senate's Committee on Banking anticipated would likely produce 6 or 7 millions out of work by the winter of 1945–1946, tangible proposals occurred mainly in foreign economic policy. "Our international policies and our domestic policies are inseparable," Secretary of State Byrnes informed the Senate on August 21, 1945. In extending its power throughout the globe, the United States hoped to save itself as well from a return of the misery of prewar experience.

From the 1932 low of $1.6 billion in exports, the United States attained $12.8 billion in 1943 and $14.3 billion in 1944, most of the new peak representing a favorable balance of trade. The figure of $14 billion in postwar exports—well over four times the 1939 level—therefore became the target of most wartime planners and their calculated precondition of continued American prosperity. Assistant Secretary of State Dean Acheson, by early 1945, publicly endorsed a $10 billion minimum figure, but Commerce Department experts thought it to be too low. Even if backlogged domestic wartime savings and demand sustained business activity for two or three years after 1946, Commerce experts warned, this alone would not prevent unemployment of as great as 4.5 million men in 1948. The most optimistic estimates calculated that the United States would not import more than $6 billion a year through 1947, and probably much less, and American private business could not, at best, profitably invest more than $3 billion a year for some time—figures that later proved much too high.

At the very least, $5 billion in annual United States loans and grants would for a time be required to attain the $14 billion export target for domestic prosperity, though some estimates ran to $8 billion. For this reason, key Washington officials publicly warned before the end of the war that the United States would have to provide ". . . the necessary financing of our foreign trade during the crucial period of reconversion at home and reconstruction abroad. . . ." From the outset, Washington set the entire question of postwar American foreign economic policy and aid in the context, as Clayton phrased it as late as November 1946, that ". . . let us admit right off that our objective has as its background the needs and interests of the people of the United States." Such a formulation was also based on the premise, as Byrnes had put it one year earlier, that "[p]olitical peace and economic warfare cannot long exist together." The failure to restore world-trade would not only affect American prosperity but in addition lead to a continua tion of the world trade restrictions which it was a prime American goal to eliminate as part of the reformation of world capitalism. For if the nations of Europe could not finance reconstruction via American aid, they would attempt to find the resources by tight exchange and import controls—in effect, continuing the status quo in the world economy inherited from the debacle of 1929. Loans would also become the key vehicle of structural change in the capitalist world. "We cannot play Santa Claus to the world but we can make loans to governments whose credit is good, provided such governments will make changes in commercial policies which will make it possible for us to increase our trade with them," Byrnes added. Trade, the reformation of foreign capitalism, and American prosperity were all seen as part of one interlocked issue.

From this viewpoint, even before America's leaders could evaluate the specific political and economic conditions of Europe—indeed, even when they were relatively sanguine—they determined on a postwar economic policy compatible with American interests. Not only, therefore, did Washington have to confront both bolshevism and the social-economic consequences of the great upheaval in the war-torn world, but it had also to redefine the nature of world capitalism as it had evolved after 1918. No responsible American leader had any illusions regarding the nation's critical role in the postwar world economy or any grave doubts as to its ability to fulfill its self-appointed role. . . .

The question of foreign economic policy was not the containment of communism, but rather more directly the extension and expansion of American capitalism according to its new economic power and needs. Primarily, America was committed to inhibiting and redirecting other forces and pressures of change abroad in the world among non-, even anti-, Soviet states. Russia and Eastern Europe were an aspect of this problem, but the rest of the world was yet more important even in 1946. . . .

Just as we insist on making an expansive American capitalism the central theme of postwar history, so, too, must we place a distinct emphasis on its relative failures—defeats the outcome and consequences of which have led to an escalation of the American attempts to master its ever more elusive self-assigned destiny. But we must also place the significance of its mounting efforts in the context of whether the multiplying undertakings were ever sufficient for the American economy's needs and for the fulfillment of its ambitious global objectives. For despite the fact that the magnitude of America's postwar program satisfied specific agricultural and industrial interests, in the largest sense it was inadequate to attain its maximum objectives. The British loan of 1946 was followed by the Marshall Plan, which in turn required massive arms aid, Point Four, and the like. By the time the intensifying transformation of the Third World, and evolution in Europe itself, could be gauged, it was evident to all in Washington that the role of capital exporter initially assigned to American business in the postwar world was woefully utopian. The state therefore undertook that key role during the first postwar decade, and wholly assumed the obligation of furnishing the political and military protection it knew an integrated world capitalism demanded. This merger of public and private power and goals, so traditional in American history, despite its vastly greater extent also fell short of the goal's monumental requirements. There were tactical successes and benefits, but the United States never attained the ideal world order it confidently anticipated during World War II.

America's leaders never fully realized the limits of American power in the world, and the use of foreign policy to express and solve the specific needs of American capitalism continued during the first postwar decade and thereafter, circumscribing the nature of American society and the process of social change throughout the globe. This interaction between a nation with universal objectives but finite power and the remainder of mankind is critical in modern history and the essence of the American experience.

Arthur M. Schlesinger, Jr.

COMMUNIST IDEOLOGY, STALINIST TOTALITARIANISM, AND AMERICAN UNIVERSALISM

Arthur M. Schlesinger, Jr., in a 1967 essay designed to refute revisionism and to defend the basic tenets of the traditionalist case, discovers the root causes of the Cold War in the Soviets' adherence to an uncompromising Leninist ideology, Moscow's totalitarianism, and Joseph Stalin's madness. The United States could have done little to change the course of events. Schlesinger concedes that Soviet Russia had significant economic recovery problems and security fears and that American policy was sometimes rigid, but he argues that Moscow caused the Cold War. To emphasize his points, he contrasts the American "universalist" view of world order with the Soviet "sphere of influence" approach.

For many years at Harvard University, and now a professor of history at the City University of New York, Schlesinger has also been an active politician in the Democratic party. He has served as an adviser to President John F. Kennedy and has written two books in praise of the Kennedys: *A Thousand Days* (1965) and *Robert Kennedy and His Times* (1978). A prolific historian, Schlesinger has also written biographies of Andrew Jackson and Franklin D. Roosevelt, as well as *The Imperial*

Arthur M. Schlesinger, Jr., "Origins of the Cold War," *Foreign Affairs* 46 (October 1967): 22–25, 26–27, 28–30, 31–32, 34–35, 42–47, 48–50, 52. Reprinted by permission of *Foreign Affairs*, Copyright © 1967 by the Council on Foreign Relations.

Presidency (1973), *The Cycles of American History* (1986), and *The Disuniting of America* (1991).

The Cold War in its original form was a presumably mortal antagonism, arising in the wake of the Second World War, between two rigidly hostile blocs, one led by the Soviet Union, the other by the United States. For nearly two somber and dangerous decades this antagonism dominated the fears of mankind; it may even, on occasion, have come close to blowing up the planet. In recent years, however, the once implacable struggle has lost its familiar clarity of outline. With the passing of old issues and the emergence of new conflicts and contestants, there is a natural tendency, especially on the part of the generation which grew up during the Cold War, to take a fresh look at the causes of the great contention between Russia and America.

Some exercises in reappraisal have merely elaborated the orthodoxies promulgated in Washington or Moscow during the boom years of the Cold War. But others, especially in the United States (there are no signs, alas, of this in the Soviet Union), represent what American historians call "revisionism"—that is, a readiness to challenge official explanations. No one should be surprised by this phenomenon. Every war in American history has been followed in due course by skeptical reassessments of supposedly sacred assumptions. So the War of 1812, fought at the time for the freedom of the seas, was in later years ascribed to the expansionist ambitions of congressional war hawks; so the Mexican War became a slaveholders' conspiracy. So the Civil War has been pronounced a "needless war," and Lincoln has even been accused of maneuvering the rebel attack on Fort Sumter. So too the Spanish-American War and the First and Second World Wars have, each in its turn, undergone revisionist critiques. It is not to be supposed that the Cold War would remain exempt.

In the case of the Cold War, special factors reinforce the predictable historiographical rhythm. The outburst of polycentrism in the Communist empire has made people wonder whether communism was ever so monolithic as official theories of the Cold War supposed. A generation with no vivid memories of Stalinism may see the Russia of the forties in the image of the relatively mild, seedy and irresolute Russia of the sixties. And for this same generation the American course of widening the war in Vietnam—which even nonrevisionists can easily regard as folly—has unquestionably stirred doubts about the wisdom of American foreign policy in the sixties which younger historians may have begun to read back into the forties.

It is useful to remember that, on the whole, past exercises in revisionism have failed to stick. Few historians today believe that the war hawks caused the War of 1812 or the slaveholders the Mexican War, or that the Civil War was needless, or that the House of Morgan brought America into the First World War or that Franklin Roosevelt schemed to produce the attack on Pearl Harbor. But this does not mean that one should deplore the rise of Cold War revisionism. For revisionism is an essential part of the process by which history, through the posing of new problems and the investigation of new possibilities, enlarges its perspectives and enriches its insights.

More than this, in the present context, revisionism expresses a deep, legitimate and tragic apprehension. As the Cold War has begun to lose its purity of definition, as the moral absolutes of the fifties become the moralistic clichés of the sixties, some have begun to ask whether the appalling risks which humanity ran during the Cold War were, after all, necessary and inevitable; whether more restrained and rational policies might not have guided the energies of man from the perils of conflict into the potentialities of collaboration. The fact that such questions are in their nature unanswerable does not mean that it is not right and useful to raise them. Nor does it mean that our sons and daughters are not entitled to an accounting from the generation of Russians and Americans who produced the Cold War.

The orthodox American view, as originally set forth by the American government and as reaffirmed until recently by most American scholars, has been that the Cold War was the brave and essential response of free men to Communist aggression. Some have gone back well before the Second World War to lay open the sources of Russian expansionism. Geopoliticians traced the Cold War to imperial Russian strategic ambitions which in the nineteenth century led to the Crimean War, to Russian penetration of the Balkans and the Middle East and to Russian pressure on Britain's "lifeline" to India. Ideologists traced it to the Communist Manifesto of 1848 ("the violent overthrow of the bourgeoisie lays the foundation for the sway of the proletariat"). Thoughtful observers (a phrase meant to exclude those who speak in Dullese about the unlimited evil of godless, atheistic, militant communism) concluded that classical Russian Imperialism and Pan-Slavism, compounded after 1917 by Leninist messianism, confronted the West at the end of the Second World War with an inexorable drive for domination.

The revisionist thesis is very different. In its extreme form, it is that, after the death of Franklin Roosevelt and the end of the Second World War, the United States deliberately abandoned the wartime policy of collaboration and, exhilarated by the possession of the atomic bomb, undertook a course of aggression of its own designed to expel all Russian influence from Eastern Europe and to establish democratic-capitalist states on the very border of the Soviet Union. As the revisionists see it, this radically new American policy—or rather this resumption by Truman of the pre-Roosevelt policy of insensate anticommunism—left Moscow no alternative but to take measures in defense of its own borders. The result was the Cold War.

Peacemaking after the Second World War was not so much a tapestry as it was a hopelessly raveled and knotted mess of yarn. Yet, for purposes of clarity, it is essential to follow certain threads. One theme indispensable to an understanding of the Cold War is the contrast between two clashing views of world order: the "universalist" view, by which all nations shared a common interest in all the affairs of the world, and the "sphere-of-influence" view, by which each great power would be assured by the other great powers of an acknowledged predominance in its own area of special interest. The universalist view assumed that national security would be guaranteed by an international organization. The sphere-of-interest view assumed that national security would be guaranteed by the balance of power. While in practice these views have by no means been incompatible (indeed, our shaky peace has been based on a combination of the two), in the abstract they involved sharp contradictions.

The tradition of American thought in these matters was universalist—i.e., Wilsonian. Roosevelt had been a member of Wilson's subcabinet; in 1920, as candidate for vice-president, he had campaigned for the League of Nations. It is true that, within Roosevelt's infinitely complex mind, Wilsonianism warred with the perception of vital strategic interests he had imbibed from [Alfred Thayer] Mahan. Moreover, his temperamental inclination to settle things with fellow princes around the conference table led him to regard the Big Three—or Four—as trustees for the rest of the world. On occasion, as this narrative will show, he was beguiled into flirtation with the sphere-of-influence heresy. But in principle he believed in joint action and remained a Wilsonian. His hope for Yalta, as he told the Congress on his return, was that it would "spell the end of the system of unilateral action, the exclusive alliances, the spheres of influence, the balances of power, and all the other expedients that have been tried for centuries—and have always failed.". . . .

It is true that critics, and even friends, of the United States sometimes noted a discrepancy between the American passion for universalism when it applied to territory far from American shores and the preeminence the United States accorded its own interests nearer home. Churchill, seeking Washington's blessing for a sphere-of-influence initiative in Eastern Europe, could not forbear reminding the Americans, "We follow the lead of the United States in South America"; nor did any universalist of record propose the abolition of the Monroe Doctrine. But a convenient myopia prevented such inconsistencies from qualifying the ardency of the universalist faith.

There seem only to have been three officials in the United States government who dissented. One was the secretary of war, Henry L. Stimson, a classical balance-of-power man, who in 1944 opposed the creation of a vacuum in Central Europe by the pastoralization of Germany and in 1945 urged "the settlement of all territorial acquisitions in the shape of defense posts which each of these four powers may deem to be necessary for their own safety" in advance of any effort to establish a peacetime United Nations. Stimson considered the claim of Russia to a preferred position in Eastern Europe as not unreasonable: As he told President Truman, "he thought the Russians perhaps were being more realistic than we were in regard to their own security." Such a position for Russia seemed to him comparable to the preferred American position in Latin America; he even spoke of "our respective orbits." Stimson was therefore skeptical of what he regarded as the prevailing tendency "to hang on to exaggerated views of the Monroe Doctrine and at the same time butt into every question that comes up in Central Europe." Acceptance of spheres of influence seemed to him the way to avoid "a head-on collision."

A second official opponent of universalism was George Kennan, an eloquent advocate from the American Embassy in Moscow of "a prompt and clear recognition of the division of Europe into spheres of influence and of a policy based on the fact of such division." Kennan argued that nothing we could do would possibly alter the course of events in Eastern Europe; that we were deceiving ourselves by supposing that these countries had any future but Russian domination; that we should therefore relinquish Eastern Europe to the Soviet Union and avoid anything which would make things easier for the Russians by giving them economic assistance or by sharing moral responsibility for their actions.

A third voice within the government against universalism was (at least after the war) Henry A. Wallace. As secretary of commerce, he stated the sphere-of-influence case with trenchancy in the famous Madison Square Garden speech of September 1946 which led to his dismissal by President Truman:

> On our part, we should recognize that we have no more business in the *political* affairs of Eastern Europe than Russia has in the *political* affairs of Latin America, Western Europe, and the United States. . . . Whether we like it or not, the Russians will try to socialize their sphere of influence just as we try to democratize our sphere of influence. . . . The Russians have no more business stirring up native Communists to political activity in Western Europe, Latin America, and the United States than we have in interfering with the politics of Eastern Europe and Russia.

Stimson, Kennan and Wallace seem to have been alone in the government, however, in taking these views. They were very much minority voices. Meanwhile universalism, rooted in the American legal and moral tradition, overwhelmingly backed by contemporary opinion, received successive enshrinements in the Atlantic Charter of 1941, in the Declaration of the United Nations in 1942 and in the Moscow Declaration of 1943.

The Kremlin, on the other hand, thought *only* of spheres of interest; above all, the Russians were determined to protect their frontiers, and especially their border to the west, crossed so often and so bloodily in the dark course of their history. These western frontiers lacked natural means of defense—no great oceans, rugged mountains, steaming swamps or impenetrable jungles. The history of Russia had been the history of invasion, the last of which was by now horribly killing up to 20 million of its people. The protocol of Russia therefore meant the enlargement of the area of Russian influence. Kennan himself wrote (in May 1944), "Behind Russia's stubborn expansion lies only the age-old sense of insecurity of a sedentary people reared on an exposed plain in the neighborhood of fierce nomadic peoples," and he called this "urge" a "permanent feature of Russian psychology. . . ."

The unconditional surrender of Italy in July 1943 created the first major test of the Western devotion to universalism. America and Britain, having won the Italian war, handled the capitulation, keeping Moscow informed at a distance. Stalin complained:

> The United States and Great Britain made agreements but the Soviet Union received information about the results . . . just as a passive third observer I have to tell you that it is impossible to tolerate the situation any longer. I propose that the [tripartite military-political commission] be established and that Sicily be assigned . . . as its place of residence.

Roosevelt, who had no intention of sharing the control of Italy with the Russians, suavely replied with the suggestion that Stalin send an officer "to General Eisenhower's headquarters in connection with the commission." Unimpressed, Stalin continued to press for a tripartite body; but his Western allies were adamant in keeping the Soviet Union off the Control Commission for Italy, and the Russians in the end had to be satisfied with a seat, along with minor Allied states, on a meaningless Inter-Allied Advisory Council. Their acquiescence in this was doubtless not unconnected with a desire to establish precedents for Eastern Europe.

Teheran in December 1943 marked the high point of three-power collaboration. Still, when Churchill asked about Russian territorial interests, Stalin replied a little ominously, "There is no need to speak at the present time about any Soviet desires, but when the time comes we will speak." In the next weeks, there were increasing indications of a Soviet determination to deal unilaterally with Eastern Europe—so much so that in early February 1944 Hull cabled Harriman in Moscow:

> Matters are rapidly approaching the point where the Soviet government will have to choose between the development and extension of the foundation of international cooperation as the guiding principle of the postwar world as against the continuance of a unilateral and

arbitrary method of dealing with its special problems even though
these problems are admittedly of more direct interest to the Soviet
Union than to other great powers.

As against this approach, however, Churchill, more tolerant of
sphere-of-influence deviations, soon proposed that, with the impending liberation of the Balkans, Russia should run things in Rumania and Britain in Greece. Hull strongly opposed this suggestion
but made the mistake of leaving Washington for a few days; and
Roosevelt, momentarily free from his Wilsonian conscience, yielded
to Churchill's pleas for a three-months' trial. Hull resumed the
fight on his return, and Churchill postponed the matter. . . .

Meanwhile Eastern Europe presented the Alliance with still
another crisis that same September. Bulgaria, which was not at war
with Russia, decided to surrender to the Western Allies while it still
could; and the English and Americans at Cairo began to discuss
armistice terms with Bulgarian envoys. Moscow, challenged by what
it plainly saw as a Western intrusion into its own zone of vital interest, promptly declared war on Bulgaria, took over the surrender negotiation and, invoking the Italian precedent, denied its Western
Allies any role in the Bulgarian Control Commission. In a long and
thoughtful cable, Ambassador Harriman meditated on the problems
of communication with the Soviet Union. "Words," he reflected,
"have a different connotation to the Soviets than they have to us.
When they speak of insisting on friendly governments' in their
neighboring countries, they have in mind something quite different
from what we would mean." The Russians, he surmised, really believed that Washington accepted "their position that although they
would keep us informed they had the right to settle their problems
with their western neighbors unilaterally." But the Soviet position
was still in flux: "the Soviet government is not one mind." The
problem, as Harriman had earlier told Harry Hopkins, was "to
strengthen the hands of those around Stalin who want to play the
game along our lines." The way to do this, he now told Hull, was to

be understanding of their sensitivity, meet them much more than
half way, encourage them and support them wherever we can, and
yet oppose them promptly with the greatest firmness where we see
them going wrong. . . . The only way we can eventually come to an
understanding with the Soviet Union on the question of noninter-

ference in the internal affairs of other countries is for us to take a
definite interest in the solution of the problems of each individual
country as they arise.

As against Harriman's sophisticated universalist strategy,
however, Churchill, increasingly fearful of the consequences of un-
restrained competition in Eastern Europe, decided in early October to carry his sphere-of-influence proposal directly to Moscow.
Roosevelt was at first content to have Churchill speak for him too
and even prepared a cable to that effect. But Hopkins, a more rigorous universalist, took it upon himself to stop the cable and warn
Roosevelt of its possible implications. Eventually Roosevelt sent a
message to Harriman in Moscow emphasizing that he expected to
"retain complete freedom of action after this conference is over."
It was now that Churchill quickly proposed—and Stalin as quickly
accepted—the celebrated division of southeastern Europe: ending
(after further haggling between [Sir Anthony] Eden and [V. M.]
Molotov) with 90 percent Soviet predominance in Rumania, 80
percent in Bulgaria and Hungary, 50–50 in Jugoslavia, 90 percent
British predominance in Greece.

Churchill in discussing this with Harriman used the phrase
"spheres of influence." But he insisted that these were only "immediate wartime arrangements" and received a highly general
blessing from Roosevelt. Yet, whatever Churchill intended, there is
reason to believe that Stalin construed the percentages as an agreement, not a declaration; as practical arithmetic, not algebra. For
Stalin, it should be understood, the sphere-of-influence idea did
not mean that he would abandon all efforts to spread communism
in some other nation's sphere; it did mean that, if he tried this and
the other side cracked down, he could not feel he had serious cause
for complaint. . . .

Yalta remains something of an historical perplexity—less,
from the perspective of 1967, because of a mythical American deference to the sphere-of-influence thesis than because of the docu-
mentable Russian deference to the universalist thesis. Why should
Stalin in 1945 have accepted the Declaration on Liberated Europe
and an agreement on Poland pledging that "the three governments will jointly" act to assure "free elections of governments re-
sponsive to the will of the people"? There are several probable

answers: that the war was not over and the Russians still wanted the Americans to intensify their military effort in the West; that one clause in the Declaration premised action on "the opinion of the three governments" and thus implied a Soviet veto, though the Polish agreement was more definite; most of all that the universalist algebra of the Declaration was plenty in Stalin's mind to be construed in terms of the practical arithmetic of his sphere-of-influence agreement with Churchill the previous October. Stalin's assurance to Churchill at Yalta that a proposed Russian amendment to the Declaration would not apply to Greece makes it clear that Roosevelt's pieties did not, in Stalin's mind, nullify Churchill's percentages. He could well have been strengthened in this supposition by the fact that *after* Yalta, Churchill himself repeatedly reasserted the terms of the October agreement as if he regarded it, despite Yalta, as controlling.

Harriman still had the feeling before Yalta that the Kremlin had "two approaches to their postwar policies" and that Stalin himself was "of two minds." One approach emphasized the internal reconstruction and development of Russia; the other its external expansion. But in the meantime the fact which dominated all political decisions—that is, the war against Germany—was moving into its final phase. In the weeks after Yalta, the military situation changed with great rapidity. As the Nazi threat declined, so too did the need for cooperation. The Soviet Union, feeling itself menaced by the American idea of self-determination and the borderlands diplomacy to which it was leading, skeptical whether the United Nations would protect its frontiers as reliably as its own domination in Eastern Europe, began to fulfill its security requirements unilaterally. . . .

The Cold War had now begun. It was the product not of a decision but of a dilemma. Each side felt compelled to adopt policies which the other could not but regard as a threat to the principles of the peace. Each then felt compelled to undertake defensive measures. Thus the Russians saw no choice but to consolidate their security in Eastern Europe. The Americans, regarding Eastern Europe as the first step toward Western Europe, responded by asserting their interest in the zone the Russians deemed vital to their security. The Russians concluded that the West was resuming its old course of capitalist encirclement; that it was purposefully laying the foundation for anti-Soviet regimes in the area defined by the blood of centuries as crucial to Russian survival. Each side believed with passion that future international stability depended on the success of its own conception of world order. Each side, in pursuing its own clearly indicated and deeply cherished principles, was only confirming the fear of the other that it was bent on aggression.

Very soon the process began to acquire a cumulative momentum. The impending collapse of Germany thus provoked new troubles: the Russians, for example, sincerely feared that the West was planning a separate surrender of the German armies in Italy in a way which would release troops for Hitler's eastern front, as they subsequently feared that the Nazis might succeed in surrendering Berlin to the West. This was the context in which the atomic bomb now appeared. Though the revisionist argument that Truman dropped the bomb less to defeat Japan than to intimidate Russia is not convincing, this thought unquestionably appealed to some in Washington as at least an advantageous side-effect of Hiroshima.

So the machinery of suspicion and countersuspicion, action and counteraction, was set in motion. But, given relations among traditional national states, there was still no reason, even with all the postwar jostling, why this should not have remained a manageable situation. What made it unmanageable, what caused the rapid escalation of the Cold War and in another two years completed the division of Europe, was a set of considerations which this account has thus far excluded.

Up to this point, the discussion has considered the schism within the wartime coalition as if it were entirely the result of disagreements among national states. Assuming this framework, there was unquestionably a failure of communication between America and Russia, a misperception of signals and, as time went on, a mounting tendency to ascribe ominous motives to the other side. It seems hard, for example, to deny that American postwar policy created genuine difficulties for the Russians and even assumed a threatening aspect for them. All this the revisionists have rightly and usefully emphasized.

But the great omission of the revisionists—and also the fundamental explanation of the speed with which the Cold War escalated—lies precisely in the fact that the Soviet Union was *not* a traditional national state. This is where the "mirror image," invoked by some psychologists, falls down. For the Soviet Union was a phenomenon very different from America or Britain: it was a totalitarian state, endowed with an all-explanatory, all-consuming ideology, committed to the infallibility of government and party, still in a somewhat messianic mood, equating dissent with treason, and ruled by a dictator who, for all his quite extraordinary abilities, had his paranoid moments.

Marxism-Leninism gave the Russian leaders a view of the world according to which all societies were inexorably destined to proceed along appointed roads by appointed stages until they achieved the classless nirvana. Moreover, given the resistance of the capitalists to this development, the existence of any non-Communist state was *by definition* a threat to the Soviet Union. "As long as capitalism and socialism exist," Lenin wrote, "we cannot live in peace: in the end, one or the other will triumph—a funeral dirge will be sung either over the Soviet Republic or over world capitalism."

Stalin and his associates, whatever Roosevelt or Truman did or failed to do, were bound to regard the United States as the enemy, not because of this deed or that, but because of the primordial fact that America was the leading capitalist power and thus, by Leninist syllogism, unappeasably hostile, driven by the logic of its system to oppose, encircle and destroy Soviet Russia. Nothing the United States could have done in 1944–45 would have abolished this mistrust, required and sanctified as it was by Marxist gospel— nothing short of the conversion of the United States into a Stalinist despotism; and even this would not have sufficed, as the experience of Jugoslavia and China soon showed, unless it were accompanied by total subservience to Moscow. So long as the United States remained a capitalist democracy, no American policy, given Moscow's theology, could hope to win basic Soviet confidence, and every American action was poisoned from the source. So long as the Soviet Union remained a messianic state, ideology compelled a steady expansion of communist power. . . .

A temporary recession of ideology was already taking place during the Second World War when Stalin, to rally his people against the invader, had to replace the appeal of Marxism by that of nationalism. ("We are under no illusions that they are fighting for us," Stalin once said to Harriman. "They are fighting for Mother Russia.") But this was still taking place within the strictest limitations. The Soviet Union remained as much a police state as ever; the regime was as infallible as ever; foreigners and their ideas were as suspect as ever. "Never, except possibly during my later experience as ambassador in Moscow," Kennan has written, "did the insistence of the Soviet authorities on isolation of the diplomatic corps weigh more heavily on me . . . than in these first weeks following my return to Russia in the final months of the war. . . . [We were] treated as though we were the bearers of some species of the plague"—which, of course, from the Soviet viewpoint, they were: the plague of skepticism.

Paradoxically, of the forces capable of bringing about a modification of ideology, the most practical and effective was the Soviet dictatorship itself. If Stalin was an ideologist, he was also a pragmatist. If he saw everything through the lenses of Marxism-Leninism, he also, as the infallible expositor of the faith, could reinterpret Marxism-Leninism to justify anything he wanted to do at any given moment. No doubt Roosevelt's ignorance of Marxism-Leninism was inexcusable and led to grievous miscalculations. But Roosevelt's efforts to work on and through Stalin were not so hopelessly naive as it used to be fashionable to think. With the extraordinary instinct of a great political leader, Roosevelt intuitively understood that Stalin was the *only* lever available to the West against the Leninist ideology and the Soviet system. If Stalin could be reached, then alone was there a chance of getting the Russians to act contrary to the prescriptions of their faith. The best evidence is that Roosevelt retained a certain capacity to influence Stalin to the end; the nominal Soviet acquiescence in American universalism as late as Yalta was perhaps an indication of that. It is in this way that the death of Roosevelt was crucial—not in the vulgar sense that his policy was then reversed by his successor, which did not happen, but in the sense that no other American could hope to have the restraining impact on Stalin which Roosevelt might for a while have had.

Stalin alone could have made any difference. Yet Stalin, in spite of the impression of sobriety and realism he made on Westerners who saw him during the Second World War, was plainly a man of deep and morbid obsessions and compulsions. When he was still a young man, Lenin had criticized his rude and arbitrary ways. A reasonably authoritative observer (N. S. Khrushchev) later commented, "These negative characteristics of his developed steadily and during the last years acquired an absolutely insufferable character." His paranoia, probably set off by the suicide of his wife in

1932, led to the terrible purges of the mid-thirties and the wanton murder of thousands of his Bolshevik comrades. "Everywhere and in everything," Khrushchev says of this period, "he saw 'enemies,' 'double-dealers' and 'spies.' " The crisis of war evidently steadied him in some way, though Khrushchev speaks of his "nervousness and hysteria . . . even after the war began." The madness, so rigidly controlled for a time, burst out with new and shocking intensity in the postwar years. "After the war," Khrushchev testifies,

> the situation became even more complicated. Stalin became even more capricious, irritable and brutal; in particular, his suspicion grew. His persecution mania reached unbelievable dimensions. . . . He decided everything, without any consideration for anyone or anything.
>
> Stalin's willfullness showed itself . . . also in the international relations of the Soviet Union. . . . He had completely lost a sense of reality; he demonstrated his suspicion and haughtiness not only in relation to individuals in the USSR, but in relation to whole parties and nations.

A revisionist fallacy has been to treat Stalin as just another Realpolitik statesman, as Second World War revisionists see Hitler as just another [Gustav] Stresemann or [Otto von] Bismarck. But the record makes it clear that in the end nothing could satisfy Stalin's paranoia. His own associates failed. Why does anyone suppose that any conceivable American policy would have succeeded?

An analysis of the origins of the Cold War which leaves out these factors—the intransigence of Leninist ideology, the sinister dynamics of a totalitarian society and the madness of Stalin—is obviously incomplete. It was these factors which made it hard for the West to accept the thesis that Russia was moved only by a desire to protect its security and would be satisfied by the control of Eastern Europe; it was these factors which charged the debate between universalism and spheres of influence with apocalyptic potentiality.

Leninism and totalitarianism created a structure of thought and behavior which made postwar collaboration between Russia and America—in any normal sense of civilized intercourse between national states—inherently impossible. The Soviet dictatorship of 1945 simply could not have survived such a collaboration. Indeed, nearly a quarter-century later, the Soviet regime, though it has meanwhile moved a good distance, could still hardly survive it without risking the release inside Russia of energies profoundly opposed to Communist despotism. As for Stalin, he may have represented the only force in 1945 capable of overcoming Stalinism, but the very traits which enabled him to win absolute power expressed terrifying instabilities of mind and temperament and hardly offered a solid foundation for a peaceful world.

Daniel Yergin

AMERICAN IDEOLOGY: THE RIGA AND YALTA AXIOMS

In his *Shattered Peace: The Origins of the Cold War and the National Security State* (1977), Daniel Yergin, like Arthur M. Schlesinger, Jr., before him, explores the long-standing debate over whether Soviet foreign policy was driven by messianic Marxist-Leninist ideology, brutal totalitarianism, or Soviet Russia's security interests. Was the Soviet Union a world revolutionary nation with which compromise was impossible? Or was it a traditional nation-state with which negotiations were possible? Yergin identifies two sets of American assumptions that clashed in the early Cold War period. The Riga axioms, named for the Latvian city where many American diplomats had studied Soviet affairs before 1933, emphasized the intractability of the ideologically bound, authoritarian Soviets. The Yalta axioms, named for the Black Sea resort where Franklin D. Roosevelt, Winston Churchill, and Joseph Stalin met in 1945, posited that Soviet-American cooperation in the postwar era could be realized through agreements that respected each side's interests. After Roosevelt's death, advisers who endorsed the Riga axioms gained influence with the new president, Harry S. Truman, who in early 1946 repudiated the Yalta axioms.

Daniel Yergin is president of Cambridge Energy Research Associates in Massachusetts. He has edited *Energy Future* (1979), *The Dependence Dilemma: Gasoline Consumption and America's Security* (1980), and *Global Insecurity* (1982). His book, *The Prize: Epic Quest for Oil, Money, and Power* (1991), **was awarded the Pulitzer Prize in 1991.**

. . . Underlying the debate [within the American elite over how to evaluate Soviet intentions and capabilities] were two related questions that have always confronted those in the West who have to shape policies toward the Soviet Union. They are the same two questions we face today.

The first was raised by the October 1917 Revolution itself. What is the connection between Marxist-Leninist ideology and Soviet foreign policy? The ideology proclaims that communism will inevitably inherit the entire world from capitalism, and calls upon Marxist-Leninists to be the conscious agents of the revolution. But the men who have ruled the Soviet Union were not and are not merely ideologues with many idle hours to dream about tomorrow's utopia. For the most part, they must concern themselves with today, with governing a powerful state that has pressing interests to protect, dangers to avoid, tasks to accomplish, and problems to solve. "There is no revolutionary movement in the West," said Stalin during the debates over the Brest-Litovsk treaty in 1918. "There are no facts; there is only a possibility, and with possibilities we cannot reckon."

The second question was brutally posed by the horrors of Stalinism, in particular by collectivization and the Great Terror of the 1930s. Does a totalitarian practice at home necessarily produce a foreign policy that is totalitarian in intent, committed to overturning the international system and to endless expansion in pursuit of world dominance? The policies of Adolf Hitler seemed to confirm that a powerful relationship did exist between such domestic practice and international behavior.

The changes wrought by the Second World War gave urgent and highest priority to these questions. What was the American response to be? Within the ensuing debate, there were two sets of generalizations, two interpretations that competed for hegemony in the American policy elite in the middle 1940s. At the heart of the first set was an image of the Soviet Union as a world revolutionary state, denying the possibilities of coexistence, committed to unrelenting ideological warfare, powered by a messianic drive for world mastery. The second set downplayed the role of ideology and the foreign policy consequences of authoritarian domestic practices, and instead saw the Soviet Union behaving like a traditional Great Power within the international system, rather than trying to overthrow it. The first set I call, for shorthand, the Riga axioms; the second, the Yalta axioms.

The Riga axioms triumphed in American policy circles in the postwar years and provided a foundation for the anticommunist consensus. Charles Bohlen summarized this outlook when he wrote to former Secretary of State Edward Stettinius in 1949. "I am quite convinced myself, and I think all of those who have been working specifically on the problems of relations with the Soviet Union are in agreement," said Bohlen, "that the reasons for the state of tension that exists in the world today between the Soviet Union and the non-Soviet world are to be found in the character and nature of the Soviet state, the doctrines to which it faithfully adheres, and not in such matters as the shutting off of Lend-Lease and the question of a loan."

With a view of this sort, the effort to make a diplomatic settlement became irrelevant, even dangerous, for the Cold War confrontation was thought to be almost genetically preordained in the revolutionary, messianic, predatory character of the Soviet Union. . . .

During the 1920s, a new "Soviet Service" developed in the State Department; it was anti-Bolshevik and opposed to diplomatic recognition of the USSR. Cohesive, with a strongly articulated sense of identity, this group advocated a policy of sophisticated anticommunism in an axiomatic form. Its outlook was based on personal experience, assessment, study, and pessimism. As U.S. leaders attempted, after World War II, to analyze Soviet policy and select an appropriate American course, this group's position provided one end of the spectrum of the debate. Eventually its axioms triumphed. Or, rather, they triumphed again, for they had held sway during most of the interwar years, when they had little competition, and before the problem of the Soviet Union had moved to the fore.

Initially, American officials saw the Bolshevik Revolution as a double betrayal. The revolutionaries made peace with the Germans at Brest-Litovsk early in 1918 and withdrew from the war, hurting the Allied cause. The Bolsheviks had also destroyed the hopes for the budding Russian democracy by overturning the liberal regime, which in its few months of existence had at last removed the Czarist stigma from the coalition meant to make the world safe for democracy. There was even the possibility of a third betrayal—that Lenin was a German agent.

American policymakers refused to recognize the new regime, in part because they hoped that it would be short-lived. The idea was shared by "practically all of us," recalled DeWitt Clinton Poole, who worked on Russian affairs in the State Department after World War I, "that the cure for Bolshevism was prosperity and good order and that Bolshevism would disappear under those conditions." There was, in Poole's words, a "breach between the Bolsheviks and the rest of the world." In an important memorandum addressed to his superiors in the State Department, in August 1919, Poole marshaled the arguments against giving diplomatic recognition to this "unconstitutional" regime: "Their aim is world-wide revolution . . . Their doctrines aim at the destruction of all governments as now constituted."

This outlook was widely accepted in the government and, instead of recognizing the Bolsheviks, the State Department set up a Division of Russian Affairs, with a mandate unusual for its time: to study and interpret the great mass of often contradictory information that made its way across the breach from this new Russia. It called upon the services of professors like Samuel Harper, of the University of Chicago, one of the first academic experts on Soviet Russia.

The U.S. maintained an observation post in the American mission in the Baltic port city of Riga, which was, through the interwar years, the capital of the independent republic of Latvia. Founded in 1201 by German merchants, tucked into a gulf at the very eastern end of the Baltic Sea, Riga still resembled a city of northern Germany, with narrow cobbled streets, gabled towers, and tiny squares. It was in this mission during the 1920s that much of the research on the Soviet Union was conducted, personnel trained, and fundamental attitudes formed and nurtured; and it was from the mission that there issued constant warnings against the international menace. For these reasons, I have associated place with ideas and linked Riga to the axiomatic outlook of the Soviet Service in the State department, although the ideas would receive further elaboration and gain new intensity in the latter half of the 1930s. . . .

The effects of the purges, with their great trials and sudden disappearances, on the image of the Soviet Union held by the

American diplomats cannot be exaggerated. The assassination of [Sergei] Kirov inaugurated a second phase of Stalinism—the orgy of terror, now directed against the apparatus of state and party. The unprecedented and spectacular show trials—conducted not only in the major cities but in almost every *oblast*—delivered their requisite output, an endless series of perfectly outlandish confessions, which "proved" that Trotskyites and foreign agents honeycombed Soviet society with their conspiracies. Millions suffered directly in this holocaust. In the simple words of Roy Medvedev, "Between 1936 and 1938 Stalin broke all records for political terror." Dread became a basic ingredient of Soviet life. By 1939 the purges had helped to establish firmly a highly centralized, bureaucratic, terror-driven totalitarian state, and the entire nation had become the servant of the state and of its ruler. . . .

Leninism had posed the first of the crucial questions about the Soviet Union—what was the relationship between its ideology and its behavior in the international system? Now Stalinism underlined in a stark fashion the second of the two questions—what was the connection between domestic totalitarianism and Soviet foreign policy? As with the first, there was no easy answer. Certainly, the American diplomats were correct in their judgment about the corruption of the Stalinist system. Indeed, if anything they were restrained, for they were able to see only the surface of the terror, for it has taken many years since for Westerners to begin to learn the full extent of Stalin's tyranny. Still, those diplomats concluded that the connection between the character of the state and its foreign policy was necessary and complete, that a totalitarian system at home meant a totalitarian foreign policy. If their answer was too categoric, even mistaken, one can understand—seeing what they did of collectivization, of the purges, of the daily life of terror and hypocrisy—why they came to it. . . .

By the end of the 1930s, the image of the revolutionary state and the ideas associated with it had become firmly fixed in the minds of the Soviet specialists and in those of people, like [Ambassador William] Bullitt, who had "learned" with them. "I am inclined to believe that all of us who have been in close contact with the thing itself gradually come to a common point of view," [Loy] Henderson observed in 1940. "There are a few exceptions among the chaps who are emotional and likely to become prejudiced." So codified had these beliefs become that we can now lay them out as axioms—though we must be careful not to confuse axioms with blinding dogma.

Doctrine and ideology and a spirit of innate aggressiveness shaped Soviet policy, the specialists believed. Thus, the USSR was committed to world revolution and unlimited expansion. In consequence, the United States, not just the countries around the Russian rim, was under siege and had to be continually vigilant. The "breach" of 1919 was still very real, to be bridged only by a major transformation.

Curiously, however, for all their fanatical devotion to ideology, the Soviet leaders were cool thinkers, much cooler than their Western counterparts. "They are realists, if ever there are any realists in this world," wrote Ambassador Laurence Steinhardt, [Joseph E.] Davies' successor, in 1940. The Soviet leaders always set their goals with supreme clarity. To an extent greater than that of most countries, Henderson wrote in 1936, Russian policy "has before it a series of definite objectives." Soviet officials are judged by "the progress" they can make "in the direction of those objectives." The Russians were always surefooted, and were masters of strategy and tactics.

The historian must here observe that the axiomatic notion that the Soviets worked by a foreign affairs plan, derived from ideology and with definite objectives, not only gave them more credit than they deserved, but also proved to be a central weakness in the assessments of Soviet policy after the war. For it led U.S. officials to exaggerate the policy coherence of the Kremlin—the role of ideology and conscious intentions. At the same time they understated the role played by accident, confusion, and uncertainty in Russian policy and also mistook mere reaction for planned action. A similar pattern, no doubt, would exist on the other side; what Americans would regard as their efforts to muddle through, in response to this or that problem, would be seen by the Soviets as part of a larger calculated policy. Indeed, one might even go further and hypothesize that there is a general tendency in international relations to exaggerate the policy coherence of an adversary. . . .

Confronted by such a potential adversary, the United States needed to adopt a stance of wariness and constant vigilance. Great patience and a counterassertiveness, an explicit "toughness," were required to cope with the Russian "personality." Steinhardt wrote to [Loy] Henderson in October 1940: "Approaches by Britain or the United States must be interpreted here as signs of weakness and the best policy to pursue is one of aloofness, indicating strength . . . As you know from your own experiences, the moment these people here get it into their heads that we are 'appeasing them, making up to them or need them,' they immediately stop being cooperative . . . My experience has been that they respond only to force and if force cannot be applied, then to straight oriental bartering or trading methods . . . That, in my opinion, is the only language they understand and the only language productive of results." The conclusion, therefore, was that diplomacy with the Soviet Union was not merely a questionable venture, but downright dangerous. . . .

The events that followed the 1939 pact—the Soviet role in the partition of Poland, the winter war in Finland, the annexation of the Balkan states and Bessarabia—all of these steps involving deportations and further extension of the terror—confirmed the Riga viewpoint, and gave its advocates the confidence to speak even more categorically. The war with Finland, in general, mobilized anti-Soviet sentiment in the United States and chilled Russo-American relations. The abhorrence that had fed DeWitt Clinton Poole's strictures two decades before returned, and with greater force.

Even at the highest levels the Riga image regained acceptance. In the middle of 1940 Loy Henderson challenged his superiors: "Is the Government of the United States to apply certain standards of judgment and conduct to aggression by Germany and Japan, and not to Soviet aggression?" The answer came now: Germany and Russia were two of a kind; they were totalitarian dictatorships. Cordell Hull, on the eve of the German invasion of Russia, summarized the knowledge gleaned in the 1930s: "Basing ourselves upon our own experiences and upon observations of the experiences of other governments," U.S. policy toward the Soviet Union called for making "no approaches to the Soviet Government," treating any Soviet approaches with reserve, and rendering "no sacrifices in principle in order to improve relations."

These axioms seemed to explain satisfactorily Russia's role in world politics and to delineate an appropriate course for the United States to follow. They dominated interpretations of events until the German invasion of Russia in the night of June 21–22, 1941. With that, the Riga axioms suffered a startling loss of relevance. A new phase began in Soviet-American relations, which led to an experience radically different from that of the Soviet Service during the interwar years. A fresh image, based upon other assumptions, came to the fore. In addition, procedures were established for handling political problems that bypassed the State Department. . . .

United States policy toward the Soviet Union was now out of the hands of the State Department. In an environment sharply transformed from that of the interwar years, the Riga School was being made obsolete by the bold new span [Franklin D.] Roosevelt was constructing to bridge the breach between America and Russia in the postwar era.

One evening in March of 1943, British Foreign Secretary Anthony Eden dined privately at the White House with President Roosevelt and Harry Hopkins. The three fell into a long, ruminating conversation that continued late into the night. With an ease available only to men who number themselves among the handful of arbiters over the world's destiny, they surveyed the outstanding political questions of the entire planet, playing with borders, shifting governments like so many chess pieces, guessing at the political shadings that would color the postwar map. "A conjuror, skillfully juggling with balls of dynamite," was the way Eden remembered Roosevelt from that night. "The big question which rightly dominated Roosevelt's mind was whether it was possible to work with Russia now and after the war," he recalled.

Roosevelt asked Eden what he thought of the "Bullitt Thesis," referring to a lengthy memorandum, based upon the Riga axioms, that Bullitt had sent to the White House several weeks earlier. Bullitt, whose enthusiasms of ten years before had long since soured into fear and alarm, predicted that the Russians would succeed in communizing the Continent—unless the United States and Britain blocked "the flow of the Red amoeba into Europe."

Eden replied that a definite answer to this question was impossible. But "even if these fears were to prove correct," he continued, "we should make the position no worse by trying to work with Russia and by assuming that Stalin meant what he said." Eden agreed with Roosevelt that it would be better to proceed on a premise contrary to Bullitt's—that it would be possible to find some system of working *with*, rather than *against*, the Soviet Union. Roosevelt also did not think that a categoric answer existed. He believed Soviet goals and methods would be partly determined by Stalin's own estimate of American and British intentions and capabilities.

Certainly the most important goal of Roosevelt's wartime diplomacy was the establishment of a basis for postwar cooperation with the Soviet Union. He had a clear conception of the postwar settlement he wanted and how it might be achieved. This conception was also governed by a number of axioms, some of which had predated the war, some of which had emerged in the course of the war. Roosevelt's axioms were always more tentative than those of Riga, but at their center point, there also lay an image—derived from experience, assessment, and optimism—of Soviet Russia. . . .

As already noted, Roosevelt believed the peace had to be based upon the realities of power, which meant that it would have to be grounded in a Great Power consortium. The British easily fit into this design. The key question concerned the role of the Soviet Union. Here Roosevelt operated on a series of axioms very different from those of the Soviet specialists in the State Department.

He believed that Russia could no longer be considered an outsider, beyond the pale of morality and international politics. What that meant in the context of the war was already obvious. The President recognized that the major land war in Europe was taking place on the Eastern Front; it was there that Germany could be defeated, with a consequent reduction in American casualties. A kind of comparative advantage set in. The Russians specialized in men, dead and wounded, while the United States pushed its industrial machine to new limits. A year after the German invasion of the Soviet Union, Roosevelt declared that "Russian endurance" was "still the main strength."

The war, which promised to bequeath a great power vacuum in Europe and at the same time erased all doubts about Russia's power and capabilities, made inevitable the emergence of the Soviet Union as a paramount and indispensable factor in the postwar international system, especially in Europe. Thus, the alternative to a broad understanding would be a postwar world of hostile coalitions, an arms race—and another war.

Some such understanding was possible because the breach that had opened at the time of the Bolshevik Revolution had narrowed and could narrow further. Roosevelt thought of the Soviet Union less as a revolutionary vanguard than as a conventional imperialist power, with ambitions rather like those of the Czarist regime. In other words, Roosevelt emphasized the imperatives of statehood in Soviet policy, rather than the role of ideology. In contrast to the Riga axioms, he proceeded on the proposition that a totalitarian domestic system did *not* inevitably and necessarily give rise to a totalitarian foreign policy. As important, he assumed less coherence and purposefulness in the Kremlin's behavior in international politics than did those who operated on the Riga axioms. Since the Soviet Union was not so much a world revolutionary state, Roosevelt believed the Grand Alliance could be continued after the war in the form of "business-like relations." He also knew that the Soviet Union would be preoccupied after the war with its vast task of reconstruction, and would be desperately interested in stability, order, and peace.

Successful collaboration among the Great Powers would necessitate the allaying of many years of Soviet hostility and suspicion. Roosevelt regarded the dissipation of distrust as one of his most important challenges. The United States could prove its good faith by sticking to its agreements. Even if the West could not deliver immediately on its promised Second Front, at least it could provide the aid it had pledged—and, in that way, also do itself a considerable favor. Again and again, Roosevelt ordered that the production and delivery of lend-lease goods be speeded up, that the quantities be increased. It was a battle down the line. "Frankly," the President sharply reminded a subordinate, "if I were a Russian, I would feel that I had been given the run-around in the United States." . . .

"Roosevelt weather" was the term applied by FDR's political staff to the favorable weather that seemed to signal victory on each of those four November days that he had been elected President. The Russians adopted the same phrase to describe the unseasonably mild climate in the first two weeks of February 1945 over the Crimea, which juts down into the Black Sea from the underside of the Ukraine. At the seaside resort of Yalta, on the southern coast of the Crimea, the last Czar had maintained his summer palace. There the Big Three gathered for their final wartime conference, between February 4 and 11, under bright, clear skies that seemed a harbinger of victory, not only in the war but also over the unfamiliar terrain of postwar international politics. FDR brought his practicality to bear, in an effort to make firm the foundations of his Grand

Design. The pleasant days and nights matched the climate of the conference itself—auguring victory for Roosevelt's foreign policy.

Marking the high tide of Allied unity, the Yalta Conference was a point of separation, a time of endings and beginnings. The conclusion of the war was at last in sight; the remaining days of the Third Reich were clearly numbered. Stalin, to the relief of the Joint Chiefs, gave further assurances that Russia would enter the war against Japan some three months after fighting ended in Europe, in exchange for certain territorial concessions in the Far East.

Aside from that central question, the major issues at Yalta concerned the politics of a postwar world. The decisions waited upon the energies of three tired men. "I think Uncle Joe much the most impressive" Alexander Cadogan, permanent undersecretary of the British Foreign Office, wrote to his wife. "The President flapped about and the P.M. boomed, but Joe just sat taking it all in and being rather amused. When he did chip in, he never used a superfluous word, and spoke very much to the point."

By and large, the Russians made more concessions than the West, and when they presented their own proposals, they were, in fact, sometimes simply returning proposals delivered to them at earlier dates by the Western powers.

The Russians, remembering their difficulties in the League of Nations, which culminated in their expulsion, were worried that they would find themselves isolated in a new international organization controlled by the United States and the United Kingdom through their allies, clients, dominions, and "Good Neighbors." The Russians accepted an American compromise, whereby the Great Powers retained a veto in the Security Council, and the Western leaders agreed to support the admission of two or three constituent Soviet republics. The British won assent to a modified Great Power role for France, including both a zone of occupation in Germany and participation on the German Control Commission.

Roosevelt successfully pushed for a "Declaration on Liberated Europe," an ill-defined lever for Western intervention in Eastern Europe, but which mainly interested Roosevelt as a device to satisfy public opinion at home. He took it up only after he had turned down a more binding State Department proposal for a High Commission on Liberated Areas because "he preferred a more flexible arrangement." Accord also followed on a number of less pressing points.

Two issues proved more difficult: the central question of Germany and the endless Polish imbroglio. Poland, the emblem of the early Cold War, took up more time than any other issue at the conference. The Allies did agree that the Russian-Polish border should be moved westward, to the Curzon Line, and, though not in very precise terms, further consented to compensation for Poland in the form of what had been German territory on its west.

More difficult was the nature of Poland's new government, that is, whether to install the Western-supported London exile government, bitterly anti-Soviet, or the Lublin government, little more than a Soviet puppet.

Britain went to war so "that Poland should be free and sovereign," said Churchill. Britain's only interest, he assured the other leaders, was "one of honor because we drew the sword for Poland against Hitler's brutal attack." Of course, he added, Polish independence could not be a cover for "hostile designs" against the Soviet Union.

Stalin, however, was still interested in practical arithmetic. "For Russia it is not only a question of honor but of security." As to honor—"We shall have to eliminate many things from the books." As to security—"Not only because we are on Poland's frontier but also because throughout history Poland has always been a corridor for attack on Russia." Twice in the last thirty years "our German enemy has passed through this corridor."

Churchill replied that he himself had little fondness for the London Poles, which was one element in the general weakness of the Western position on the Polish question. "Admittedly," a British diplomat commented, "Uncle Joe's masterly exposition of the Russian attitude over Poland sounded sincere, and as always was hyperrealistic."

At last, the Allies agreed to "reorganize" the Lublin government with some men from London and from the Polish underground, but details were left to Molotov and the two Allied ambassadors in Moscow to work out.

For Germany, the Russians pushed for dismemberment; in substance, their proposal was the suggestion Roosevelt had made at Tehran. The two Western governments went along, reluctantly.

The Russians also insisted on receiving reparations from Germany. Postwar planning in the U.S. had generally rejected reparations. America certainly had no need for reparations; and reparations had been in bad repute in both Britain and the United States since J. M. Keynes' *Economic Consequences of the Peace*, published shortly after the First World War. "We are against reparations," Roosevelt had bluntly said before Yalta.

At Yalta, however, the Western countries met a Soviet Union urgently determined to exact reparations. As early as September 1941, in conversations with Averell Harriman and Lord Beaverbrook, Stalin had asked flatly: "What about getting the Germans to pay for the damage?" Stalin's "second revolution" had been an industrial revolution, an upheaval that had cost much in human life and in the manner in which the survivors lived. Stalin's interest in reparations was compensatory as well as punitive; he wanted help in the huge task of reconstruction that lay ahead. By 1945, the Germans had wrought enormous destruction. Twenty million people had been killed— though it was years before the Kremlin revealed the full magnitude. Seven million horses had been lost, as were 20 out of 23 million pigs. Destroyed were 4.7 million houses, 1710 towns, and 70,000 villages. Twenty-five million people were homeless. Sixty-five thousand kilometers of railway tracks had been ruined; 15,800 locomotives and 428,000 freight cars had been either demolished or damaged.

Here, however, the Soviet concern went beyond the simple arithmetic of devastation. Reading through the minutes of meeting upon meeting during the war and after, the historian must conclude that reparations were not only a central issue, but also a highly significant symbol in Moscow's postwar vision—although always only of peripheral interest to the Americans. Perhaps the Russians could never understand the nature of American concern for Eastern Europe; similarly, the Americans could never comprehend the emotional intensity the Russians attached to reparations. Reparations may well have been as much a "test case" for the Russians as Eastern Europe was to become for the Americans.

At Yalta, Churchill adamantly opposed reparations, warning that England "would be chained to a dead body of Germany." Concerned about economic consequences and criticism at home, Roosevelt wavered until Hopkins shoved him a note: "The Russians have given in so much at this conference that I don't think we should let them down." The President finally agreed to set $20 billion, half for the Russians, as the basis for further discussions, though with the understanding that reparations were to be in goods, production, and equipment, and not in cash. . . .

Roosevelt was a realist; he knew that everything depended upon implementation of the accords, and that, in turn, would depend upon intentions and future alignments. He was gambling. He hinted at this caution in a note he scribbled to his wife the day he left Yalta: "We have wound up the conference—successfully I think."

That said, there can be no question but that Roosevelt departed the Crimea optimistic and satisfied. Basing his conclusions on conversations with Roosevelt, Admiral [William] Leahy decided that Roosevelt had "no regrets about what the Russians were to get. He thought they were valid claims." But FDR's satisfaction extended beyond the agreements themselves. He regarded the conference as a hopeful answer to the question about postwar cooperation with Russia that he had posed to Eden two years earlier, in the course of their after-dinner survey. This summit meeting in the Crimea had been a testing and, more important, a confirmation of what we might thus call Franklin Roosevelt's "Yalta axioms."

Stalin himself had gone out of his way to endorse the premise that underlay FDR's Grand Design. The dictator had pointed to "a more serious question" than an international organization. One should not worry too much about small nations. "The greatest danger was conflict between the three Great Powers." The main task was to prevent their quarreling and "secure their unity for the future."

It is true that Roosevelt, once home, delivered a speech to Congress, pure in its Wilsonianism, in which he declared that Yalta spelled the end of unilateral action, exclusive alliances, spheres of influence, power blocs, and "all other expedients that had been tried for centuries—and have always failed."

But, out of public earshot, he continued to stress the realities of power and the basic structure of a Great Power consortium. Two days after his speech to Congress, talking privately about Germany, he said, "Obviously the Russians are going to do things their own way in the areas they occupy." But he hoped that a general framework of collaboration would prevent the Soviet sphere of influence from becoming a sphere of control. . . .

[V. M.] Molotov saw the President [Truman] at five-thirty on April 23, [1945]. Struggling to follow Davies' advice in an unexpectedly tense situation, he tried to outline the Russian case, especially on the Polish question.

The President, however, was in no mood for ambiguities. Three days before, having discussed matters with Harriman and Stettinius, he had declared: "We could not, of course, expect to get 100 percent of what we wanted," but he felt that "on important matters . . . we should be able to get 85 percent." Now, bent on obtaining that chunk, Truman brushed over Molotov's statement and instead lectured the Russian in what Leahy described as "plain American language." The Russians had to stick to their agreements, as interpreted in Washington. Relations could no longer be "on the basis of a one-way street."

Molotov turned white at the dressing down. "I have never been talked to like that in my life," he said.

"Carry out your agreements and you won't get talked to like that," Truman replied curtly.

Those who had urged their views on Truman were pleased by his performance. Leahy noted in his diary that the "President's strong American stand" left the Russians only two courses of action: "either to approach closely to our expressed policy in regard to Poland" or to drop out of the new international organization. He went on to add: "The President's attitude was more than pleasing to me, and I believe it will have a beneficial effect on the Soviet attitude toward the rest of the world. They have always known we have the power, and now they should know that we have the determination to insist upon the declared right of all people to choose their own form of government." On the same day, Eden had assured Churchill that "the new President is not to be bullied by the Soviets."

Melvyn P. Leffler

AMERICA'S NATIONAL SECURITY POLICY: A SOURCE OF COLD WAR TENSIONS

Melvyn P. Leffler challenges the once popular view that American lead-ers were largely reactive as they devised postwar foreign policy. On the contrary, he asserts, American diplomatic, military, and intelligence offi-cials—including President Harry S Truman himself—had formulated a concept of national security that propelled America abroad. American leaders became especially concerned about the geopolitical balance of power in Europe and Asia, where it seemed communists might make gains during a time of economic crisis and political unrest. American of-ficials became more interventionist abroad not so much in reaction to Soviet military capabilities or diplomatic demands, argues Leffler, but because of their fears for the survival of United States overseas interests. If the economic and political turmoil in Eurasia persisted and American power faltered, American analysts prophesied, the Soviet Union might come to control vast resources and threaten American political and eco-nomic principles. Leffler concludes that American officials exaggerated the benefits that would accrue to the Soviet Union and that America's global pursuit of security made Moscow apprehensive.

Melvyn P. Leffler is a professor of history at the University of Virginia. He is the author of *The Elusive Quest: America's Pursuit of European Sta-bility and French Security, 1919–1933* (1979), *A Preponderance of Power: National Security, the Truman Administration, and the Cold War* (1992), and *The Specter of Communism* (1994).

In an interview with Henry Kissinger in 1978 on "The Lessons of the Past," Walter Laqueur observed that during World War II "few if any people thought . . . of the structure of peace that would follow the war except perhaps in the most general terms of friend-ship, mutual trust, and the other noble sentiments mentioned in

"The American Conception of National Security and the Beginnings of the Cold War, 1945–48," by Melvyn P. Leffler, *American Historical Review*, vol. LXXXIX, no. 2, pp. 346–81, April 1984. Reprinted by permission of the author.

wartime programmatic speeches about the United Nations and related topics." Kissinger concurred, noting that no statesman, except perhaps Winston Churchill, "gave any attention to what
would happen after the war." Americans, Kissinger stressed, "were
determined that we were going to base the postwar period on
good faith and getting along with everybody."

That two such astute and knowledgeable observers of international policies were so uninformed about American planning at
the end of the Second World War is testimony to the enduring
mythology of American idealism and innocence in the world of
Realpolitik. It also reflects the state of scholarship on the interrelated areas of strategy, economy, and diplomacy. Despite the publication of several excellent overviews of the origins of the Cold War,
despite the outpouring of incisive monographs on American foreign policy in many areas of the world, and despite some first-rate
studies on the evolution of strategic thinking and the defense establishment, no comprehensive account yet exists of how American
defense officials defined national security interests in the aftermath
of World War II. Until recently, the absence of such a study was
understandable, for scholars had limited access to records pertain-
ing to national security, strategic thinking, and war planning. But
in recent years documents relating to the early years of the Cold
War have been declassified in massive numbers.

This documentation now makes it possible to analyze in
greater depth the perceptions, apprehensions, and objectives of
those defense officials most concerned with defining and defend-
ing the nation's security and strategic interests. This essay seeks
neither to explain the process of decision making on any particular
issue nor to dissect the domestic political considerations and fiscal
constraints that narrowed the options available to policy makers.
Furthermore, it does not pretend to discern the motivations
and objectives of the Soviet Union. Rather, the goal here is to elu-
cidate the fundamental strategic and economic considerations that
shaped the definition of American national security interests in the
postwar world. Several of these considerations—especially as they
related to overseas bases, air transit rights, and a strategic sphere of
influence in Latin America—initially were the logical result of technological developments and geostrategic experiences rather than
directly related to postwar Soviet behavior. But American defense
officials also considered the preservation of a favorable balance of

power in Eurasia as fundamental to U.S. national security. This objective impelled defense analysts and intelligence officers to appraise and reappraise the intentions and capabilities of the Soviet Union. Rather modest estimates of the Soviets' ability to wage war against the United States generated the widespread assumption that the Soviets would refrain from military aggression and seek to avoid war. Nevertheless, American defense officials remained greatly preoccupied with the geopolitical balance of power in Europe and Asia, because that balance seemed endangered by communist exploitation of postwar economic dislocation and social and political unrest. Indeed, American assessments of the Soviet threat were less a consequence of expanding Soviet military capabilities and of Soviet diplomatic demands than a result of growing apprehension about the vulnerability of American strategic and economic interests in a world of unprecedented turmoil and upheaval. Viewed from this perspective, the Cold War assumed many of its most enduring characteristics during 1947–48, when American officials sought to cope with an array of challenges by implementing their own concepts of national security.

American officials first began to think seriously about the nation's postwar security during 1943–44. Military planners devised elaborate plans for an overseas base system. Many of these plans explicitly contemplated the breakdown of the wartime coalition. But, even when strategic planners postulated good postwar relations among the Allies, their plans called for an extensive system of bases. These bases were defined as the nation's strategic frontier. Beyond this frontier the United States would be able to use force to counter any threats or frustrate any overt acts of aggression. Within the strategic frontier, American military predominance had to remain inviolate. Although plans for an overseas base system went through many revisions, they always presupposed American hegemony over the Atlantic and Pacific oceans. These plans received President Franklin D. Roosevelt's endorsement in early 1944. After his death, army and navy planners presented their views to President Harry S Truman, and Army Chief of Staff George C. Marshall discussed them extensively with Secretary of State James F. Byrnes.

Two strategic considerations influenced the development of an overseas base system. The first was the need for defense in depth. Since attacks against the United States could only emanate from Europe and Asia, the Joint Chiefs of Staff concluded as early as November 1943 that the United States must encircle the Western Hemisphere with a defensive ring of outlying bases. In the Pacific this ring had to include the Aleutians, the Philippines, Okinawa, and the former Japanese mandates. Recognizing the magnitude of this strategic frontier, Admiral William E. Leahy, chief of staff to the president, explained to Truman that the joint chiefs were not thinking of the immediate future when, admittedly, no prospective naval power could challenge American predominance in the Pacific. Instead, they were contemplating the long term, when the United States might require wartime access to the resources of southeast Asia as well as "a firm line of communications from the West Coast to the Asiatic mainland, plus denial of this line in time of war to any potential enemy." In the Atlantic, strategic planners maintained that their minimum requirements included a West African zone, with primary bases in the Azores or Canary Islands. Leahy went even further, insisting on primary bases in West Africa itself—for example, at Dakar or Casablanca. The object of these defensive bases was to enable the United States to possess complete control of the Atlantic and Pacific oceans and keep hostile powers far from American territory.

Defense in depth was especially important in light of the Pearl Harbor experience, the advance of technology, and the development of the atomic bomb. According to the Joint Chiefs of Staff, "Experience in the recent war demonstrated conclusively that the defense of a nation, if it is to be effective, must begin beyond its frontiers. The advent of the atomic bomb reemphasizes this requirement. The farther away from our own vital areas we can hold our enemy through the possession of advanced bases . . . , the greater are our chances of surviving successfully an attack by atomic weapons and of destroying the enemy which employs them against us." Believing that atomic weapons would increase the incentive to aggression by enhancing the advantage of surprise, military planners never ceased to extol the utility of forward bases from which American aircraft could seek to intercept attacks against the United States.

The second strategic consideration that influenced the plan for a comprehensive overseas base system was the need to project American power quickly and effectively against any potential adversary. In conducting an overall examination of requirements for base rights in September 1945, the Joint War Plans Committee stressed that World War II demonstrated the futility of a strategy of static defense. The United States had to be able to take "timely" offensive action against the adversary's capacity and will to wage war. New weapons demanded that advance bases be established in "areas well removed from the United States, so as to project our operations, with new weapons or otherwise, nearer the enemy." Scientists, like Vannevar Bush, argued that, "regardless of the potentialities of these new weapons [atomic energy and guided missiles], they should not influence the number, location, or extent of strategic bases now considered essential." The basic strategic concept underlying all American war plans called for an air offensive against a prospective enemy from overseas bases. Delays in the development of the B-36, the first intercontinental bomber, only accentuated the need for these bases.

In October 1945 the civilian leaders of the War and Navy departments carefully reviewed the emerging strategic concepts and base requirements of the military planners. Secretary of the Navy James Forrestal and Secretary of War Robert P. Patterson discussed them with Admiral Leahy, the Joint Chiefs of Staff, and Secretary of State Byrnes. The civilian secretaries fully endorsed the concept of a far-flung system of bases in the Atlantic and Pacific oceans that would enhance the offensive capabilities of the United States. Having expended so much blood and effort capturing Japanese-held islands, defense officials, like Forrestal, naturally wished to devise a base system in the Pacific to facilitate the projection of American influence and power. The Philippines were the key to southeast Asia, Okinawa to the Yellow Sea, the Sea of Japan, and the industrial heartland of northeast Asia. From these bases on America's "strategic frontier," the United States could preserve its access to vital raw materials in Asia, deny these resources to a prospective enemy, help preserve peace and stability in troubled areas, safeguard critical sea lanes, and, if necessary, conduct an air offensive against the industrial infrastructure of any Asiatic power, including the Soviet Union. . . .

In the immediate postwar years American ambitions for an elaborate base system encountered many problems. Budgetary constraints compelled military planners to drop plans for many secondary and subsidiary bases, particularly in the South Pacific and Caribbean. These sacrifices merely increased the importance of those bases that lay closer to a potential adversary. By early 1948, the joint chiefs were willing to forego base rights in such places as Surinam, Curacoa-Aruba, Cayenne, Nounea, and Vivi-Levu if "joint" or "participating" rights could be acquired or preserved in Karachi, Tripoli, Algiers, Casablanca, Dharan, and Monrovia. Budgetary constraints, then, limited the depth of the base system but not the breadth of American ambitions. Furthermore, the governments of Panama, Iceland, Denmark, Portugal, France, and Saudi Arabia often rejected or abolished the exclusive rights the United States wanted and sometimes limited the number of American personnel on such bases. Washington, therefore, negotiated a variety of arrangements to meet the objections of host governments. By early 1948, for example, the base in Iceland was operated by a civilian company under contract to the United States Air Force; in the Azores, the base was manned by a detachment of Portuguese military personnel operating under the Portuguese flag, but an air force detachment serviced the American aircraft using the base. In Port Lyautey, the base was under the command of the French navy, but under a secret agreement an American naval team took care of American aircraft on the base. In Saudi Arabia, the Dharan air strip was cared for by 300 U.S. personnel and was capable of handling B-29s. Because these arrangements were not altogether satisfactory, in mid-1948 Secretary of Defense Forrestal and Secretary of the Army Kenneth Royall advocated using American economic and military assistance as levers to acquire more permanent and comprehensive base rights; particularly in Greenland and North Africa.

Less well known than the American effort to establish a base system, but integral to the policymakers' conception of national security, was the attempt to secure military air transit and landing rights. Military planners wanted such rights at critical locations not only in the Western Hemisphere but also in North Africa, the Middle East, India, and southeast Asia. To this end they delineated a route from Casablanca through Algiers, Tripoli, Cairo, Dharan, Karachi, Delhi, Calcutta, Rangoon, Bangkok, and Saigon to Manila. In closing out the African-Middle East theater at the conclusion of the war, General H. W. Aurand, under explicit instructions from the secretary of war, made preparations for permanent rights at seven airfields in North Africa and Saudi Arabia. According to a study by the Joint Chiefs of Staff, "Military air transit rights for the United States along the North African-Indian route were most desirable in order to provide access to and familiarity with bases from which offensive and defensive action might be conducted in the event of a major war, and to provide an alternate route to China and to United States Far Eastern bases." In other words, such rights would permit the rapid augmentation of American bases in wartime as well as the rapid movement of American air units from the eastern to the western flank of the U.S. base system. In order to maintain these airfields in a state of readiness, the United States would have to rely on private airlines, which had to be persuaded to locate their operations in areas designated essential to military air transit rights. In this way, airports "in being" outside the formal American base system would be available for military operations in times of crisis and war. Assistant Secretary [of War John] McCloy informed the State Department at the beginning of 1945 that a "strong United States air transport system, international in scope and readily adapted to military use, is vital to our air power and future national security." Even earlier, the joint chiefs had agreed not to include South American air bases in their strategic plans so long as it was understood that commercial fields in that region would be developed with a view to subsequent military use. . . .

From the closing days of World War II, American defense officials believed that they could not allow any prospective adversary to control the Eurasian land mass. This was the lesson taught by two world wars. Strategic thinkers and military analysts insisted that any power or powers attempting to dominate Eurasia must be regarded as potentially hostile to the United States. Their acute awareness of the importance of Eurasia made Marshall, Thomas Handy, George A. Lincoln, and other officers wary of the expansion of Soviet influence there. Cognizant of the growth in Soviet strength, General John Deane, head of the United States military mission in Moscow, urged a tougher stand against Soviet demands even before World War II had ended. While acknowledging that the increase in Soviet power stemmed primarily from the defeat of Germany and Japan, postwar assessments of the Joint Chiefs of Staff emphasized the importance of deterring further Soviet aggrandizement in Eurasia. Concern over the consequences of Russian domination of Eurasia helps explain why in July 1945 the joint chiefs decided to oppose a Soviet request for bases in the Dardanelles; why during March and April 1946 they supported a firm stand against Russia in Iran, Turkey, and Tripolitania; and why in the summer of 1946 Clark Clifford and George Elsey, two White House aides, argued that Soviet incorporation of any parts of Western Europe, the Middle East, China, or Japan into a communist orbit was incompatible with American national security. . . .

Studies by the Joint Chiefs of Staff stressed that, if Eurasia came under Soviet domination, either through military conquest or political and economic "assimilation," America's only potential adversary would fall heir to enormous natural resources, industrial potential, and manpower. By the autumn of 1945, military planners already were worrying that Soviet control over much of Eastern Europe and its raw materials would abet Russia's economic recovery, enhance its warmaking capacity, and deny important foodstuffs, oil, and minerals to Western Europe. By the early months of 1946, Secretary Patterson and his subordinates in the War Department believed that Soviet control of the Ruhr-Rhineland industrial complex would constitute an extreme threat. Even more dangerous was the prospect of Soviet predominance over the rest of Western Europe, especially France. Strategically, this would undermine the impact of any prospective American naval blockade and would allow Soviet military planners to achieve defense in depth. The latter possibility had enormous military significance, because American war plans relied so heavily on air power and strategic bombing, the efficacy of which might be reduced substantially if the Soviets acquired outlying bases in Western Europe and the Middle East or if they "neutralized" bases in Great Britain.

Economic considerations also made defense officials determined to retain American access to Eurasia as well as to deny Soviet predominance over it. [Secretary of War Henry L.] Stimson, Patterson, McCloy, and Assistant Secretary Howard C. Peterson agreed with Forrestal that long-term American prosperity required open markets, unhindered access to raw materials, and the rehabilitation of much—if not all—of Eurasia along liberal capitalist lines. In late 1944 and 1945, Stimson protested the prospective industrial emasculation of Germany, lest it undermine American economic well-being, set back recovery throughout Europe, and unleash forces of anarchy and revolution. Stimson and his subordinates in the Operations Division of the army also worried that the spread of Soviet power in northeast Asia would constrain the functioning of the free enterprise system and jeopardize American economic interests. A report prepared by the staff of the Moscow embassy and revised in mid-1946 by Ambassador (and former General) Walter Bedell Smith emphasized that "Soviet power is by nature so jealous that it has already operated to segregate from world economy almost all of the areas in which it has been established." While Forrestal and the navy sought to contain Soviet influence in the Near East and to retain American access to Middle East oil, Patterson and the War Department focused on preventing famine in occupied areas, forestalling communist revolution, circumscribing Soviet influence, resuscitating trade, and preserving traditional American markets especially in Western Europe. But American economic interests in Eurasia were not limited to Western Europe, Germany, and the Middle East. Military planners and intelligence officers in both the army and navy expressed considerable interest in the raw materials of southeast Asia, and, as already shown, one of the purposes of the bases they wanted was to maintain access to those resources and deny them to a prospective enemy.

While civilian officials and military strategists feared the loss of Eurasia, they did not expect the Soviet Union to attempt its military conquest. In the early Cold War years, there was nearly universal agreement that the Soviets, while eager to expand their influence, desired to avoid a military engagement. In October 1945, for example, the Joint Intelligence Staff predicted that the Soviet Union would seek to avoid war for five to ten years. . . . In March 1947, while the Truman Doctrine was being discussed in Congress, the director of army intelligence maintained that the factors operating to discourage Soviet aggression continued to be decisive. In September 1947, the CIA concluded that the Soviets would not seek to conquer Western Europe for several reasons: they would recognize their inability to control hostile populations; they would fear triggering a war with the United States that could not be won; and they would prefer to gain hegemony by political and economic means. In October 1947, the Joint Intelligence Staff maintained that for three years at least the Soviet Union would take no action that would precipitate a military conflict.

Even the ominous developments during the first half of 1948 did not alter these assessments. Despite his alarmist cable of March 5, designed to galvanize congressional support for increased defense expenditures, General Lucius Clay, the American military governor in Germany, did not believe war imminent. A few days later, the CIA concluded that the communist takeover in Czechoslovakia would not increase Soviet capabilities significantly and reflected no alteration in Soviet tactics. On March 16, the CIA reported to the president, "The weight of logic, as well as evidence, also leads to the conclusion that the Soviets will not resort to military force within the next sixty days." While this assessment was far from reassuring, army and navy intelligence experts concurred that the Soviets still wanted to avoid war, the question was whether war would erupt as a result of "miscalculation" by either the United States or Russia. After talking to Foreign Minister V. M. Molotov in June, Ambassador Smith concluded that Soviet leaders would not resort to active hostilities. During the Berlin blockade, army intelligence reported few signs of Soviet preparations for war; naval intelligence maintained that the Soviets desired to avoid war yet consolidate their position in East Germany. In October 1948, the Military Intelligence Division of the army endorsed a British appraisal that "all the evidence available indicates that the Soviet Union is not preparing to go to war in the near future." In December Acting Secretary of State Robert Lovett summed up the longstanding American perspective when he emphasized that he saw "no evidence that Soviet intentions run toward launching a sudden military attack on the western nations at this time. It would not be in character with the tradition or mentality of the Soviet leaders to resort to such a measure unless they felt themselves either politically extremely weak, or militarily extremely strong."

Although American defense officials recognized that the Soviets had substantial military assets, they remained confident that the Soviet Union did not feel extremely strong. Military analysts studying Russian capabilities noted that the Soviets were rapidly mechanizing infantry units and enhancing their firepower and mobility. It was estimated during the winter of 1946–47 that the Soviets could mobilize six million troops in thirty days and twelve million in six months, providing sufficient manpower to overrun all important parts of Eurasia. The Soviets were also believed to be utilizing German scientists and German technological know-how to improve their submarine force, develop rockets and missiles, and acquire knowledge about the atomic bomb. During 1947 and 1948, it was reported as well that the Soviets were making rapid progress in the development of high performance jet fighters and already possessed several hundred intermediate range bombers comparable to the American B-29.

Even so, American military analysts were most impressed with Soviet weaknesses and vulnerabilities. The Soviets had no long-range strategic air force, no atomic bomb, and meager air defenses. Moreover, the Soviet navy was considered ineffective except for its submarine forces. The Joint Logistic Plans Committee and the Military Intelligence Division of the War Department estimated that the Soviet Union would require approximately fifteen years to overcome wartime losses in manpower and industry, ten years to redress the shortage of technicians, five to ten years to develop a strategic air force, fifteen to twenty-five years to construct a modern navy, ten years to refurbish military transport, ten years (or less) to quell resistance in occupied areas, fifteen to twenty years to establish a military infrastructure in the Far East, three to ten years to acquire the atomic bomb, and an unspecified number of years to remove the vulnerability of the Soviet rail-net and petroleum industry to long-range bombing. For several years at least, the Soviet capability for sustained attack against North America would be very limited. In January 1946 the Joint Intelligence Staff concluded that "the offensive capabilities of the United States are manifestly superior to those of the U.S.S.R. and any war between the U.S. and the USSR would be far more costly to the Soviet Union than to the United States.". . .

If American defense officials did not expect a Soviet military attack, why, then, were they so fearful of losing control of Eurasia? The answer rests less in American assessments of Soviet military capabilities and short-term military intentions than in appraisals of economic and political conditions throughout Europe and Asia. Army officials in particular, because of their occupation roles in Germany, Japan, Austria, and Korea, were aware of the postwar plight of these areas. Key military men—Generals Clay, Douglas MacArthur, John Hilldring, and Oliver P. Echols and Colonel Charles H. Bonesteel—became alarmed by the prospects of famine, disease, anarchy, and revolution. They recognized that communist parties could exploit the distress and that the Russians could capitalize upon it to spread Soviet influence. As early as June 1945, Rear Admiral Ellery Stone, the American commissioner in Italy, wrote that wartime devastation had created fertile soil for the growth of communism in Italy and the enlargement of the Soviet sphere. MacArthur also feared that, if the Japanese economy remained emasculated and reforms were not undertaken, communism would spread. Clay, too, was acutely aware that German communists were depicting themselves and their beliefs as their country's only hope of salvation. In the spring of 1946 military planners, working on contingency plans for the emergency withdrawal of American troops from Germany, should war with Russia unexpectedly occur, also took note of the economic turmoil and political instability in neighboring countries, especially France. Sensitivity to the geopolitical dimensions of the socioeconomic crisis of the postwar era impelled Chief of Staff Eisenhower to give high priority in the army budget to assistance for occupied areas. . . .

In brief, during 1946 and 1947, defense officials witnessed a dramatic unraveling of the geopolitical foundations and socioeconomic structure of international affairs. Britain's economic weakness and withdrawal from the eastern Mediterranean, India's independence movement, civil war in China, nationalist insurgencies in Indo-China and the Dutch East Indies, Zionist claims to Palestine and Arab resentment, German and Japanese economic paralysis, communist inroads in France and Italy—all were ominous developments. Defense officials recognized that the Soviet Union had not created these circumstances but believed that Soviet leaders would exploit them. Should communists take power, even without direct Russian intervention, the Soviet Union, it was assumed, would gain predominant control of the resources of these areas because of the postulated subservience of communist parties everywhere to the Kremlin. Should nationalist uprisings persist, communists seize power in underdeveloped countries, and Arabs revolt against American support of a Jewish state, the petroleum and raw materials of critical areas might be denied the West. The imminent possibility existed that, even without Soviet military aggression, the resources of Eurasia could fall under Russian control. With these resources, the Soviet Union would be able to overcome its chronic economic weaknesses, achieve defense in depth, and challenge American power—perhaps even by military force.

In this frightening postwar environment American assessments of Soviet long-term intentions were transformed. When World War II ended, military planners initially looked upon Soviet aims in foreign affairs as arising from the Kremlin's view of power politics, Soviet strategic imperatives, historical Russian ambitions, and Soviet reactions to moves by the United States and Great Britain. American intelligence analysts and strategic planners most frequently discussed Soviet actions in Eastern Europe, the Balkans, the Near East, and Manchuria as efforts to establish an effective security system. Despite enormous Soviet gains during the war, many assessments noted that, in fact, the Soviets had not yet achieved a safe security zone, especially on their southern periphery. While Forrestal, Deane, and most of the planners in the army's Operations Division possessed a skeptical, perhaps even sinister, view of Soviet intentions, the still prevailing outlook at the end of 1945 was to dismiss the role of ideology in Soviet foreign policy yet emphasize Soviet distrust of foreigners; to stress Soviet expansionism but acknowledge the possibility of accommodation; to abhor Soviet domination of Eastern Europe but discuss Soviet policies elsewhere in terms of power and influence; and to dwell upon the Soviet preoccupation with security yet acknowledge doubt about ultimate Soviet intentions.

This orientation changed rapidly during 1946. In January, the Joint War Plans Committee observed that "the long-term objective [of the Soviet Union] is deemed to be establishment of predominant influence over the Eurasian land mass and the strategic approaches thereto." Reports of the new military attaché in Moscow went further, claiming that "the ultimate aim of Soviet foreign policy seems to be the dominance of Soviet influence throughout the world" and "the final aim . . . is the destruction of the capitalist system." Soon thereafter, [George F.] Kennan's "long telegram" was widely distributed among defense officials, on whom it had considerable impact. Particularly suggestive was his view that Soviet leaders needed the theme of capitalist encirclement to justify their autocratic rule. Also influential were Kennan's convictions that the Soviet leaders aimed to shatter the international authority of the United States and were beyond reason and conciliation. . . .

Yet these assessments did not seriously grapple with contradictory evidence. While emphasizing Soviet military capabilities, strategic ambitions, and diplomatic intransigence, reports like the Clifford-Elsey memorandum of September 1946 and the Joint Chiefs of Staff report 1696 (upon which the Clifford-Elsey memorandum heavily relied) disregarded numerous signs of Soviet weakness, moderation, and circumspection. During 1946 and 1947 intelligence analysts described the withdrawal of Russian troops from northern Norway, Manchuria, Bornholm, and Iran (from the latter under pressure, of course). Numerous intelligence sources reported the reduction of Russian troops in Eastern Europe and the extensive demobilization going on within the Soviet Union. In October 1947 the Joint Intelligence Committee forecast a Soviet army troop strength during 1948 and 1949 of less than two million men. Soviet military expenditures appeared to moderate. Other reports dealt with the inadequacies of Soviet transportation and bridging equipment for the conduct of offensive operations in Eastern Europe. And, as already noted, assessments of the Soviet economy revealed persistent problems likely to restrict Soviet adventurism.

Experience suggested that the Soviet Union was by no means uniformly hostile or unwilling to negotiate with the United States. In April 1946, a few days after a State-War-Navy subcommittee issued an alarming political estimate of Soviet policy (for use in American military estimates), Ambassador Smith reminded the State Department that the Soviet press was not unalterably critical of the United States, that the Russians had withdrawn from Bornholm, that Stalin had given a moderate speech on the United Nations, and that Soviet demobilization continued apace. The next month General Lincoln, who had accompanied Byrnes to Paris for the meeting of the council of foreign ministers, acknowledged that the Soviets had been willing to make numerous concessions regarding Tripolitania, the Dodecanese, and Italian reparations. In the spring of 1946, General Echols, General Clay, and Secretary Patterson again maintained that the French constituted the major impediment to an agreement on united control of Germany. At the same time the Soviets ceased pressing for territorial adjustments with Turkey. After the diplomatic exchanges over the Dardanelles in the late summer of 1946 the Soviets did not again ask for either a revision of the Montreux Convention or the acquisition of bases in the Dardanelles. In early 1947 central intelligence delineated more than a half-dozen instances of Soviet moderation or concessions. In April the Military Intelligence Division noted that the Soviets had limited their involvement in the Middle East, diminished their ideological rhetoric, and given only moderate support to Chinese communists. In the months preceding the Truman Doctrine, Soviet behavior—as noted by American military officials and intelligence analysts—hardly justified the inflammatory rhetoric [Dean] Acheson and Truman used to secure congressional support for aid to Greece and Turkey. Perhaps this is why General Marshall, as secretary of state, refrained from such language himself and preferred to focus on the socioeconomic aspects of the unfolding crisis.

In their overall assessments of Soviet long-term intentions, however, military planners dismissed all evidence of Soviet moderation, circumspection, and restraint. In fact, as 1946 progressed, these planners seemed to spend less time analyzing Soviet intentions and more time estimating Soviet capabilities. Having accepted the notion that the two powers were locked in an ideological struggle of indefinite duration and conscious of the rapid demobilization of American forces and the constraints on American defense expenditures, they no longer explored ways of accommodating a potential adversary's legitimate strategic requirements or pondered how American initiatives might influence the Soviet Union's definition of its objectives. Information not confirming prevailing assumptions either was ignored in overall assessments of Soviet intentions or was used to illustrate that the Soviets were shifting tactics but not altering objectives. Reflective of the emerging mentality was a report from the Joint Chiefs of Staff to the president in July 1946 that deleted sections from previous studies that had outlined Soviet weaknesses. A memorandum sent by Secretary Patterson to the president at the same time was designed by General Lauris Norstad, director of the War Department's Plans and Operations Division, to answer questions about relations with the Soviet Union "without ambiguity." Truman, Clark Clifford observed many years later, liked things in black and white.

During 1946 and early 1947, the conjunction of Soviet ideological fervor and socioeconomic turmoil throughout Eurasia contributed to the growth of a myopic view of Soviet long-term policy objectives and to enormous apprehension lest the Soviet Union gain control of all the resources of Eurasia, thereby endangering the national security of the United States. American assessments of Soviet short-term military intentions had not altered; Soviet military capabilities had not significantly increased, and Soviet foreign policy positions had not greatly shifted. But defense officials were acutely aware of America's own rapidly diminishing capabilities, of

Britain's declining military strength, of the appeal of communist doctrine to most of the underdeveloped world, and of the opportunities open to communist parties throughout most of Eurasia as a result of prevailing socioeconomic conditions. War Department papers, studies of the joint chiefs, and intelligence analyses repeatedly described the restiveness of colonial peoples that had sapped British and French strength, the opportunities for communist parties in France, Italy, and even Spain to capitalize upon indigenous conditions, and the ability of the Chinese communists to defeat the nationalists and make the resources and manpower of Manchuria and North China available to the Soviet Union. In this turbulent international arena, the survival of liberal ideals and capitalist institutions was anything but assured. "We could point to the economic benefits of Capitalism," commented one important War Department paper in April 1946, "but these benefits are concentrated rather than widespread, and, at present, are genuinely suspect throughout Europe and in many other parts of the world.". . .

During late 1946 and early 1947, the Truman administration assumed the initiative by creating German Bizonia, providing military assistance to Greece and Turkey, allocating massive economic aid to Western Europe, and reassessing economic policy toward Japan. These initiatives were aimed primarily at tackling the internal sources of unrest upon which communist parties capitalized and at rehabilitating the industrial heartlands of Eurasia. . . .

Yet if war should unexpectedly occur, the United States had to have the capability to inflict incalculable damage upon the Soviet Union. Accordingly, Truman shelved (after some serious consideration) proposals for international control of atomic energy. The Baruch Plan, as it evolved in the spring and summer of 1946, was heavily influenced by defense officials and service officers who wished to avoid any significant compromise with the Soviet Union. They sought to perpetuate America's nuclear monopoly as long as possible in order to counterbalance Soviet conventional strength, deter Soviet adventurism, and bolster American negotiating leverage. When negotiations at the United Nations for international control of atomic energy languished for lack of agreement on its implementation, the way was clear for the Truman administration gradually to adopt a strategy based on air power and atomic weapons. This strategy was initially designed to destroy the adversary's will and capability to wage war by annihilating Russian industrial, petroleum, and urban centers. After completing their study of the 1946 Bikini atomic tests, the Joint Chiefs of Staff in July 1947 called for an enlargement of the nuclear arsenal. While Truman and Forrestal insisted on limiting military expenditures, government officials moved vigorously to solve problems in the production of plutonium, to improve nuclear cores and assembly devices, and to increase the number of aircraft capable of delivering atomic bombs. After much initial postwar disorganization, the General Advisory Committee to the Atomic Energy Commission could finally report to the president at the end of 1947 that "great progress" had been made in the atomic program. From June 30, 1947, to June 30, 1948, the number of bombs in the stockpile increased from thirteen to fifty. Although at the time of the Berlin crisis the United States was not prepared to launch a strategic air offensive against the Soviet Union, substantial progress had been made in the development of the nation's air-atomic capabilities. By the end of 1948, the United States had at least eighteen nuclear-capable B-50s, four B-36s, and almost three times as many nuclear-capable B-29s as had been available at the end of 1947.

During late 1947 and early 1948, the administration also responded to pleas of the Joint Chiefs of Staff to augment the overseas base system and to acquire bases in closer proximity to the Soviet Union. Negotiations were conducted with the British to gain access to bases in the Middle East and an agreement was concluded for the acquisition of air facilities in Libya. Admiral [Richard L.] Conolly made a secret deal with the French to secure air and communication rights and to stockpile oil, aviation gas, and ammunition in North Africa. Plans also were discussed for post-occupation bases in Japan, and considerable progress was made in refurbishing and constructing airfields in Turkey. During 1948 the Turks also received one hundred eighty F-47 fighter-bombers, thirty B-26 bombers, and eighty-one C-47 cargo planes. The F-47s and B-26s, capable of reaching the vital Ploesti and Baku oil fields, were more likely to be used to slow down a Soviet advance through Turkey or Iran, thereby affording time to activate a strategic air offensive from prospective bases in the Cairo-Suez area.

Despite these developments, the joint chiefs and military planners grew increasingly uneasy with the budgetary constraints under which they operated. They realized that American initiatives, however necessary, placed the Soviet Union on the defensive, created an incendiary situation, and made war more likely—though still improbable. In July 1947, intelligence analysts in the War Department maintained that the Truman Doctrine and the Marshall Plan had resulted in a more aggressive Soviet attitude toward the United States and had intensified tensions. "These tensions have caused a sharper line of demarcation between West and East tending to magnify the significance of conflicting points of view, and reducing the possibility of agreement on any point." Intelligence officers understood that the Soviets would perceive American efforts to build strategic highways, construct airfields, and transfer fighter bombers to Turkey as a threat to Soviet security and to the oilfields in the Caucasus. The latter, noted the director of naval intelligence, "lie within easy air striking range of countries on her southern flank, and the Soviet leaders will be particularly sensitive to any political threat from this area, however remote." Intelligence analysts also recognized that the Soviets would view the Marshall Plan as a threat to Soviet control in Eastern Europe as well as a death-knell to communist attempts to capture power peacefully in Western Europe. And defense officials were well aware that the Soviets would react angrily to plans for currency reform in German Trizonia and to preparations for a West German republic. "The whole Berlin crisis," army planners informed Eisenhower, "has arisen as a result of . . . actions on the part of the Western Powers." In sum, the Soviet clampdown in Eastern Europe and the attempt to blockade Berlin did not come as shocks to defense officials, who anticipated hostile and defensive Soviet reactions to American initiatives.

The real consternation of the Joint Chiefs of Staff and other high-ranking civilian and military officials in the defense agencies stemmed from their growing conviction that the United States was undertaking actions and assuming commitments that now required greater military capabilities. Recognizing that American initiatives, aimed at safeguarding Eurasia from further communist inroads, might be perceived as endangering Soviet interests, it was all the more important to be ready for any eventuality. Indeed, to the extent that anxieties about the prospects of war escalated in March and April 1948, these fears did not stem from estimates that the Soviets were planning further aggressive action after the communist seizure of power in Czechoslovakia but from apprehensions that ongoing American initiatives might provoke an attack. . . .

Having conceived of American national security in terms of Western control and of American access to the resources of Eurasia outside the Soviet sphere, American defense officials now considered it imperative to develop American military capabilities to meet a host of contingencies that might emanate from further Soviet encroachments or from indigenous communist unrest. Such contingencies were sure to arise because American strategy depended so heavily on the rebuilding of Germany and Japan, Russia's traditional enemies, as well as on air power, atomic weapons, and bases on the Soviet periphery. Such contingencies also were predictable because American strategy depended so heavily on the restoration of stability in Eurasia, a situation increasingly unlikely in an era of nationalist turmoil, social unrest, and rising economic expectations. Although the desire of the national military establishment for large increments in defense expenditures did not prevail in the tight budgetary environment and presidential election year of 1948, the mode of thinking about national security that subsequently accelerated the arms race and precipitated military interventionism in Asia was already widespread among defense officials.

Indeed, the dynamics of the Cold War after 1948 are easier to comprehend when one grasps the breadth of the American conception of national security that had emerged between 1945 and 1948. This conception included a strategic sphere of influence within the Western Hemisphere, domination of the Atlantic and Pacific oceans, an extensive system of outlying bases to enlarge the strategic frontier and project American power, an even more extensive system of transit rights to facilitate conversion of commercial air bases to military use, access to the resources and markets of most of Eurasia, denial of those resources to a prospective enemy, and the maintenance of nuclear superiority. Not every one of these ingredients, it must be emphasized, was considered vital. Hence, American officials could acquiesce, however grudgingly, to a Soviet sphere in Eastern Europe and could avoid direct intervention in China. But cumulative challenges to these concepts of national security were certain to provoke a firm American response. This occurred initially in 1947–48 when decisions were made in favor of the Truman Doctrine, Marshall Plan, military assistance, Atlantic alliance, and German and Japanese rehabilitation. Soon thereafter, the "loss" of China, the Soviet detonation of an atomic bomb, and the North Korean attack on South Korea intensified the perception of threat to prevailing concepts of national security. The Truman administration responded with military assistance to southeast Asia, a decision to build the hydrogen bomb, direct military intervention in Korea, a commitment to station troops permanently in Europe, expansion of the American alliance system, and a massive rearmament program in the United States. Postulating a long-term Soviet intention to gain world domination, the American conception of national security, based on geopolitical and economic imperatives, could not allow for additional losses in Eurasia, could not risk a challenge to its nuclear supremacy, and could not permit any infringement on its ability to defend in depth or to project American force from areas in close proximity to the Soviet homeland.

To say this is neither to exculpate the Soviet government for its inhumane treatment of its own citizens nor to suggest that Soviet foreign policy was idle or benign. Indeed, Soviet behavior in Eastern Europe was often deplorable; the Soviets sought opportunities in the Dardanelles, northern Iran, and Manchuria; the Soviets hoped to orient Germany and Austria toward the East; and the Soviets sometimes endeavored to use communist parties to expand Soviet influence in areas beyond the periphery of Russian military power. But, then again, the Soviet Union had lost twenty million dead during the war, had experienced the destruction of seventeen hundred towns, thirty-one thousand factories, and one hundred thousand collective farms, and had witnessed the devastation of the rural economy with the Nazi slaughter of twenty million hogs and seventeen million head of cattle. What is remarkable is that after 1946 these monumental losses received so little attention when American defense analysts studied the motives and intentions of Soviet policy; indeed, defense officials did little to analyze the threat perceived by the Soviets. Yet these same officials had absolutely no doubt that the wartime experiences and sacrifices of the United States, though much less devastating than those of Soviet Russia, demonstrated the need for and entitled the United States to oversee the resuscitation of the industrial heartlands of Germany and Japan, establish a viable balance of power in Eurasia, and militarily dominate the Eurasian rimlands, thereby safeguarding American access to raw materials and control over all sea and air approaches to North America.

To suggest a double standard is important only insofar as it raises fundamental questions about the conceptualization and implementation of American national security policy. If Soviet pol-. icy was aggressive, bellicose, and ideological, perhaps America's reliance on overseas bases, air power, atomic weapons, military al- liances, and the rehabilitation of Germany and Japan was the best course to follow, even if the effect may have been to exacerbate So- viet anxieties and suspicions. But even when one attributes the worst intentions to the Soviet Union, one might still ask whether American presuppositions and apprehensions about the benefits that would accrue to the Soviet Union as a result of communist (and even revolutionary nationalist) gains anywhere in Eurasia tended to simplify international realities, magnify the breadth of American interests, engender commitments beyond American ca- pabilities, and dissipate the nation's strength and credibility. And, perhaps even more importantly, if Soviet foreign policies tended to be opportunist, reactive, nationalistic, and contradictory, as some recent writers have claimed and as some contemporary analysts suggested, then one might also wonder whether America's own conception of national security tended, perhaps unintentionally, to engender anxieties and to provoke countermeasures from a proud, suspicious, insecure, and cruel government that was at the same time legitimately apprehensive about the long-term implications arising from the rehabilitation of traditional enemies and the devel- opment of foreign bases on the periphery of the Soviet homeland.

Vladislav Zubok and Constantine Pleshakov

STALIN'S ROAD TO THE COLD WAR

Russian scholars Vladislav Zubok and Constantine Pleshakov explore the complex roots of Stalin's foreign policy in this excerpt from their prize- winning book, *Inside the Kremlin's Cold War* (1996). Drawing on previ- ously unavailable Soviet archival sources, they sketch a picture of Soviet foreign policy during the early Cold War period that stands at odds with much Western scholarship—traditionalist and revisionist alike. Zubok and Pleshakov contend that Stalinist foreign policy cannot be seen either

as inexorably expansionist, as traditionalist scholars claim, or as strictly reactive, as many revisionist scholars suggest. Rather, they argue that three interrelated factors shaped the Soviet road to Cold War confrontation with the West: the personalities of Soviet leaders, of whom the suspicious and insecure Stalin proved by far the most decisive; the peculiar blend of ideological and security compulsions found in all top Soviet leaders of the era; and the actions of the Western powers, most especially those of the United States. A "revolutionary-imperial paradigm," they propose, best explains postwar Soviet behavior.

Vladislav Zubok and Constantine Pleshakov have both written widely on the Soviet Union and the Cold War. Zubok is currently a fellow at the National Security Archive in Washington, D.C. and has been extremely active in the Washington-based Cold War International History Project. Pleshakov is a historian at the Institute of the USA and Canada, Russian Academy of Sciences, Moscow.

Late on the morning of June 24, 1945, the golden clocks on the Kremlin's Spasskaya Tower chimed and everyone in the Soviet Union with a radio listened to those familiar sounds. The great Parade of Victory was about to begin. All along Red Square and the area surrounding it, victorious troops in decorated uniforms, with captured Nazi banners, in formations and in the turrets of tanks, all perfectly still, waited for a signal to march. Thousands of people crowded into the guest stalls. Suddenly, thunderous applause spread through the crowd as the ruling State Committee of Defense emerged from the Kremlin and began to climb the stairs of Lenin's Mausoleum. It was this group that had replaced the Communist Politburo during the four years of the most devastating war in the world's history. Leading the others, walking at some distance from them, was Joseph Stalin, the head of the USSR.

In just a few years the same leaders who celebrated the triumph over Nazi Germany would clash with their former allies, the United States and Great Britain, in a costly and protracted struggle. To understand how the Soviets perceived a conflict with the West, one has to understand what happened in the deep recesses of the Kremlin. Joseph Stalin and his lieutenants were rulers of a special type—tyrannical, cruel, and certainly loathsome in many ways—who defined their legitimacy in the terms they themselves set and harshly imposed on the people of the USSR. Nevertheless, in 1945, with the defeat of Nazi Germany still fresh in everyone's mind, these men were united in victory with the people they ruled.

The Kremlin leaders and their regime experienced their golden hour representing the triumphant forces of history. They carried on the legacy of Russia as the savior of the world, a legacy willingly shared by millions of their countrymen. In order to understand the Cold War from the Soviet perspective, one must understand the importance of that moment and the larger historic legacy of Russia and the Russian Revolution, vindicated by the victory of 1945.

The Soviet worldview had been shaped by a history that was dramatically different from that of the West. The legacy of czarist history, the Bolshevik revolution, the Civil War, and the experience of World War II all contributed to a unique Soviet perspective. Another, important factor that significantly shaped the Soviet perspective was that Russia represented not only a nation but also a distinctive imperial civilization. One could argue that, with the exception of the period of the Mongol yoke (thirteenth-fifteenth centuries), Russia has always been an empire. And even during the Mongol interlude, when its land had become a province of a grandiose nomandic mega-state, Russia still remained in the imperial framework. The traditional imperial legacy was an insurmountable obstacle to Russia's becoming an "ordinary" nation-state. Despite their intentions to build a brave new world from scratch, Russian Communists simply could not break with the imperial mode of thinking.

At the end of the fifteenth century the concept of Moscow as the Third Rome had emerged; two previous Romes had fallen, for they had sinned, and (after the collapse of Constantinople) it was now time for Moscow to be the eternal keeper of the Christian faith. This Russian messianism became the spiritual backbone of the expanding Russian empire, which perceived itself as nothing short of sacred. After the revolution of 1917, however, Soviet Russia assumed the responsibility of spreading the Marxist message. Now, as the keeper of the Marxist faith, it would emancipate mankind rather than Orthodox Christianity.

History gave the Russians more concrete reasons to see themselves as saviors of the world. Russians credited themselves with having rescued Europe from two invading powers—the Mongols in the thirteenth century and Napoleon's army in the early nineteenth century. The belief that Russia was the protector of mankind against a militant anti-Christ was strongly reinforced by the victory over the Nazis in 1945. In the European war theater the Soviet contribution to victory was decisive and costly. The enormous sacrifice of the Russian people in the Second World War had led the Soviet leaders to believe that the Allies owed them a great deal.

The fact that the Soviet regime had been founded by Communist revolutionaries further alienated Russia from the West and contributed to its messianic legacy. The proletarian revolution, as envisaged by Marx and Engels, was meant to create an unprecedented universal proletarian empire. By the end of the nineteenth century, however, Marxism in Western Europe was becoming more and more national, and was being transformed into the Social-Democratic projects of a welfare nation-state. The Socialists of France and Germany and even of Russia supported World War I as a war between nation-states. V. I. Lenin, the founder of bolshevism, found himself alone when he called for transforming the imperialist European war into a civil class war. His call, after the defeat of a leftist revolution in Germany in 1918, failed to ignite any other nations. Only in Russia, where the concept of a nation state had totally failed, did Lenin lead the people to the utopia of a universal proletarian empire without borders. The imperial implications of both Marxist thought and Russian history provide the broad background and context for understanding Soviet involvement in the Cold War.

The origins of Cold War thinking from the Soviet side are often interpreted in the West in a simplistic manner: Stalin wanted to conquer the world and so switched from cooperation to confrontation. The American revisionist school generally regards the Cold War as a bilateral process, with Stalin reacting to certain assertive actions by Washington. In the case of Stalin's leadership, however, we are facing something more complicated than just expansionism or "reactions." Stalin and generations of Soviet bureaucrats who grew up with him or under his rule shared a complex attitude toward the outside world that had its roots in Russian history, Marxism, and, in its modified version, Leninism. It would be wrong to interpret Communist behavior in the world arena in terms of either geopolitics or ideology. We prefer to conceive of this conduct as the result of the symbiosis of imperial expansionism and ideological proselytism.

When Lenin came to power in 1917, he was driven by a utopian dream that the fire of the world revolution, having started in Russia, would engulf the world. In this context in 1918 he attempted to abandon the world of geopolitics. If Russia were to prevail over Germany in the First World War, any regime in Russia would have to collaborate with the Allies. Instead, Lenin signed a separate peace treaty (the Treaty of Brest-Litovsk) with Kaiser Germany in which he sacrificed the most developed areas of European Russia, even those that Germany had not yet occupied. The loss of these crucial territories—a geopolitical catastrophe—could have been averted only through military cooperation with the major allies of czarist Russia: Great Britain, France, and the United States. But this was unacceptable to Lenin, for the leader of the Russian Revolution had his eyes only on consolidation of the new regime— and for a particular purpose. Preserving Russia as the headquarters of world revolution promised the spread of the revolutionary ideology around the globe, or at least in Eastern and Central Europe.

In 1922, after signing the Treaty of Rapallo with Germany, Lenin switched to a more complex model of Marxist state behavior, coming very close to elaborating the revolutionary-imperial paradigm. But the father of the Russian Revolution did not have the slightest intention of canceling ideology as a motivation in the making of foreign policy. The result was a strange amalgam of ideological proselytism and geopolitical pragmatism that began to evolve in Soviet Russia in the early 1920s. Marxism was a utopian teaching, but since it proclaimed that the goal of the material transformation of the world was to be realized in a violent confrontation with its opponents, Communist proselytes developed a whole set of highly effective political institutions. Utopian ideals gave way to a ruthless and cynical interpretation of the realpolitik tradition.

The combination of traditional Russian messianism and Marxist ideology produced something larger (though more fragile) than its parts taken separately. The two phenomena became completely blurred in the USSR by the 1920s and remained that way until the collapse of the Soviet regime in 1991. Together they provide a theoretical explanation of Soviet foreign policy behavior—the revolutionary-imperial paradigm.

Lenin's comrades-in-arms, such as Stalin and Molotov, and even the younger generation of Soviet leaders represented by [Nikita] Khrushchev, would inherit this ambivalent worldview.

Each of them would make his own intricate Cold War journey, guided by the two misleading suns of empire and revolution. . . .

Instrumental to any society, leaders were the driving force of the USSR. The changing society and the international environment at some points were even ignored by the Soviet demigods, though none of them could disregard entirely the world around them. Stalin throughout his life carefully monitored the possible dangerous consequences of Western ideological influence on his regime. Similarly, the problem of international security was never ignored during the Cold War years. The ominous and almost lethal German invasion of Russia in 1941 took the Soviet leadership by surprise and taught them a tragic lesson. The nuclear issue in particular was one of the major factors predetermining the actions of all members of the Kremlin leadership. . . .

Another major issue concerns the extent to which the Soviet Union wanted the Cold War. Without a doubt the imperial tradition of Russia, reinforced by Marxist globalism, predestined Soviet expansionism. But the Cold War emerged from the ruins of World War II, and this hard fact raises three problems. First, there was the issue of the appropriate rewards for the Soviet contribution to the war. Of paramount importance in Europe and recognized as such by Britain and the United States, the Soviet war effort had almost unimaginable costs. More than twenty-seven million people died— the majority of them young men between the ages of eighteen and thirty, but also women and children. The European sphere of the USSR was devastated by the German war machine. Shouldn't Stalin's leadership expect special treatment from Western powers after such a sacrifice? And how did this expectation affect Soviet relations with the West after 1945—be it concerning economic assistance (generous reparations from Germany, direct American aid) or recognized spheres of influence for the Soviet Union in Europe (each territory—Poland, Hungary, and Czechoslovakia—having been fertilized with Soviet blood)?

Second, given the scale of human and material losses, the Soviet Union, though it had troops almost all over Eurasia from Germany to Manchuria, could not sustain the stress of another war. In this respect, it is hard to imagine that Stalin could have deliberately chosen to pursue brinkmanship with the West. The nuclear disability of the Soviet Union in 1945–1949 also argues for the belief that Stalin's original intention of 1945–1947 was to proceed with some kind of partnership with the West.

Third, there was the issue of complete Soviet cooperation with the United States and Britain during the war. The tension this cooperation often engendered did not preclude a search for solutions and even unilateral concessions on both sides. Stalin disbanded the Comintern in 1943; Roosevelt and Churchill formally recognized the Soviet zone of security in Eastern Europe in 1943–1945. Could Stalin have believed that this intense interaction was to end abruptly as soon as the war was won? Or did this new mode of understanding based upon mutual compromise imply postwar cooperation? Could Stalin—especially given his fascination with the Russian imperial past—envisage some sort of jointly managed system of international relations, not unlike that which followed the Napoleonic Wars? We do have evidence that Stalin identified himself with Alexander I, a victorious emperor and a postwar partner of his wartime allies at the Vienna Congress of 1815.

The Soviet wartime experience did not in itself regulate Stalin's attitude toward the West. There was also the xenophobic nature of Stalin's regime, which had deep roots in the past. Stalin was aware that any openness toward the outside world could mean the seeds of political opposition in the USSR. Russian czarist history taught a lesson from the Napoleonic Wars, after which Russian officers, having seen Europe, did try to abolish autocracy in their own country in the Decembrists' mutiny of 1825. . . .

In February 1945, in the Palace of Livadia at Yalta, the Western Allies did something that millions of people, including thousands of politicians and dozens of historians in the West, would for decades after regret and criticize: they acknowledged that the enormous Soviet sacrifices and successes in the war entitled the Soviet Union to a preeminent role in Eastern Europe. This was reflected in a number of key decisions that during the Cold War would be called "the treason of Yalta" or the "Yalta agreements." The Western Allies recognized the Soviet-made Provisional Government of National Unity in Poland on the condition that some members of the government-in-exile in London and of the Polish Home Army underground be added to it, and that free and unfettered elections take place as soon as possible. Roosevelt and Churchill also agreed to Stalin's plans to move Poland eastward by annexing the lands up to the Curzon line and compensating the

Poles with Germany's Eastern Silesia, part of Saxony, and Western Prussia. This meant that Eastern Prussia would belong to the Soviet Union, a new geopolitical fact that Stalin confirmed later at Potsdam. Even before the Soviet leader promised to join the fighting in the Far East, he found that the Western leaders supported his interest in long-sought spheres of influence there. The Yalta Conference advocated the status quo in Outer Mongolia, thus leaving it within the Soviet domain and outside China. When U.S. Ambassador Harriman asked Stalin what he wanted in exchange for Russia's entry in the war against Japan, Stalin brought out a map and said that "the Kurile Islands and the lower Sakhalin should be returned to Russia." He then "drew a line around the southern part of the Liaotung Peninsula, including Port Arthur and Dairen, saying that the Russians wished again [as before 1905] to lease these ports and the surrounding area." Roosevelt and Churchill complied with these demands as well.

In expectation of this moment Stalin refrained from promoting revolutionary Marxist-oriented movements or unilateral expansion. The commitments to Soviet security interests that he extracted from the Allies in Teheran and especially Yalta for some time looked to him to be the surest way to create a protective territorial belt around the USSR, to neutralize the resurgence of its traditional geopolitical rivals, Germany and Japan. The USSR had to digest its territorial and geopolitical gains and heal its terrible wounds. Stalin, when he analyzed the world in terms of the last interwar period (1918–1939), had ample reason to expect that there would be a protracted period of "capitalist stabilization," a return of the United States to isolationism, and a struggle of European powers for preservation of their vast imperial possessions. Thus a number of considerations led him to believe after V-Day in Europe that some mode of cooperation with the United States and Great Britain could be imaginable after the war as well.

The empirical evidence confirmed for Stalin that his country had been fully recognized as a partner in managing the world. The diplomacy of the Grand Alliance of the war years seemed to have started a new chapter in international relations. The Soviet Union had been accepted as a great power, equaled only by the United States and Great Britain. This equality manifested itself in the Soviet Union's full participation in preparing the outlines for the postwar world. The Big Three were steadily coming to a mutual understanding on spheres of influence in Europe and Asia. The territories annexed by Stalin in 1939–1940 during his alliance with Hitler were recognized de facto as part of the Soviet Union. Later, in the Cold War days, the United States would insist that it had never recognized the incorporation of the Baltics into the USSR. In 1943–1945, during the Big Three meetings, however, the three leaders and their foreign ministers had spent hours discussing the problem of elections in Poland and of the legitimacy of the Poles' "London" government, but the issue of free elections in Estonia, Latvia, and Lithuania was tacitly omitted.

As for the countries of Eastern Europe, the Allies were step by step agreeing to the introduction of Soviet influence there. These countries were not supposed to be Sovietized, but Churchill did agree with Stalin on the percentage of influence that the USSR and Britain should get in each country in Eastern Europe. The Polish issue had been the most acute one and did cause quarrels and antagonisms among the Big Three. But in Yalta and Potsdam, London and Washington were supporting the "London Poles" with much less vigor than in 1944.

Even the United Nations, which was created by the Big Three, met Stalin's expectations. The permanent members of the Security Council, where the United States, the USSR, and Great Britain were to dominate (for France was hardly tolerated as a great power and China was infinitely weak), would form the elite club for managing the globe. In late 1944 to early 1945 Stalin took the task of organizing the United Nations as seriously as did Litvinov. To ensure that the U.N. Security Council would, in fact, be a club of great powers, Stalin did much to see that the United States would not stay out. With Stalin's blessing, Molotov and another Soviet diplomat, Dmitry Manuilsky, cooperated with the American drafters on the U.N. Charter—which became for decades a model document in the Wilsonian tradition. To the same end the Kremlin leader also supported New York over Geneva, Vienna, or Prague as the future headquarters of the United Nations, because he wanted the United States to be actively engaged in a future organization of united nations. Simultaneously, Stalin persistently sought and, to his satisfaction, obtained the agreement of Roosevelt and Churchill to grant the Soviet Union veto power in the U.N. Security Council.

By 1945 one could find some rudiments of the revolutionary-imperial paradigm in Stalin's foreign policy, but he was fully prepared to shelve ideology, at least for a time, and adhere only to the concept of a balance of power. Stalin ardently believed in the inevitability of a postwar economic crisis of the capitalist economy and of clashes within the capitalist camp that would provide him with a lot of space for geopolitical maneuvering in Europe and Asia—all within the framework of general cooperation with capitalist countries.

Yet just one year after Yalta, in his first postwar speech in the Bolshoi Theater, on February 9, 1946, Stalin emphasized the importance of ensuring Soviet security unilaterally—through renewed mobilization of domestic resources, belt-tightening, and rearmament. There was only a dying echo of the early hopes for a possible model of peaceful coexistence. He said, "It might be possible to avoid military catastrophes, if there were a way of periodically reapportioning raw materials and markets among the countries according to their economic weight—taking concerted and peaceful decisions." But, he added, "this is impossible to fulfill in the contemporary capitalist conditions of world economic development."

Stalin meant a possible settlement of disputes among the great powers through the redistribution of spheres of influence, but he could not be that explicit. This was the part of his "election" speech addressed to party functionaries, and thus Stalin's point went totally unnoticed. The American embassy in its report on the speech omitted this point completely. George Kennan wrote his famous "long telegram" explaining to officials in the Truman administration that it would be simply impossible to find a modus vivendi with the USSR, the revolutionary heir to the security-obsessed czarist Russia. In another message Kennan wrote, "That suspicion in one degree or another is an integral part of [the] Soviet system, and will not yield entirely to any form of rational persuasion or assurance." From that moment many in the United States regarded Stalin's speech as the declaration of the Cold War. . . .

The shift in Stalin's attitude toward postwar cooperation in 1945–1946 can be attributed in part to his "deep and morbid obsessions and compulsions," which had lain dormant for a while but eventually pushed him to guarantee Soviet security in expectation of the total collapse of relations between the USSR and the Western democracies. These compulsions were of immense international significance, since the power to dictate Soviet foreign policy—and domestic policy as well—belonged to Stalin alone.

One such compulsion was to retain his totalitarian control over the state and society once the war was over. Stalin, reflected the Soviet writer Konstantin Simonov, had "feared a new Decembrism. He had shown Ivan to Europe and Europe to Ivan, as Alexander I did in 1813–1814." Indeed, many Soviet soldiers who participated in the liberation of Europe were appalled at how poorly the standard of living in the Soviet Union compared with that of Europe. Many veterans no longer feared the Soviet secret police and would not be silenced. Some, according to an NKVD (secret police) report to Stalin on January 27, 1946, made anti-Soviet remarks, clashed with local authorities, and even distributed anti-Soviet leaflets.

Stalin, true to form, moved to eradicate this mood before it could develop into even the slightest threat to his power. Upon their return, millions of the Soviets who had stayed abroad, as prisoners of war or in the forces of European resistance groups, were screened—some were eventually shot, and others were sent to the Gulag to be cleansed of any European influence. All this was done when the "popular" legitimacy of Stalin's regime was at its peak, and when, for quite a few Soviet citizens, patriotism and preoccupation with Truman's America, armed with the atomic bomb, overshadowed the frustrations of everyday life.

Another of Stalin's compulsions was his deep suspicion of the motives of the Western Allies. Stalin, as the Yugoslav Communist Milovan Djilas has noted, feared that "the imperialists" would never tolerate great Soviet advances during the war. As pleased as he was with the outcome of Yalta and Potsdam, he looked forward to the struggle ahead. . . .

Two events dramatically altered Stalin's view of the diplomatic landscape and loosed his demons of suspicion: the first was the death of Roosevelt; the second was America's dropping of the A-bomb on Hiroshima.

When Stalin had hoped to encourage London and Washington to resolve recurrent tensions by "redistributing spheres of influence," his dream partner had been Franklin D. Roosevelt. William Taubman correctly sees Roosevelt's death as "a turning point in Soviet-American relations," but fails to appreciate how important Roosevelt was to the Soviet dictator. He was the only president whom Stalin accepted as a partner, even when he felt that FDR was scheming behind his back. In April 1945, when Soviet intelligence informed Stalin of Nazi attempts to conclude a separate peace with the Americans, his faith in the possibility of a partnership with the West was not shaken. As long as the two Western leaders did not, in Stalin's opinion, "gang up" on him, there remained the chance for an international regime of cooperation.

When Roosevelt died and Churchill was not reelected—a total surprise to the Kremlin—Stalin lost his two equals, the opponents with whom he knew he could play a grand game with a good chance of success. There was no longer a common threat or the great cauldron of European war to forge a strong relationship of equals between Stalin and the new Western politicians. Truman, James Byrnes, Clement Attlee, and Ernest Bevin were obviously not powerful enough (and probably also not cynical enough) for Stalin's game. In a matter of months what looked like a classic trilateral diplomacy deteriorated before Stalin's eyes into a hopeless international morass, where many expectations were swept aside by a host of new faces and factors. This must have been stunning to Stalin, who was used to dealing with a maximum of three players. During the party infighting of 1923–1929 it was Stalin and the Kamenev-Zinoviev group against Trotsky, then Stalin and Bukharin against Kamenev-Zinoviev. This pattern of very few players had continued in the international arena in 1939–1944. Now all was changed.

Truman in particular seemed to be an unknown entity: a rookie president was easy prey for crafty manipulators. Yet Stalin did not abandon his hopes for a grand game or "détente." He tested Truman at Potsdam and, after hard bargaining, "got what [he] wanted" on two key issues: reparations from Germany and the future of Poland. Many years later Molotov admitted that, at that moment, "the Americans provided us with a way out that reduced tension between us and our Western allies." Yet this was not to be.

It was the atomic bombardment of Japan and the abrupt end of the war in the Pacific that convinced Stalin that his dream of a postwar partnership was not to be fulfilled. The old demons of insecurity were back. The atomic bomb threw the Kremlin leader off balance—and eventually back into the curse of tyrants: neurotic solitude. . . .

For those who conceive of the despotic Soviet regime as static, consistent, and expansionist at all times, we have argued otherwise. Like all political systems, even the one built by Stalin had a human face and limitations. Three major factors shaped the Kremlin's view of the post-World War II order and later of the Cold War: the personalities of the key Soviet leaders, their peculiar blend of ideological and geopolitical motivations, which we have labeled the revolutionary-imperial paradigm, and the policies of the West, primarily the United States.

Of these three factors, the Soviet leadership was by far the most dynamic and variable. Soviet leaders possessed impressive qualities and suffered terrible delusions and weaknesses. They could be brutal and unreasonable but also prudent, cautious, and patient. Raised in an autocratic state, they were influenced by its dictates and in turn challenged them. Not all of the leaders were die-hard dogmatics. Their whims and innovations, complexes and phobias, shaped a malleable view of the Cold War from the Soviet shore. Sometimes they even enjoyed more flexibility in their roles than their Western counterparts. Yet the messianic prescriptions of revolutionary-imperial ideology loomed large in the political environment in which Soviet leaders struggled, rose, and fell. Ideology was neither the servant nor the master of Soviet foreign policy. But it was the *delirium tremens* of Soviet statesmen, the core of the regime's self-legitimacy, a terrifying delusion they could never shake off.

It is tempting to lay total blame for the Cold War on the delusions of Stalin and his lieutenants. A closer look at the Cold War from the Soviet side reveals, however, that they were not the only culprits in the conflict. We cannot disregard other, complex factors, such as the crass nature of power politics, choices of U.S. and British policy-makers, and the deeper causes of hostility and mistrust between dictatorship and democracy in an uncertain world. Stalin, notwithstanding his reputation as a ruthless tyrant, was not prepared to take a course of unbridled unilateral expansionism after World War II. He wanted to avoid confrontation with the West. He was even ready to see cooperation with the Western powers as a preferable way of building his influence and solving contentious international issues. Thus, the Cold War was not his choice or his brainchild.

The arrangements at Yalta for Eastern Europe, and the critical victories of the Red Army in the Allies' ultimate triumph over the Axis powers, led Stalin to expect that the cooperative regulation of international relations would be possible. For this, by 1945, Stalin was ready to diminish the role of ideology in his postwar diplomacy with the West to a minimal level. He was ready to observe the limits on Soviet spheres of influence in Europe and Asia, and he was prepared to keep in power "transitional" regimes in Eastern Europe that would be acceptable to the West. That did not mean that Stalin would cease to be the dreadful dictator and the pontiff of the Communist world. It did mean, however, that the Kremlin leader believed he needed years of peace in order to bring the USSR from its wartime destruction, when six out of the fifteen Soviet republics were occupied and devastated by the Germans, to the status of an economic and military superpower.

After the death of Roosevelt, which signaled the end of the wartime bonds of amity between Stalin and the Western leaders, and particularly after the atomic bomb was dropped on Hiroshima, Stalin began to have increasing doubts about postwar cooperation. His probes in Turkey and in Iran, "gray areas" between the Soviet and British zones of influence, had evoked fierce resistance on the part of the United States. Step by step, the revolutionary-imperial paradigm began to resurface in Stalin's thought and actions.

Stalin's foreign and domestic priorities were limited in nature, and yet they led to tension with the West. Stalin wanted not only to restore order and strength to a country torn apart by war, but also to maximize the fruits of victory. He refrained from flying red flags all over the Soviet spheres of domination, yet he was determined to exploit Central Europe for his rearmament program. The brutality of the Soviet regime and Stalin's cruel, scheming, and maniacally suspicious nature, which served these ends, looked first unacceptable and then sinister to the West.

Stalin's road to the Cold War, in the years from 1946 to 1950, was strewn with miscalculations. He did not want to provoke American and British "imperialism," yet he overreacted to any perceived threat of it in Germany and in Eastern Europe. In response to the Marshall Plan, Stalin began to consolidate a Soviet security zone in Eastern Europe by ruthless police methods and intensive Communist propaganda. Trying to stop Western separatist policies in Germany, he triggered the Berlin blockade crisis. Stalin's biggest diplomatic triumph in the chilling years after the Second World War was an alliance with Communist China in February 1950. Yet this strategic success did not survive the Korean conflict, where the Kremlin leader grossly misjudged the international situation and, by sanctioning the North Korean aggression, subjected the Koreans, his Chinese ally, and the rest of the world to a bloody and protracted war that contained the real danger of a global conflagration. In short, Stalin's postwar foreign policy was more defensive, reactive, and prudent than it was the fulfillment of a master plan. Yet instead of postponing a confrontation with the United States and gaining a much-needed respite for recovery, he managed to draw closer to it with every step. The explanation of this seeming paradox can best be found in Stalin's mentality as well as in his increasing reliance on the logic and dictates of the revolutionary-imperial paradigm to which he had committed himself.

It is no secret that Stalin ran Soviet foreign policy more or less single-handedly, without the benefit of advice from his close circle of friends. Molotov and Zhdanov, two oligarchs at Stalin's side, never acted on their own while Stalin was alive. These men, their perceptions and activities, point to the real source of the impressive achievements, yet ultimate folly and debacle, of Soviet foreign policy under Stalin—the totalitarian way in which it was conceived, directed, and implemented. Molotov's diplomacy was exactly what Stalin hoped Soviet diplomacy could be: a combination of blunt pressure and exploitation of "imperialist contradictions" among Western countries. Molotov was always prudent and even more cautious than Stalin. He had a strong sense of how far the Soviets could probe Western strength and resolve. For Molotov, the growth of Soviet power was the most certain and infallible road toward the global triumph of the Communist order. Disastrous miscalculations, policies that cost millions of lives, were just tactical slips en route to ultimate triumph and mattered little to him. After Stalin's death, Molotov became the guardian of the revolutionary-imperial paradigm that his predecessor and idol sought to shape and that was embodied in the conquests of the USSR during the Second World War.

Zhdanov's activities testify to his subservient role as a keeper of ideological orthodoxy in Soviet foreign policy under Stalin. Zhdanov cannot be associated with a "party diplomacy" or anything distinct from the diplomacy of Stalin and Molotov. All attempts of the Communist party's propaganda staff to expand its responsibilities came to naught in the face of Stalin's personal diplomacy. Zhdanov, however, became one of the main and most talented players, when in the summer of 1947 Stalin decided to use Communist propaganda and ideology to legitimize Soviet control over Eastern Europe and resuscitate the Comintern's "fifth column" throughout Western Europe. Through Zhdanov, Stalin announced the concept of "two camps" and accepted the worldview of Manichean bipolarity long before this bipolarity acquired its deadly nuclear reality. Until his premature death, Zhdanov remained an obedient keeper of the ideological goals that only Stalin had the power to implement.

Stalin cast a long shadow on the Cold War from the Soviet shore and on the foreign policy of his successors. The challengers to Stalin's legacy, Beria, Malenkov, and finally Khrushchev, fought against the West, and had to face the formidable military threat of the United States, rearmed and bristling with nuclear weapons as a result of Stalin's provocations in Berlin and Korea. But, equally, they fought against Stalin's immortality, the enormous burden of protecting his legacy inside the Soviet Union and worldwide. All their strategies for détente with the United States were severely constrained and eventually shattered by America's hard line, but also by the determination of the vast majority of Soviet elites to prevent a roll-back of Soviet power and influence in the world. The only possible course, in this climate, was to achieve a truce with the West from a position of strength.

It is tempting to argue that, in this sense, the Cold War tensions and the revolutionary-imperial paradigm, shared by most of Stalin's successors, fed off each other. The magnitude of the U.S. challenge served to unite the Soviet leadership and elites in their determination to spare no resources in fending off the war threat. Also, it may explain why, long after Stalin was dead, there was no outbreak of mass discontent in the Soviet Union over the issue of "guns versus butter": most in that generation of Russians, Ukrainians, Byelorus, and others, having experienced the Nazi invasion, did not question the Kremlin's military and foreign policies, so long as they appeared to provide protection, however illusory, against the nightmare of another major war.

Yet, Stalin's death changed much in the Cold War from the Soviet side. None of his successors could afford to wage the Cold War with the same large-scale mobilization of resources. Nor were most of them as ruthless as Stalin had been. . . .

Thomas G. Paterson

INEVITABLE CONFLICT: THE UNSTABLE INTERNATIONAL SYSTEM

The debate between traditionalist and revisionist historians tended to bypass questions about the system or structure of international relations. In his book *On Every Front: The Making and Unmaking of the Cold War* (1992), Thomas G. Paterson argues that an unstable international system contributed significantly to Cold War tensions. While any international system is conflict-ridden by nature, the unprecedented physical destruction of the Second World War, with its attendant economic dislocations, social turmoil, and political chaos, intensified conflict. The complex process of creating a new structure of international relations out of the ashes of the old thus made some form of Soviet-American confrontation inevitable. Although he does not ascribe exclusive weight to this factor, Paterson contends that the characteristics of the volatile international system cannot be ignored in explanations of the origins of the Cold War.

A professor of history at the University of Connecticut, Paterson has written numerous works in the field of foreign relations and has served as president of the Society for Historians of American Foreign Relations. His books include *Soviet-American Confrontation* (1973), *American Foreign Relations: A History* (1995), *Meeting the Communist Threat* (1988), *Kennedy's Quest for Victory: American Foreign Policy, 1961–1963* (1989), and *Contesting Castro* (1994).

The Hiroshima tragedy was but one chapter in the story of massive, war-induced destruction. This story, with all its horrid details, must be recounted not because it shocks or sensationalizes but because it illustrates how massive and daunting were the problems of the postwar world, how shaky the scaffolding of the international order. Hitler had once said about his warmongering pursuits that "we may be destroyed, but if we are, we shall drag a world with us—a world in flames." Because he largely satisfied his prophecy, the Second World War, like any war of substantial duration, served as an agent of conspicuous international changes. The conflagration of 1939–1945 was so wrenching, so total, so profound, that a world was overturned—not simply a material world of crops, buildings, and rails, not simply a human world of healthy and productive laborers, farmers, merchants, financiers, and intellectuals, not simply a secure world of close-knit families and communities, not simply a military world of Nazi storm troopers and Japanese kamikazes, but all that and more. The war also unhinged the world of stable politics, inherited wisdom, traditions, institutions, alliances, loyalties, commerce, and classes.

When Acting Secretary of State Dean Acheson surveyed the fragile condition of the postwar world and identified the primary problems that faced American foreign policy in the postwar era, he saw "social *disintegration*, political *disintegration*, the loss of faith by people in leaders who have led them in the past, and a great deal of economic *disintegration*." How could this alarming condition be reversed? The question preoccupied people in all countries; they worried that the war-induced dislocations would perpetuate rather than diminish the extremism that had led to the Second World War. American leaders asked themselves in particular how safe the United States could be in such a disorderly world. How secure would be America's core values of liberal capitalism and political democracy and its global economic and strategic interests—all of which in the past had guaranteed most Americans a comparatively high standard of living and national security?

Leaders of all political persuasions, as they witnessed the immensity of the destruction, spoke of a new age without knowing its dimensions. "The world was fluid and about to be remade," remembered the American journalist Theodore H. White. The normal way of doing things now seemed inappropriate, although as creatures of the past the survivors remained attached to ideas and institutions that seemed to provide security through familiarity. They sensed the seriousness and the enormity of the tasks of cleaning up the rubble, of putting the broken world back together again, of shaping an orderly international system. But imponderables abounded. Would peoples in the long-restive colonized countries, for example, rebel against their foreign masters at the very time that the once-mighty imperial nations themselves suffered internal political upheavals? Few people could say with confidence that they knew the configuration of the postwar world. What lay ahead was a tortuous time of experimenting, of trial and error, of stumbling and striving, of realized and dashed hopes, of contests among competing formulas for a stable world order.

Few nations or individuals had the material resources, talent, and desire—the sheer energy, guts, and money—to mold a brave new world out of the discredited and crumbled old. If the reconstruction tasks seemed Herculean, however, the opportunities appeared boundless for the ambitious, the hearty, and the caring. One vigorous, optimistic, well-intentioned, competitive voice sounded above the rubble that constituted London, Berlin, Warsaw, Minsk, and Tokyo. That voice echoed with power from the United States, the wartime "arsenal of democracy."

At war's end President Truman declared a two-day national holiday. Horns, bells, and makeshift noisemakers sounded across the nation. Paraders in Los Angeles played leapfrog on Hollywood Boulevard; farther north, jubilant sailors broke windows along San Francisco's Market Street. In New York City office workers tossed tons of paper from the windows of skyscrapers on cheering crowds below. Stock market prices shot up. A five-year-old boy recorded the August 1945 moment: "This is the best year. The war is over. Two wars are over. Everyone is happy. Tin cans are rolling. Everything is confused. And little pieces of paper." Not only had the dying subsided, but also the United States had emerged from the global conflict in the unique position of an unscathed belligerent. No bombs had fallen on American cities. No armies had ravaged the countryside. No American boundaries had been redrawn. Factories stood in place, producing goods at an impressive rate. In August, at the General Motors plant in Moraine, Ohio, shiny new Frigidaire refrigerators and airplane propeller blades moved along parallel assembly lines. Farm fields were rich in crops, and full employment during the war years had buoyed family savings. "The American people," remarked the director of the Office of War Mobilization and Reconversion, "are in the pleasant predicament of having to learn to live 50 percent better than they have ever lived before."

Whereas much of Europe and Asia confronted a massive task of "reconstruction," the United States faced "reconversion"— adjusting the huge war machine to peacetime purposes. Automobile plants had to convert production from tanks to cars, a delightful prospect for auto manufacturers, who knew that Americans were eager to spend their wartime earnings on consumer goods once again. With great pride Americans applauded their good fortune. They were different. They had no rubble to clear. The Soviets knew, said Joseph Stalin in a grand understatement, that "things are not bad in the United States.". . .

Even the death count for Americans in uniform, about four hundred thousand, appeared merciful when compared with staggering figures elsewhere. Indeed, the *Saturday Evening Post* editorialized in 1945 that "we Americans can boast that we are not as other men are." The war had overturned a world, and many Americans believed that they were now on top of it. A new international system for the postwar era was in the making, and the United States intended to be its primary architect.

In the rubble-strewn postwar world, international relations changed markedly from prewar interactions. Any historical period, such as the Cold War, is identified by a particular structure of relationships among the world's leading nations—by, in short, the international "system." Bipolarism, for example, characterized the Napoleonic era of the late eighteenth and early nineteenth centuries; Great Britain and France vied for world mastery, established alliances with lesser powers, frequently clashed in war, and managed far-flung empires. The period between the Congress of Vienna in 1815 and the outbreak of World War I in 1914 was multipolar, with a number of leading actors on the international stage who preferred diplomatic negotiations to military combat and who deliberately set about to create a balance of power for the maintenance of a conservative, imperial, antirevolutionary world. Systems are always in flux, and they change dramatically when shocked by brash newcomers, devastating wars, and economic depressions.

Any international system in any age is conflict-ridden. Anarchy more than peace is a system's most consistent feature, and this characteristic in turn compels most governments to worry about insecurity and to strive for security. The attempts that nations have made to reduce the anarchy constitute our diplomatic history. Conflict is inherent in any international system simply because peoples and countries seldom share common goals, interests, cultures, and ideologies. "This is a lawless world," University of Chicago Professor Herman Finer told a postwar radio audience, "because it is a world without a common morality or a common superior. Nationalisms and moralities collide." The ways that politics, economies, and societies are organized, and the ideas that sustain them, are different from one corner of the world to the other. Core values clash. A few nations are ruled by monarchs; some suffer under dictators; others enjoy popularly elected governments. Some people prefer public ownership of property; others champion private enterprise. Some societies are centered on simple, rural, peasant life; others are marked by mass-production industries located in sprawling metropolises. Buddhist, Christian, Jewish, Muslim, Hindu, and countless other religions contend for followers in holy crusades that accentuate the fragmentation of the international system. Intense ethnic and racial differences—witness the Turks and the Armenians or the white and black South Africans—disturb the peace as well. Civil wars, social revolutions, new technologies, economic recessions, famines, natural disasters, environmental abuses—they, too, push the international system toward disorder.

Some nations are more powerful or influential than others and flaunt their superiority. Strong nations tend to expand; large and small countries alike will resist. Historical examples abound of peoples who fervently believe they possess superior ideas and institutions that must be exported to the less fortunate—in essence, that they must replicate their domestic systems at the international level. Some nations have what others want—territory, food, water, minerals, labor, and a multitude of things over which peoples have squabbled for centuries. Great nations are always looking for friends who will join them in formal or informal alliances to check the growth of those states they consider unfriendly or potentially so. Small nations have to be wary of the major actors, who may cast longing eyes on them and exploit their vulnerability. Some countries become dependent upon others for their prosperity and security, and the dependent inevitably develop resentments against the metropole that profits from the dependency relationship. Nations wishing to remain "neutral" or unaligned are wooed or cajoled.

The leading powers, whether aligned or at loggerheads, watch one another suspiciously, on the assumption that in international politics, as in business, one can supposedly trust friends seldom, enemies never. Slight shifts in the distribution of power—of resources—arouse concern. What one government considers defense, another labels "offense." The construction of a military base, the testing of a new weapon, a request to alter a boundary, the signing of a treaty—all may be defined as both defensive or offensive, depending upon one's point of view. A rifle is a defensive weapon if seen from the butt, but it is a weapon of attack if one is staring into the muzzle. Suspicion and fear undermine trust and prompt countermeasures. Leaders may assume evil intentions on the part of other nations and then, playing it safe, plan for the worst. Governments feel compelled to match the decisions of their adversaries. Failure to develop a new weapon, for example, might entail risk, for an enemy might gain some advantage by producing it.

Leaders also fear falling dominoes, chain reactions, colliding rows of bowling pins, mud slides, rising tides, the snowballing effect, or the spread of contagious diseases—to name some oft-heard metaphors—that begin far from their homes but that may come cascading toward them through momentum. Economic chain reactions, tariff wars, economic downturns, competition for raw materials—also prompt alarm. Military interventions abroad or the political manipulation of another nation seem imperative to break the momentum of such calamities. For great powers, the containment of foreign threats ranks high, and therefore, lines need to be drawn far from home. In such a threatening and disorderly world, leaders often exaggerate danger and thus escalate chances for war. The degree and kind of conflict may vary, but there is always conflict.

Higher degrees of conflict are reached when the international system undergoes significant change, when it transforms into a new or revised system. Such was the case after World War II. Change, by definition, is destabilizing. Some postwar leaders, even though immersed in day-to-day decision making, pondered the general characteristics of the international system. They knew that significant changes had altered the configuration of power. As participants in and shapers of a new age they were "present at the creation." But the outline of the new system was only vaguely evident. The process of creating a new system out of the ashes of the discredited prewar system intensified the conflict inherent in any international structure. . . .

[A] macroanalytic view of the international system will enable us to identify the opportunities and constraints which faced the major actors. Like a menu, this systemic level of analysis outlines the choices available, as well as the limits of choice. It sketches the "big picture," so that the disparate components of the postwar system may be examined in proper relationship. Exploration of the broad international context reveals which nations held real or potential power and why, ultimately, they jettisoned international cooperation and moved toward a divided world of competing spheres of influence.

Yet analysis of the characteristics of the international system alone does not go far enough to explain the origins of the Cold War. While it is true that a nation's foreign policy responds to the prevailing features of the international system, each nation will react differently according to its peculiar domestic order. If the Soviet-American confrontation were simply the inevitable product of the conflict-ridden international system, there would be little purpose in studying the leaders, ideas, policies, economics, politics, or societies of particular nations because, this logic would have it, events would be largely beyond their control. Under this interpretation the system would dictate antagonistic relations, leaving few alternatives for reconciling differences. It would not matter whether different personalities or different national policies existed. But of course, leaders make choices, even if they only dimly understand their consequences, and they choose policies they think will protect their nations' interests. Franklin D. Roosevelt, Harry S. Truman, Winston Churchill, Clement Attlee, Joseph Stalin, Ho Chi Minh, Mao Zedong, and many others helped create the international system to which they had to react. To fathom the beginnings of the Cold War, then, we must discuss not only the traits of the international system but also the dynamics of particular nations and the individuals who led them. Later chapters will develop these ingredients of conflict. Here we will explore the birth and nature of the postwar international system.

The Second World War visited wrenching changes upon the old international system and spawned new characteristics that produced conflict. One conspicuous characteristic was the redistribution of power. The defeat of Germany, Italy, and Japan left power

vacuums. Britain, nearly bankrupt, dependent, and unable to police its empire, was reduced to a resentful second-rate power;
France, much of whose territory had been occupied by the Germans during the war, continued to suffer from unstable politics
and no longer mustered international respect. In the colonial
world nationalist insurgencies bargained for power with these
weakened imperial states and fought to make the world less Eu-
rope-centered. In short, many of the nations which had wielded
authority in the multipolar system of the 1930s had fallen from
their elevated status.

Two nations with quite different ideologies emerged from
the rubble of World War II to claim high rank. The United States
and the Soviet Union, eager to realize their universalist visions of
the postwar world and to seize opportunities for extending their
respective influence, tried to fill vacuums of power. With the old
barriers to American and Soviet expansion gone, Washington and
Moscow clashed over occupation policies in Germany, Italy, Japan,
Austria, and Korea. They squabbled over which political groups
should replace the Nazi regimes in Eastern Europe. The competitive interaction between the United States and the Soviet Union—
"like two big dogs chewing on a bone," said Senator J. William
Fulbright—shaped the bipolarism or bipolarity of the immediate
postwar years. "Not since Rome and Carthage," Dean Acheson
claimed, "had there been such a polarization of power on this
earth." This new bipolar structure replaced the multipolar system
of the 1930s, wherein at least six nations had been active, influential participants. By the late 1940s decisions made in the imperial
capitals of Washington and Moscow often determined whether
people in other nations voted, where they could travel, how much
they ate, and what they could print.

To say that the world was bipolar, however, is not to suggest
that the two poles were equal in power. They were not. An asymmetry—not a balance—of power existed. In fact, the United States
held preponderant power and flexed its multidimensional muscle
to build even more power. As the only major nation not devastated
by the war, the United States so outdistanced other nations in almost every measurement of power—from industrial production to
domestic political stability—that it enjoyed hegemony. Hegemony
exists when one nation possesses superior economic, military, and
political power in the world system. The first ingredient is a

prerequisite for the other two. No nation can aspire to hegemony or achieve that Olympian status unless its economy is strong—and stronger than any other's. More than statistics established American supremacy. World conditions did so. The United States was powerful because almost every other nation was war-weakened.

Both the United States and the Soviet Union emerged from the war as powers, but only one at that time was a superpower—the United States. The Soviet Union was certainly not weak. Although handicapped by its economic wreckage, the huge nation held predominant postwar power over its neighbors in Eastern Europe. Still, the Soviet Union was a regional, not a global, power before the early 1950s. The characteristic of hegemony meant that the United States had more opportunities and resources than other nations to shape the postwar system. By exercising their preponderant global power—through military occupations, foreign aid and loans, and domination of the World Bank and United Nations Organization, for example—U.S. officials pushed the world toward the American postwar goal of a nonradical, capitalist, free trade international order in the mold of domestic America.

The United States, as we shall see, did not get all that it wanted (hegemonic powers seldom do) because a host of obstacles thrown up by allies and foes alike sometimes obstructed American hopes and plans, and resources were finite. "We cannot scatter our shots equally all over the world," Acheson remonstrated. "We just haven't got enough shots to do that. . . ." American power, however superior, had limits and suffered failures. More serious, in the long run, any hegemon like the United States risks traveling a path toward decline because it cannot afford to be both global economic master and global policeman. The latter, a very expensive role, strains the domestic economy, undermines the infrastructure (by underfunding education and technological research, for example), and ultimately diminishes the nation's competitiveness in the international marketplace. A globe-circling superpower ultimately experiences insecurity because it becomes a worldwide target. "Imperial overstretch" undercuts hegemonic power. But this theme of decline jumps ahead of the story here. However circumscribed, American hegemony was conspicuous in the international system of the early Cold War period.

Another prominent characteristic of the international system that unleashed conflict was the destruction of economies in many parts of the world. The war cut an ugly scar across Europe and Asia. "If Hitler succeeds in nothing else," mused Office of Strategic Services officer Allen Dulles, "like Samson, he may pull down the pillars of the temple and leave a long and hard road of reconstruction." The postwar task was forbidding. Not only did cities have to be rebuilt, factories opened, people put back to work, rails repaired, rivers and roads made passable, and crop yields increased, but the flow of international commerce and finance had to be reestablished if nations were to raise through exports the money needed to buy the imports required for recovery. Many old commercial and financial patterns had been broken, and given the obstacle of economic disarray, new exchanges were difficult to establish. Where would Germany's vital coal and steel go? Would industrial Western Europe and agricultural Eastern Europe recreate old commercial ties? Would the restrictive trade practices of the 1930s, especially the tariff barriers, continue into the 1940s? Would colonies continue to provide raw materials to their imperial lords? Could international cooperation and organizations like the General Agreement on Tariffs and Trade (1948) curb economic nationalism? Would trade be conducted on a multilateral, "open door" basis, as the United States preferred, or by bilateral or preferential methods, as many others, such as Britain and the Soviet Union, practiced? Would the economic disorders spawned by the Great Depression be repeated to produce political chaos, aggression, and war?

The answers to these questions helped define the international system of the post-1945 era. The new international system, it was hoped, would enjoy stable economic conditions to ensure pacific international relations. Yet the very effort to reconstruct economies and create economic order engendered conflict because different models and formulas—Communist? socialist? capitalist? mixed economy?—competed to define the future. At the same time the asymmetrical distribution of power persuaded weaker nations that they faced the danger of economic coercion.

The Second World War also bequeathed domestic political turmoil to the new international system. The governments of the 1930s, now discredited, vied with insurgent groups for governing power in many states. Socialists, Communists, and other varieties of the political left, many of whom had fought in the underground resistance movements and had thus earned some popular respect and following, challenged the more entrenched, conservative elites, many of whom had escaped into exile when the German armies goose-stepped into their countries. In Poland the Communist, Soviet-sponsored Lublin Poles successfully undercut the political authority of the Poles who had fled to London. The conservative Dutch government-in-exile watched warily as leftist resistance groups gradually rallied political support. Political confusion in the Netherlands was heightened by the wartime loss of voting lists. In Greece a coalition of leftists in the National Liberation Front (EAM) fought the return to power of a British-created government and the unpopular Greek monarchy of King George. The civil war that rocked Greece until fall 1949 claimed some 158,000 lives and ended in an American-backed conservative government. In France Charles de Gaulle gained ascendancy after vying for power with the Communists. The Chinese civil war, which had raged for years between the Communists of Mao Zedong and the Nationalists of Jiang Jieshi (Chiang Kai-shek), flared up again at the close of the war. That internecine struggle ended in a Communist victory in 1949. Yugoslavia was also the scene of political battle between Josip Broz Tito's ultimately successful Partisans and a group headed by Dr. Ivan Šubašić of the London émigré government, which in turn suffered strained ties with King Peter. In the occupied nations of Germany, Austria, and Korea, moreover, the victors created competitive zones, postponing the formation of central governments. In the defeated countries of Japan and Italy, American officials decided who would rule, whereas in parts of Eastern Europe, Soviet officials placed Communists in strategic positions of power.

The major powers, in short, intervened abroad to exploit the political opportunities created by the destructive scythe of World War II. The stakes seemed high. A change in a nation's political orientation might presage a change in its international alignment. The great powers tended to ignore local conditions, especially nationalism, which might and often did mitigate against alignment with an outside power. Americans nonetheless feared that a leftist or Communist Greece would look to the East and permit menacing Soviet bases on Greek territory or open the door to a Soviet naval presence in the Mediterranean. Moscow dreaded a conservative anti-Soviet Polish government led by the London faction, for it might prove so weak and so hostile to Moscow as to permit a revived Germany to send storm troopers once again through the Polish corridor into the heart of Russia or block the Soviet Union's efforts to contain a resurgent Germany. A Communist China, thought Americans, might align with the Soviet Union; a Nationalist China would remain in the American camp. All in all, the rearranging of political structures within nations drew the major powers into competition, accentuating the conflict inherent in the postwar international system.

Just as the war threw politics into chaos, so it hastened the disintegration of empires. The Japanese movement into French Indochina and drive for Dutch East Indies oil had led to Pearl Harbor in 1941. The initially successful Japanese expansion demonstrated to many Asian nationalists that their white imperial masters could be defeated. In a spirit of Pan-Asianism, some nationalists collaborated with Tokyo during the war. The Japanese, in need of administrators to manage occupied areas, trained and armed some indigenous leaders. Japan granted Burma considerable autonomy in 1942, for example, and after the war the Burmese became determined to push the British out. Other nationalists gained organizational unity, élan, and experience by battling the Japanese invaders. At the end of the war the European powers, exhausted and financially hobbled, had to struggle to reestablish mastery over rebellious colonies. The appeal of the self-determination principle, still echoing from the days of Woodrow Wilson and given new emphasis by the Atlantic Charter (1941) and the United Nations Charter (1945), became far-reaching. The long process of "regime collapse" in what became known as the Third World gained momentum. "There are many peoples who are clamoring for freedom from the colonial powers," American Undersecretary of State Sumner Welles remarked during the war. He predicted "trouble" unless these peoples got what they wanted. Failure to plan for the transfer of power to them, he warned, "would be like failing to install a safety valve and then waiting for the boiler to blow up." There were too many boilers and too few safety valves.

No empire was immune to decolonization. The United States granted the Philippines independence in 1946, but that new nation became a client state where U.S. officials helped the government resist a peasant revolt led by the Huks. The British, worn low by the war and by the challenges of nationalist groups demanding independence, retreated in 1947 from India, which then descended into civil war between Hindus and Muslims. The two new nations of India and Pakistan were thus born amid massacres and a massive uprooting of people. The following year Britain also relinquished Burma (Myanmar) and Ceylon (Sri Lanka). Israel, carved out of British-governed Palestine, became a new independent state in 1948. The British also found it difficult to maintain their sphere of influence in Iran, Greece, and Egypt and began retreats from those politically unsteady states. The French clung to Indochina, where nationalist forces led by Ho Chi Minh had declared an independent Vietnam by quoting the American Declaration of Independence. "If those gooks want a fight," boasted French General Étienne Valluy, "they'll get it." Bloody battle ensued, ultimately forcing French withdrawal in 1954. The French empire also came under siege in Africa; in early 1947 Malagasy insurgents in the island colony of Madagascar rebelled. Ninety thousand people died as French troops crushed the insurrection the next year (France finally granted the Malagasy Republic independence in 1960). The Dutch also decided to fight, but after four debilitating years of combat they pulled out of Indonesia in 1949. The defeated Japanese were forced to give up their claims to Formosa and Korea, as well as to Pacific island groups. Italy departed from Ethiopia and lost its African colonies of Tripolitania (Libya) and Eritrea. In the Middle East, Lebanon, Syria, and Jordan, areas once managed by Europeans, gained independence in 1943, 1944, and 1946 respectively.

The world map, as after World War I, was redrawn. The emergence of so many new states, and the instability associated with the transfer of authority, shook the very foundations of the international system. Power was being redistributed. In varying degrees the United States and Soviet Union competed for the allegiance of the new governments, meddled in colonial rebellions, and generally sought to exploit opportunities for an extension of their influence. In the case of Vietnam the powers supported different sides: Washington, without relish, backed the ruling French, and Moscow endorsed the Vietminh insurgency. The stakes seemed high. President Roosevelt told an adviser near the end of the war that more than one billion "brown people" yearned for independence—and "1,100,000,000 potential enemies are dangerous." The emerging nations could serve as strategic bases, markets for exports, sources of vital raw materials, sites for investments, and votes in international organizations; conversely, they could deny powerful nations such assets. As a Central Intelligence Agency report emphasized, the resource-rich Third World and the reconstruction of hobbled Western Europe were intricately linked: "The continuance of unsettled conditions [in colonial or former colonial areas] hinders economic recovery and causes a diversion of European strength into efforts to maintain or reimpose control by force". . . .

The new atomic bomb and the ensuing nuclear arms race further destabilized the postwar international system. As the two bickering major powers groped for ways to deal with "the bomb" and spurred their atomic development programs, people everywhere held their breaths, harboring thoughts about doomsday. Nuclear weapons were not simply dangerous to enemies; they threatened apocalypse for humankind. Cartoonists sketched pictures of uncontrollable monsters that the scientists had created. "All the scientists are frightened—frightened for their lives—and frightened for *your* life," a Nobel Prize-winning chemist wrote in early 1946 in a popular magazine. About the same time a French radio station broadcast a make-believe story about an atomic storm engulfing the earth after radioactive atoms had escaped from a U.S. research laboratory. Many Parisians thought they heard truth and panicked. One observer suggested that a Soviet-American war "might not end with *one* Rome but with *two* Carthages."

The atomic bomb, uncontrolled, envied, copied, and brandished, became a major obstacle to a peaceful postwar international system. The "most terrible weapon ever known in human history," Secretary of War Henry L. Stimson quietly told the president, unsettled the world community, for it was an agent of massive human destruction, and "in a world atmosphere already extremely sensitive to power, the introduction of this weapon has profoundly affected political considerations in all sections of the globe." Nations that possessed *the* bomb seemed to hold an advantage in international politics, for it could serve as a deterrent against an adversary as well as a means to annihilate an enemy. When combined with air power and a long-range delivery capability, the atomic bomb also hurdled geographical boundaries, rendering them useless as protective elements in a nation's security shield. With the perfecting of air warfare in World War II, "the roof blew off the territorial state."

The question that dogged the peacemakers was: How were they to control the development, spread, and use of atomic energy? There had been arms races before, and disarmament conferences in the 1920s and 1930s, but the postwar nuclear race moved at a far different and more dangerous level. The atomic bomb was the "absolute weapon," not only more violent but also capable of speedy delivery, rapid retaliation, immediate cataclysm, and lingering death-dealing radioactivity. Americans worried that they would lose their monopoly—that nuclear proliferation would leave them vulnerable, too. Such fears intensified when the Soviet Union successfully produced its own bomb in 1949. While from the start some people appealed for a world government to put the atomic genie back in the bottle—"world state or world doom"—others began to marvel over the new armament's potential value as a diplomatic weapon to pry concessions from adversaries or as a deterrent to keep them at bay.

Some scholars have argued that the advent of nuclear weapons, because of their deterrent role, as well as the bipolarity of the Cold War, served to stabilize the postwar international system. But this interpretation suffers from a narrow definition of peace and stability, concentrates almost solely on Soviet-American relations, and confines itself to the strategic-military realm. Because the militaries of the United States and the Soviet Union did not directly clash or because the two nations did not destroy each other in a nuclear holocaust, "peace" prevailed. Such an assumption discounts too much history, a history hardly peaceful or stable.

One of the reasons why the Soviets kept their troops in Eastern Europe—conceivably ready to pounce on America's European allies if necessary—was the immediate postwar U.S. atomic monopoly and "atomic diplomacy"; in short, the Soviet Union deployed conventional forces in its sphere to deter superior American nuclear and air power. Since the much-disputed presence of the Red Army in Eastern Europe contributed considerably to the coming of the Cold War and the division of the continent, American atomic weapons accentuated instability, not stability. In addition, numerous wars fought by the client or dependent states of the two powers, as well as great-power military interventions and covert activities, repeatedly disturbed the peace for decades after 1945. And they took the lives of millions of people in Korea, Vietnam, Guatemala, Hungary, Czechoslovakia, Angola, and Afghanistan, among many others. It would come as a surprise to most world leaders in the period since 1945, furthermore, that they presided over a "long peace." Many of them knew anxious moments of a "long war"—severe crises, nuclear brinkmanship, events spinning out of control, accidents, missed signals, poor communications, and stress, as the confrontations in Berlin and Cuba attest.

Huge economic costs are also neglected in the "long peace" argument. Nuclear weapons and their delivery systems, military establishments, and interventions consumed trillions of dollars. The spending of such monumental sums on armaments and wars meant that the money was not spent on economic development, environmental protection, education, medical research and health, famine relief, and a host of other undertakings that might better have served international stability. No, as Stimson suggested, nuclear weapons brought neither peace nor stability to the postwar international system, and certainly not in the early years of the Cold War.

Any exploration of the causes of the Cold War must give prominence to another new characteristic of the international system: the shrinkage of the globe and the related emergence of a global outlook for most peoples and nations. Geography had not changed, but ways of moving across it and of thinking about it had. Observers began to speak not only of an "atomic age" but of an "air age" and a "global age." Remarkable advances in communications and transportation, especially in aviation, brought nations closer to one another. "We are for all time de-isolated," noted one analyst. The world seemed more compact and accessible. President Truman described a "much smaller earth—an earth whose broad oceans have shrunk and whose national protections have been taken away by new weapons of destruction."

People had to think now not only in traditional land miles but also in flying hours. "Starvation and over-production, bloated wealth and extreme poverty on a national scale cannot co-exist, only hours apart, without developing pressures far more intense than those of other days when time and distance served as safety valves," General Dwight D. Eisenhower told a postwar meeting in New York City. In a popularization for schoolchildren, N. L. Englehardt, Jr., urged his young readers to think "air thoughts" and titled one of his chapters "How the World Has Shrunk." Because the Atlantic Ocean could be traversed easily and quickly by flying over it, that once-prominent barrier between the Old and New worlds disappeared. The Canadian minister of national defence noted, too, that "only the top of the world separates us [Canada and the USSR], and that means we're next-door neighbors in this modern flying age." The British also recognized the significant change; sea power, they regretted, no longer served to defend their island fortress, now vulnerable to air attack. Stimson perceived that the United States could never again "be an island to herself. No private program and no public policy, in any sector of our national life can now escape from the compelling fact that if it is not framed with reference to the world, it is framed with perfect futility." Geographical isolation was gone with the past. In a world contracted by science, events in lands once considered distant or tangential now held greater significance than ever before for all peoples.

Because frontiers had been extended, because nations were brought nearer one another, and because the world had shrunk, the major powers coveted bases far from home, much as the United States had sought and acquired bases in the Caribbean in the early twentieth century to protect the Panama Canal. By drawing peoples and nations closer to one another, by making some fearful of surprise attack and others concerned that their security was threatened by faraway events, the airplane drew the great powers into confrontations as never before. The shrinkage of the world and the globalist perspective and interdependence that followed this phenomenon ensured international conflict.

Such was the postwar international system—with its opportunities and constraints, with its many characteristics that generated conflict. The makers of the postwar order grappled with immense, new problems, and they strove to reduce the systemic instability. Their decisions, however, exacerbated conflict. The reason why the leaders of the postwar world made bad conditions worse is clear: Sensing danger from the volatile international system to their domestic systems, they sought to build their nations' power, to enlarge their spheres of influence. The conflict inherent in any international system, especially one struggling to make the transition from full-scale war to postwar peace, hardened into a four-decade-long Cold War.

II

The Origins of the Cold War in Europe

Barton J. Bernstein

SAVING AMERICAN LIVES AND PRESSING THE SOVIETS: THE ATOMIC BOMB DECISION

President Truman's explanation for his decision in August 1945 to annihilate the Japanese cities of Hiroshima and Nagasaki with atomic bombs was characteristically brief and pointed: to end the Second World War as quickly as possible in order to save American lives. The following essay does not dispute Truman's point. Indeed, Barton J. Bernstein emphasizes that the decision to use the bomb did *not* prompt troubling doubts, moral or otherwise, on the part of Truman or most of his top advisers. American leaders had well before 1945 begun treating enemy civilians as legitimate targets of aerial warfare, and were by then most anxious to end the war as expeditiously as possible. Yet Bernstein adds another important, if not determinative, reason for dropping the bomb. Both Roosevelt and Truman, he insists, believed that the atomic bomb would serve as a bargaining lever—a diplomatic bonus—in dealing with the Soviets by making them more manageable, especially in Eastern Europe. The atomic bomb, according to Bernstein, thus stands as one of the root causes of Soviet-American mistrust.

Barton J. Bernstein is a professor of history at Stanford University and co-chair of the International Relations Program and the International Policy Studies Program. He is the editor of *Politics and Policies of the Truman Administration* (1970) and *The Atomic Bomb* (1975), and has written numerous essays about nuclear and foreign policy issues during the Cold War era.

Fifty years ago, during a three-day period in August 1945, the United States dropped two atomic bombs on Japan, killing more than 115,000 people and possibly as many as 250,000, and injuring at least another 100,000. In the aftermath of the war, the bombings raised both ethical and historical questions about why and how they were used. Would they have been used on Germany? Why were cities targeted so that so many civilians would be killed?

Barton J. Bernstein, "The Atomic Bombings Reconsidered," *Foreign Affairs*, 74 (January/February 1995), pp. 135–152. Reprinted by permission of *Foreign Affairs*, Copyright 1995 by the Council on Foreign Relations.

Were there likely alternative ways to end the war speedily and avoid the Allies' scheduled November 1, 1945, invasion of Kyushu?

Such questions often fail to recognize that, before Hiroshima and Nagasaki, the use of the A-bomb did not raise profound moral issues for policymakers. The weapon was conceived in a race with Germany, and it undoubtedly would have been used against Germany had the bomb been ready much sooner. During the war, the target shifted to Japan. And during World War II's brutal course, civilians in cities had already become targets. The grim Axis bombing record is well known. Masses of noncombatants were also intentionally killed in the later stages of the American air war against Germany; that tactic was developed further in 1945 with the firebombing of Japanese cities. Such mass bombing constituted a transformation of morality, repudiating President Franklin D. Roosevelt's prewar pleas that the warring nations avoid bombing cities to spare civilian lives. Thus, by 1945, American leaders were not seeking to avoid the use of the A-bomb on Japan. But the evidence from current archival research shows that by pursuing alternative tactics instead, they probably could still have obviated the dreaded invasion and ended the war by November.

In 1941, urged by émigré and American scientists, President Roosevelt initiated the atomic bomb project—soon code-named the Manhattan Project—amid what was believed to be a desperate race with Hitler's Germany for the bomb. At the beginning, Roosevelt and his chief aides assumed that the A-bomb was a legitimate weapon that would be used first against Nazi Germany. They also decided that the bomb project should be kept secret from the Soviet Union, even after the Soviets became a wartime ally, because the bomb might well give the United States future leverage against the Soviets.

By mid-1944, the landscape of the war had changed. Roosevelt and his top advisers knew that the likely target would now be Japan, for the war with Germany would undoubtedly end well before the A-bomb was expected to be ready, around the spring of 1945. In a secret September 1944 memorandum at Hyde Park, Roosevelt and British Prime Minister Winston Churchill ratified the shift from Germany to Japan. Their phrasing suggested that, for the moment anyway, they might have had some slight doubts about actually using the bomb, for they agreed that "it might *per-*

haps, after mature consideration, be used against the Japanese" (my emphasis).

Four days later, mulling over matters aloud with a visiting British diplomat and chief U.S. science adviser Vannevar Bush, Roosevelt briefly wondered whether the A-bomb should be dropped on Japan or whether it should be demonstrated in America, presumably with Japanese observers, and then used as a threat. His speculative notion seemed so unimportant and so contrary to the project's long-standing operating assumptions that Bush actually forgot about it when he prepared a memo of the meeting. He only recalled the president's remarks a day later and then added a brief paragraph to another memorandum.

Put in context alongside the dominant assumption that the bomb would be used against the enemy, the significance of F.D.R.'s occasional doubts is precisely that they were so occasional—expressed twice in almost four years. All of F.D.R.'s advisers who knew about the bomb always unquestioningly assumed that it would be used. Indeed, their memoranda frequently spoke of "after it is used" or "when it is used," and never "*if* it is used." By about mid-1944, most had comfortably concluded that the target would be Japan.

The bomb's assumed legitimacy as a war weapon was ratified bureaucratically in September 1944 when General Leslie Groves, the director of the Manhattan Project, had the air force create a special group—the 509th Composite Group with 1,750 men—to begin practicing to drop atomic bombs. So dominant was the assumption that the bomb would be used against Japan that only one high-ranking Washington official, Undersecretary of War Robert Patterson, even questioned this notion after V-E Day. He wondered whether the defeat of Germany on May 8, 1945, might alter the plans for dropping the bomb on Japan. It would not.

The Manhattan Project, costing nearly $2 billion, had been kept secret from most cabinet members and nearly all of Congress. Secretary of War Henry L. Stimson, a trusted Republican, and General George C. Marshall, the equally respected army chief of staff, disclosed the project to only a few congressional leaders. They smuggled the necessary appropriations into the War Department budget without the knowledge—much less the scrutiny—of most congressmen, including most members of the key appropriations committees. A conception of the national interest agreed upon by a few men from the executive and legislative branches had revised the normal appropriations process.

In March 1944, when a Democratic senator heading a special investigating committee wanted to pry into this expensive project, Stimson peevishly described him in his diary as "a nuisance and pretty untrustworthy . . . He talks smoothly but acts meanly." That man was Senator Harry S. Truman. Marshall persuaded him not to investigate the project, and thus Truman did not learn any more than that it involved a new weapon until he was suddenly thrust into the presidency on April 12, 1945.

In early 1945, James F. Byrnes, then F.D.R.'s "assistant president" for domestic affairs and a savvy Democratic politician, began to suspect that the Manhattan Project was a boondoggle. "If [it] proves a failure," he warned Roosevelt, "it will be subjected to relentless investigation and criticism." Byrnes' doubts were soon overcome by Stimson and Marshall. A secret War Department report, with some hyperbole, summarized the situation: "If the project succeeds, there won't be any investigation. If it doesn't, they won't investigate anything else."

Had Roosevelt lived, such lurking political pressures might have powerfully confirmed his intention to use the weapon on the enemy—an assumption he had already made. How else could he have justified spending roughly $2 billion, diverting scarce materials from other war enterprises that might have been even more useful, and bypassing Congress? In a nation still unprepared to trust scientists, the Manhattan Project could have seemed a gigantic waste if its value were not dramatically demonstrated by the use of the atomic bomb.

Truman, inheriting the project and trusting both Marshall and Stimson, would be even more vulnerable to such political pressures. And, like F.D.R., the new president easily assumed that the bomb should and would be used. Truman never questioned that assumption. Bureaucratic developments set in motion before he entered the White House reinforced his belief. And his aides, many inherited from the Roosevelt administration, shared the same faith.

Groves, eager to retain control of the atomic project, received Marshall's permission in early spring 1945 to select targets for the new weapon. Groves and his associates had long recognized that they were considering a weapon of a new magnitude, possibly equivalent to the "normal bombs carried by [at least] 2,500 bombers." And they had come to assume that the A-bomb would be "detonated well above ground, relying primarily on blast effect to do material damage, [so that even with] minimum probable efficiency, there will be the maximum number of structures (dwellings and factories) damaged beyond repair."

On April 27, the Target Committee, composed of Groves, army air force men like General Lauris Norstad, and scientists including the great mathematician John Von Neumann, met for the first time to discuss how and where in Japan to drop the bomb. They did not want to risk wasting the precious weapon, and decided that it must be dropped visually and not by radar, despite the poor weather conditions in Japan during the summer, when the bomb would be ready.

Good targets were not plentiful. The air force, they knew, "was systematically bombing out the following cities with the prime purpose . . . of not leaving one stone lying on another: Tokyo, Yokohama, Nagoya, Osaka, Kyoto, Kobe, Yawata, and Nagasaki . . . The air force is operating primarily to laying |sic| waste all the main Japanese cities . . . Their existing procedure is to bomb the hell out of Tokyo."

By early 1945, World War II—especially in the Pacific—had become virtually total war. The firebombing of Dresden had helped set a precedent for the U.S. air force, supported by the American people, to intentionally kill mass numbers of Japanese citizens. The earlier moral insistence on noncombatant immunity crumbled during the savage war. In Tokyo, during March 9–10, a U.S. air attack killed about 80,000 Japanese civilians. American B-29s dropped napalm on the city's heavily populated areas to produce uncontrollable firestorms. It may even have been easier to conduct this new warfare outside Europe and against Japan because its people seemed like "yellow subhumans" to many rank-and-file American citizens and many of their leaders.

In this new moral context, with mass killings of an enemy's civilians even seeming desirable, the committee agreed to choose "large urban areas of not less than three miles in diameter existing in the larger populated areas" as A-bomb targets. The April 27 discussion focused on four cities: Hiroshima, which, as "the largest untouched target not on the 21st Bomber Command priority list," warranted serious consideration; Yawata, known for its steel industry; Yokohama; and Tokyo, "a possibility [though] now practically all bombed and burned out and . . . practically rubble with only the palace grounds left standing." They decided that other areas warranted more consideration: Tokyo Bay, Kawasaki, Yokohoma, Nagoya, Osaka, Kobe, Kyoto, Hiroshima, Kure, Yawata, Kokura, Shimonoseki, Yamaguchi, Kumamoto, Fukuoka, Nagasaki, and Sasebo.

The choice of targets would depend partly on how the bomb would do its deadly work—the balance of blast, heat, and radiation. At their second set of meetings, during May 11–12, physicist J. Robert Oppenheimer, director of the Los Alamos laboratory, stressed that the bomb material itself was lethal enough for perhaps a billion deadly doses and that the weapon would give off lethal radioactivity. The bomb, set to explode in the air, would deposit "a large fraction of either the initial active material or the radioactive products in the immediate vicinity of the target; but the radiation . . . will, of course, have an effect on exposed personnel in the target area." It was unclear, he acknowledged, what would happen to most of the radioactive material: it could stay for hours as a cloud above the place of detonation or, if the bomb exploded during rain or in high humidity and thus caused rain, "most of the active material will be brought down in the vicinity of the target area." Oppenheimer's report left unclear whether a substantial proportion or only a small fraction of the population might die from radiation. So far as the skimpy records reveal, no member of the Target Committee chose to dwell on this matter. They probably assumed that the bomb blast would claim most of its victims before the radiation could do its deadly work.

In considering targets, they discussed the possibility of bombing the emperor's palace in Tokyo and "agreed that we should not recommend it but that any action for this bombing should come from authorities on military policy." They decided to gather information on the effectiveness of using the bomb on the palace.

The Target Committee selected their four top targets: Kyoto, Hiroshima, Yokohama, and Kokura Arsenal, with the implication that Niigata, a city farther away from the air force 509th group's Tinian base, might be held in reserve as a fifth. Kyoto, the ancient former capital and shrine city, with a population of about a million, was the most attractive target to the committee. "From the psychological point of view," the committee minutes note, "there is the advantage that Kyoto is an intellectual center for Japan and [thus] the people there are more apt to appreciate the significance of such a weapon." The implication was that those in Kyoto who survived the A-bombing and saw the horror would be believed elsewhere in Japan.

Of central importance, the group stressed that the bomb should be used as a terror weapon—to produce "the greatest psychological effect against Japan" and to make the world, and the U.S.S.R. in particular, aware that America possessed this new power. The death and destruction would not only intimidate the surviving Japanese into pushing for surrender, but, as a bonus, cow other nations, notably the Soviet Union. In short, America could speed the ending of the war and by the same act help shape the postwar world.

By the committee's third meeting, two weeks later, on May 28, they had pinned down matters. They chose as their targets (in order) Kyoto, Hiroshima, and Niigata, and decided to aim for the center of each city. They agreed that aiming for industrial areas would be a mistake because such targets were small, spread on the cities' fringes, and quite dispersed. They also knew that bombing was imprecise enough that the bomb might easily miss its mark by a fifth of a mile, and they wanted to be sure that the weapon would show its power and not be wasted.

The committee understood that the three target cities would be removed from the air force's regular target list, reserving them for the A-bomb. But, the members were informed, "with the current and prospective rate of . . . bombings, it is expected to complete strategic bombing of Japan by 1 Jan 46 so availability of future [A-bomb] targets will be a problem." In short, Japan was being bombed out.

On May 28, 1945, physicist Arthur H. Compton, a Nobel laureate and member of a special scientific panel advising the high-level Interim Committee newly appointed to recommend policy about the bomb, raised profound moral and political questions about how the atomic bomb would be used. "It introduces the question of mass slaughter, really for the first time in history," he wrote. "It carries with it the question of possible radioactive poison over the area bombed. Essentially, the question of the use . . . of the new weapon carries much more serious implications than the introduction of poison gas."

Compton's concern received some independent support from General Marshall, who told Secretary Stimson on May 29 that the A-bomb should first be used not against civilians but against military installations—perhaps a naval base—and then possibly against large manufacturing areas after the civilians had received ample warnings to flee. Marshall feared "the opprobrium which might follow from an ill considered employment of such force." A graduate of Virginia Military Institute and a trained soldier, Marshall struggled to retain the older code of not *intentionally* killing civilians. The concerns of Compton the scientist and Marshall the general, their values so rooted in an earlier conception of war that sought to spare noncombatants, soon gave way to the sense of exigency, the desire to use the bomb on people, and the unwillingness or inability of anyone near the top in Washington to plead forcefully for maintaining this older morality.

On May 31, 1945, the Interim Committee, composed of Stimson, Bush, Harvard President James Conant, physicist and educator Karl T. Compton, Secretary of State designate James F. Byrnes, and a few other notables, discussed the A-bomb. Opening this meeting, Stimson, the aged secretary of war who had agonized over the recent shift toward mass bombing of civilians, described the atomic bomb as representing "a new relationship of man to the universe. This discovery might be compared to the discoveries of the Copernican theory and the laws of gravity, but far more important than these in its effects on the lives of men."

Meeting, as they were, some six weeks before the first nuclear test at Alamogordo, they were still unsure of the power of this new weapon. Oppenheimer told the group that it would have an explosive force of between 2,000 and 20,000 tons of TNT. Its visual effect would be tremendous. "It would be accompanied by a brilliant luminescence which would rise to a height of 10,000 to 20,000 feet," Oppenheimer reported. "The neutron effect [radiation] would be dangerous to life for a radius of at least two-thirds of a mile." He estimated that 20,000 Japanese would be killed.

According to the committee minutes, the group discussed "various types of targets and the effects to be produced." Stimson "expressed the conclusion, on which there was general agreement, that we could not give the Japanese any warning; that we could not concentrate on a civilian area; but that we should seek to make a profound psychological impression on as many of the inhabitants as possible. At the suggestion of Dr. Conant, the secretary agreed that the most desirable target would be a vital war plant employing a large number of workers and closely surrounded by workers' houses."

Directed by Stimson, the committee was actually endorsing terror bombing—but somewhat uneasily. They would not focus exclusively on a military target (the older morality), as Marshall had recently proposed, nor fully on civilians (the emerging morality). They managed to achieve their purpose—terror bombing—without bluntly acknowledging it to themselves. All knew that families—women, children, and, even in the daytime, during the bomb attack, some workers—dwelled in "workers' houses."

At the committee's morning or afternoon session, or at lunch, or possibly at all three times—different members later presented differing recollections—the notion of a noncombat demonstration of the A-bomb came up. The issue of how to use the bomb was not even on Stimson's agenda, nor was it part of the formal mandate of the Interim Committee, but he may have showed passing interest in the subject of a noncombat demonstration. They soon rejected it. It was deemed too risky for various reasons: the bomb might not work, the Japanese air force might interfere with the bomber, the A-bomb might not adequately impress the Japanese militarists, or the bomb might incinerate any Allied POWs whom the Japanese might place in the area. . . .

The bomb had been devised to be used, the project cost about $2 billion, and Truman and Byrnes, the president's key political aide, had no desire to avoid its use. Nor did Stimson. They even had additional reasons for wanting to use it: the bomb might *also* intimidate the Soviets and render them tractable in the postwar period.

Stimson emphasized this theme in a secret memorandum to Truman on April 25: "If the problem of the proper use of this weapon can be solved, we should then have the opportunity to bring the world into a pattern in which the peace of the world and our civilization can be saved." Concern about the bomb and its relationship to the Soviet Union dominated Stimson's thinking in the spring and summer of 1945. And Truman and Byrnes, perhaps partly under Stimson's tutelage, came to stress the same hopes for the bomb.

During 1945, Stimson found himself presiding, with agony, over an air force that killed hundreds of thousands of Japanese civilians. Usually, he preferred not to face these ugly facts, but sought refuge in the notion that the air force was actually engaged in precision bombing and that somehow this precision bombing was going awry. Caught between an older morality that opposed the intentional killing of noncombatants and a newer one that stressed virtually total war, Stimson could neither fully face the facts nor fully escape them. He was not a hypocrite but a man trapped in ambivalence.

Stimson discussed the problem with Truman on June 6. Stimson stressed that he was worried about the air force's mass bombing, but that it was hard to restrict it. In his diary, Stimson recorded: "I told him I was anxious about this feature of the war for two reasons: first, because I did not want to have the United States get the reputation of outdoing Hitler in atrocities; and second, I was a little fearful that before we could get ready the air force might have Japan so thoroughly bombed out that the new weapon would not have a fair background to show its strength." According to Stimson, Truman "laughed and said he understood."

Unable to reestablish the old morality and wanting the benefits for America of the new, Stimson proved decisive—even obdurate—on a comparatively small matter: removing Kyoto from Groves' target list of cities. It was not that Stimson was trying to save Kyoto's citizens; rather, he was seeking to save its relics, lest the Japanese become embittered and later side with the Soviets. As Stimson explained in his diary entry of July 24: "The bitterness which would be caused by such a wanton act might make it impossible during the long postwar period to reconcile the Japanese to us in that area rather than to the Russians. It might thus . . . be the means of preventing what our policy demanded, namely, a sympathetic Japan to the United States in case there should be any aggression by Russia in Manchuria."

Truman, backing Stimson on this matter, insisted privately that the A-bombs would be used only on military targets. Apparently the president wished not to recognize the inevitable—that a weapon of such great power would necessarily kill many civilians. At Potsdam on July 25, Truman received glowing reports of the vast destruction achieved by the Alamogordo blast and lavishly recorded the details in his diary: a crater of 1,200 feet in diameter, a steel tower destroyed a half mile away, men knocked over six miles away. "We have discovered," he wrote in his diary, "the most terrible bomb in the history of the world. It may be the fire destruction prophesied." But when he approved the final list of A-bomb targets, with Nagasaki and Kokura substituted for Kyoto, he could write in his diary, "I have told Sec. of War . . . Stimson to use it so that military objectives and soldiers and sailors are the target and not women and children. Even if the Japs are savages, ruthless, merciless, and fanatic . . . [t]he target will be a purely military one." Truman may have been engaging in self-deception to make the mass deaths of civilians acceptable.

Neither Hiroshima nor Nagasaki was a "purely military" target, but the official press releases, cast well before the atomic bombings, glided over this matter. Hiroshima, for example, was described simply as "an important Japanese army base." The press releases were drafted by men who knew that those cities had been chosen partly to dramatize the killing of noncombatants.

On August 10, the day after the Nagasaki bombing, when Truman realized the magnitude of the mass killing and the Japanese offered a conditional surrender requiring continuation of the emperor, the president told his cabinet that he did not want to kill any more women and children. Rejecting demands to drop more atomic bombs on Japan, he hoped not to use them again. After two atomic bombings, the horror of mass death had forcefully hit the president, and he was willing to return partway to the older morality—civilians might be protected from A-bombs. But he continued to sanction the heavy conventional bombing of Japan's cities, with the deadly toll that napalm, incendiaries, and other bombs produced. Between August 10 and August 14—the war's last day, on which about 1,000 American planes bombed Japanese cities, some delivering their deadly cargo after Japan announced its surrender—the United States probably killed more than 15,000 Japanese.

Before August 10, Truman and his associates had not sought to avoid the use of the atomic bomb. As a result, they had easily dismissed the possibility of a noncombat demonstration. Indeed, the post-Hiroshima pleas of Japan's military leaders for a final glorious battle suggest that such a demonstration probably would not have produced a speedy surrender. And American leaders also did not pursue other alternatives: modifying their unconditional surrender demand by guaranteeing the maintenance of the emperor, awaiting the Soviet entry into the war, or simply pursuing heavy conventional bombing of the cities amid the strangling naval blockade.

Truman and Byrnes did not believe that a modification of the unconditional surrender formula would produce a speedy surrender. They thought that guaranteeing to maintain the emperor would prompt an angry backlash from Americans who regarded Hirohito as a war criminal, and feared that this concession might embolden the Japanese militarists to expect more concessions and thus prolong the war. As a result, the president and his secretary of state easily rejected Stimson's pleas for a guarantee of the emperor.

Similarly, most American leaders did not believe that the Soviet entry into the Pacific war would make a decisive difference and greatly speed Japan's surrender. Generally, they believed that the U.S.S.R.'s entry would help end the war—ideally, before the massive invasion of Kyushu. They anticipated Moscow's intervention in mid-August, but the Soviets moved up their schedule to August 8, probably because of the Hiroshima bombing, and the Soviet entry did play an important role in producing Japan's surrender on August 14. Soviet entry without the A-bomb *might* have produced Japan's surrender before November.

The American aim was to avoid, if possible, the November 1 invasion, which would involve about 767,000 troops, at a possible cost of 31,000 casualties in the first 30 days and a total estimated American death toll of about 25,000. And American leaders certainly wanted to avoid the second part of the invasion plan, an assault on the Tokyo plain, scheduled for around March 1, 1946, with an estimated 15,000–21,000 more Americans dead. In the spring and summer of 1945, no American leader believed—as some later falsely claimed—that they planned to use the A-bomb to save half a million Americans. But, given the patriotic calculus of the time, there was no hesitation about using A-bombs to kill many Japanese in order to save the 25,000–46,000 Americans who might otherwise have died in the invasions. Put bluntly, Japanese life—including civilian life—was cheap, and some American leaders, like many rank-and-file citizens, may well have savored the prospect of punishing the Japanese with the A-bomb.

Truman, Byrnes, and the other leaders did not have to be reminded of the danger of a political backlash in America if they did not use the bomb and the invasions became necessary. Even if they had wished to avoid its use—and they did not—the fear of later public outrage spurred by the weeping parents and loved ones of dead American boys might well have forced American leaders to drop the A-bomb on Japan.

No one in official Washington expected that one or two atomic bombs would end the war quickly. They expected to use at least a third, and probably more. And until the day after Nagasaki, there had never been in their thinking a choice between atomic bombs and conventional bombs, but a selection of both—using mass bombing to compel surrender. Atomic bombs and conventional bombs were viewed as supplements to, not substitutes for, one another. Heavy conventional bombing of Japan's cities would probably have killed hundreds of thousands in the next few months, and might have produced the desired surrender before November 1.

Taken together, some of these alternatives—promising to retain the Japanese monarchy, awaiting the Soviets' entry, and even more conventional bombing—very probably could have ended the war before the dreaded invasion. Still, the evidence—to borrow a phrase from F.D.R.—is somewhat "iffy," and no one who looks at the intransigence of the Japanese militarists should have full confidence in those other strategies. But we may well regret that these alternatives were not pursued and that there was not an effort to avoid the use of the first A-bomb—and certainly the second.

Whatever one thinks about the necessity of the first A-bomb, the second—dropped on Nagasaki on August 9—was almost certainly unnecessary. It was used because the original order directed the air force to drop bombs "as made ready" and, even after the Hiroshima bombing, no one in Washington anticipated an imminent Japanese surrender. Evidence now available about developments in the Japanese government—most notably the emperor's then-secret decision shortly before the Nagasaki bombing to seek peace—makes it clear that the second bomb could undoubtedly have been avoided. At least 35,000 Japanese and possibly almost twice that number, as well as several thousand Koreans, died unnecessarily in Nagasaki.

Administration leaders did not seek to avoid the use of the A-bomb. They even believed that its military use might produce a powerful bonus: the intimidation of the Soviets, rendering them, as Byrnes said, "more manageable," especially in Eastern Europe. Although that was not the dominant purpose for using the weapon, it certainly was a strong confirming one. Had Truman and his associates, like the dissenting scientists at Chicago, foreseen that the A-bombing of Japan would make the Soviets intransigent rather than tractable, perhaps American leaders would have questioned their decision. But precisely because American leaders expected that the bombings would also compel the Soviet Union to loosen its policy in Eastern Europe, there was no incentive to question their intention to use the atomic bomb. Even if they had, the decision would probably have been the same. In a powerful sense, the atomic bombings represented the implementation of an assumption—one that Truman comfortably inherited from Roosevelt. Hiroshima was an easy decision for Truman.

Only years later, as government archives opened, wartime hatreds faded, and sensibilities changed, would Americans begin seriously to question whether the atomic bombings were necessary, desirable, and moral. Building on the postwar memoirs of Admiral William Leahy and General Dwight D. Eisenhower, among others, doubts began to emerge about the use of the atomic bombs against Japan. As the years passed, Americans learned that the bombs, according to high-level American military estimates in June and July 1945, probably could not have saved a half million American lives in the invasions, as Truman sometimes contended after Nagasaki, but would have saved fewer than 50,000. Americans also came slowly to recognize the barbarity of World War II, especially the mass killings by bombing civilians. It was that redefinition of morality that made Hiroshima and Nagasaki possible and ushered in the atomic age in a frightening way.

That redefinition of morality was a product of World War II, which included such barbarities as Germany's systematic murder of six million Jews and Japan's rape of Nanking. While the worst atrocities were perpetrated by the Axis, all the major nation-states sliced away at the moral code—often to the applause of their leaders and citizens alike. By 1945 there were few moral restraints left in what had become virtually a total war. Even F.D.R.'s prewar concern for sparing enemy civilians had fallen by the wayside. In that new moral climate, any nation that had the A-bomb would probably have used it against enemy peoples. British leaders as well as

Joseph Stalin endorsed the act. Germany's and Japan's leaders surely would have used it against cities. America was not morally unique—just technologically exceptional. Only it had the bomb, and so only it used it.

To understand this historical context does not require that American citizens or others should approve of it. But it does require that they recognize that pre- and post-Hiroshima dissent was rare in 1945. Indeed, few then asked why the United States used the atomic bomb on Japan. But had the bomb not been used, many more, including numerous outraged American citizens, would have bitterly asked that question of the Truman administration.

In 1945, most Americans shared the feelings that Truman privately expressed a few days after the Hiroshima and Nagasaki bombings when he justified the weapon's use in a letter to the Federal Council of Churches of Christ. "I was greatly disturbed over the unwarranted attack by the Japanese on Pearl Harbor and their murder of our prisoners of war," the president wrote. "The only language they seem to understand is the one we have been using to bombard them. When you have to deal with a beast you have to treat him as a beast."

Robert H. Ferrell

REORIENTING AMERICAN FOREIGN POLICY: HARRY S. TRUMAN'S ACHIEVEMENTS

In the following essay, a selection from his biography of Harry S Truman, historian Robert H. Ferrell stresses the singular importance of the president in moving the United States from isolationism to active engagement in world affairs during the early postwar years. Truman, according to Ferrell, deserves the lion's share of the credit for the major U.S. policy achievements of the 1947–1949 period: the Truman Doctrine, the

Reprinted from *Harry S. Truman: A Life* by Robert H. Ferrell, by permission of the University of Missouri Press, pp. 246–253, 254–257, 264–267. Copyright © 1994 by the Curators of the University of Missouri.

Marshall Plan, the North Atlantic Treaty Organization (NATO), and the broader strategy for containing the Soviet Union of which they formed so central a part. Not only did Truman correctly identify the gravity of the Soviet threat and devise strategies appropriate to derailing it, Ferrell writes, but he deftly transformed an American tradition of abstention from European affairs into the more appropriate role of full participation in global politics. Ferrell praises and defends American Cold War decisions in a manner reminiscent of Arthur Schlesinger's earlier essay, reaffirming a traditionalist perspective.

A longtime professor of history at Indiana University, Robert H. Ferrell has written widely on modern American politics and foreign relations. Among his numerous books are *Peace in Their Time: The Origins of the Kellogg-Briand Pact* (1952), *American Diplomacy in the Great Depression* (1957), *Harry S. Truman and the Modern American Presidency* (1983), and *Woodrow Wilson and World War I: 1917–1921* (1985).

The principal accomplishment of Harry S. Truman during his nearly eight years in the presidency was to change the foreign policy of the United States, from abstention to participation in the affairs of Europe and the world. To say such a thing after decades of participation seems almost pretentious. As Americans of the present day look back on their country's history, they see not only the nation's incessant moves of policy since Truman's time but also the two world wars of our century. In their minds' eyes they equate the world wars with participation, and in a kind of lapse of thought they are willing to affirm that their government and its citizenry have devoted the entire twentieth century to contemplating and if necessary resolving the confusions and conflicts—what President George Washington in his farewell address described as the combinations and collisions—of powers outside the Western Hemisphere.

Still, the truth is that until 1947, in the midst of Truman's first term, the principal American way with foreign policy was that of Presidents Washington, Jefferson, and Monroe: the old-time view that there was a New World and an Old World; that Almighty God had sifted the choice grain and sent it to the New; and that the interests of humankind—survival of the choice grain—lay in nonintervention in, abstention from, the affairs of the Old. Americans of this earlier time deemed participation in the world wars a temporary proposition. For them, World War I was a matter of "paying the debt to Lafayette." Although President Wilson desired the country to enter the League of Nations, popular support for such an arrangement lasted a very short time, and, as everyone knows, Wilson lost out with the Senate, and his proposed Democratic successor, Governor James M. Cox of Ohio, lost out with the American people. Similarly, after World War II few Americans expected the nation to continue its commitments abroad. President Roosevelt told Stalin at Yalta he did not expect American troops to remain in Europe more than two years.

This outlook came to an end during the Truman administration. The president of that time presided over the change. And more, he guided the change through the toils of political opposition and popular confusion. He did not always do right. In the Truman Doctrine he overstated the need to oppose the Soviet Union to get a large appropriation for Greece and Turkey through Congress, and he persuaded some Americans to consider the USSR a sort of bogey rather than another, if large and important, opponent in the long series of nations that have disliked the United States and sought its discomfiture. Such exaggeration led to the belief that the United States committed itself to oppose communism everywhere. In the Marshall Plan the administration may have thought too much of its assistance to European stability, which for Western Europe was only 10 or 20 percent of aggregate capital formation. The plan's cost was no burden, considering America's economic domination of the world: in the late 1940s the United States possessed half of the world's productive capacity. In the case of the North Atlantic Treaty the administration misestimated the intentions of the Soviet Union, espying a Soviet desire to conquer Western Europe. Still, there were extenuating circumstances for such miscalculation. Taken altogether the achievement from March 1947 to April 1949 was very large.

The first move was the Truman Doctrine, a statement of American purpose announced by the president in a speech before Congress on March 12, 1947. A logical procession of moves ensued—the doctrinal statement preceding the economic and military programs—although at the moment the administration did not see matters developing in this clear, careful manner.

The origins of the Truman Doctrine lay in immediate post-war relations with the Soviet Union, in which the current ruler of the USSR chose to reject friendship with the United States and substitute what he had known within Russia since his youth, manipulation and pressure. This course, he must have hoped, would bring the rewards in foreign policy it had produced in domestic affairs. But even while ending coalition governments in Eastern Europe, turning them into communist governments, actions that the Western nations could have considered a legacy of the war, the Soviets began to close off Western influence in Iran, Turkey, and Greece. Simultaneously with refusal to evacuate the northern provinces of Iran had come what both the Turkish and American governments assumed was an attack on Turkish independence: demands to change the Montreux Convention governing the straits into a joint military occupation and for cession of border territories lost after World War I. The Turkish government was vulnerable to this sort of pressure. Turkey had a population of 19 million, an army of five hundred thousand, and a long border with the USSR. The Soviets apparently were attempting to bring the country into the same relationship as they had managed with Poland. All the while the situation in Greece was turning serious. The government that the British army installed in Athens in 1944–1945 went from bad to worse, using its budget for the army and police, inflating the currency, failing to deal with an insurgency on its borders. Despite a pledge to Churchill that the West would have a 90 percent influence in Greece, Stalin encouraged the insurgent leader, General Markos Vafiades, to offer border concessions to Yugoslavia, Albania, and Bulgaria, in return for military assistance ("giving them what they wanted at our expense, so that we might get what we needed to achieve power").

The movement toward a new American policy for Europe gained momentum in the first full year of peace, 1946, with two full-dress analyses of Soviet-American relations. The initial review was George F. Kennan's "long telegram" from Moscow on February 1946, an eight-thousand-word account of Russian policy. The state department had asked for the cable, though doubtless it had no idea Kennan, who was chargé d'affaires, would send such a long explanation. In arousing government officials its importance was undoubted—it came to the attention of Secretary of the Navy Forrestal, who sent copies to friends, and Washington officials began to sense a historical dimension to Soviet behavior. Its influence upon President Truman was less clear. Years later, when Kennan had become well known both as a diplomat and as an author of books and articles, including the "X" article in the journal *Foreign Affairs* in the summer of 1947 that set out the idea of "containment" of the Soviet Union, the diplomat-historian said wistfully that he was not sure Truman had known who he was, even though he briefed the president. "I met with [Truman] once or twice during this period. . . . I suspect he was vaguely aware that there was a young fellow over in the State Department who had written a good piece on the Russians—I doubt whether Truman ever really read anything I wrote, though. Certainly I don't think he grasped my position." The president does not seem to have read the long telegram, nor perhaps ever heard of it.

In September of the same year George Elsey of the White House staff produced a second, somewhat similar, statement of U.S.-Soviet problems, to which after a few emendations the president's special counsel, Clifford, put his own name. Based on information gathered throughout the government, including the long telegram, it was a much more authoritative commentary. Printed and bound in book form, as nicely written as Kennan's essay, it was an impressive seventy-nine pages, offering chapters on agreements with the Soviets, violations, reparations, and Soviet actions affecting American security. The first sentence of its first page established the theme: "The gravest problem facing the United States today is that of American relations with the Soviet Union." Negotiation, it predicted, would not get far: "The general pattern of the Soviet system is too firmly established to be altered suddenly by any individual—even Stalin." That Americans could persuade the Soviets to "change the character of their philosophy and society" appeared highly improbable. The United States needed to stand up to the Soviet Union by assisting friendly governments wherever possible.

Truman's first reaction to the Clifford-Elsey report was to call in all twenty numbered copies and put them under lock and key. The morning after reading it he told Clifford to bring them to him. He may have noticed two indiscreet statements. One was on the Middle East, "an area of great strategic interest to the Soviet Union because of the shift of Soviet industry to southeastern Russia, within range of air attack from much of the Near East." This might have encouraged the U.S. Army Air Forces, about to become independent in the Defense Act of the next year, to open a campaign to station bombers in the Middle East. The other was a flat-out remark that "to maintain our strength at a level which will be effective in restraining the Soviet Union, the United States must be prepared to wage atomic and biological warfare." In any event it was dangerous to put America's Russian policy between two covers, easily available perhaps to some supporter of Henry Wallace, not to mention a Russian spy.

How seriously the president otherwise took the report is difficult to say. He was still unwilling to come out against the Soviet Union. The report was dated September 24; three days earlier he had written former vice president of the United States John Garner that "there is too much loose talk about the Russian situation. We are not going to have any shooting trouble with them but they are tough bargainers and always ask for the whole earth, expecting maybe to get an acre." Some months afterward he wrote his daughter that he had required a year and a half after Potsdam to change his mind about the Soviets. Until the time of the Truman Doctrine he clearly continued to think things over, to see what he could do.

In considering how the president made up his mind about the Soviet Union and prepared himself for his doctrine, evidence other than those two reports lies in two statements he himself drew up, one at the beginning of 1946, the other a year later. The letter to Byrnes of January 5, 1946, related not only how Byrnes should keep the president informed but also what he, Truman, thought about Soviet-American relations. Russian behavior in Iran, he told himself in the letter and perhaps said to Byrnes, was "parallel to the program of Russia in Latvia, Estonia and Lithuania." It was in line with Russia's "highhanded and arbitrary" actions in Poland. At Potsdam the Soviets had faced him down with an accomplished fact in regard to Poland, almost forcing him to agree to Russian occupation of eastern Poland and occupation by the Poles of the area between the Eastern and Western Neisse rivers. At that time the United States had been anxious for Russian entry into the Far Eastern war, and "[o]f course we found later that we didn't need Russia there and the Russians have been a headache to us ever since." The United States, he wrote, should refuse to recognize the governments of Romania and Bulgaria until those regimes complied with the Yalta Declaration on Eastern Europe. The United States should insist on internationalization of Europe's waterways. In the Pacific it should maintain complete control of Japan and the island groups captured in the Pacific war. "We should rehabilitate China and create a strong central government there. We should do the same for Korea." The United States should also force return of lend-lease ships given Russia, and indeed of the entire lend-lease debt. "There isn't a doubt in my mind that Russia intends an invasion of Turkey and the seizure of the Black Sea Straits to the Mediterranean. Unless Russia is faced with an iron fist and strong language another war is in the making. Only one language do they understand—'How many divisions have you?'"

The beginning of the new year, 1947, brought a similar statement. By this time he was writing that he would not allow the Soviet regime to "bulldoze" the United States. He made a list of things to do:

1. Present Russian ambassador to U.S.A. persona non grata, a stable boy who ought to stay in a stable. Does not belong in Washington.
2. Urge Stalin to pay us a visit. We'll send the battleship *Missouri* for him if he'll come, either to Odessa or Leningrad and bring his guard
3. Settle Korean question on the basis of Moscow agreement [of December 1945] or better, give Koreas a government of their own.
4. Settle the Manchurian question [the Communist Chinese were in occupation, supported by the Soviets] on the basis of the Sino-Russian treaty and support Chiang Kai-shek for a strong China.
5. Agree to a discussion of Russia's lend-lease debt to the United States. Vital.
6. Agree to a commercial air treaty on a reciprocal basis.
7. Make it plain that we have no territorial ambitions. That we only want peace, but we'll fight for it!

The projects varied in importance, but point seven was a good summary. The president thereupon explained himself in a little essay:

The smart boys, columnists, radio commentators etc. wonder why Russia is more amenable to reason now than a year ago. None of them have thought to say either in print or over the air that perhaps someone sent them word that an agreement could be made on a peaceable basis if they wanted it. But if a peaceable basis was not what Russia wanted the U.S.A. would meet them on any other basis. The president stated at the meeting in Berlin in July, 1945, that a free Danube is necessary to Central European peace and Central European economy. That Trieste should be a free port for all Central Europe. That the Dardanelles, Kiel Canal, and the Rhine-Danube waterway should all be free on the same basis to all nations. That Manchuria should be Chinese, that Dairen should be a free port, that Russia should have Kuriles and Sakhalin, that we would control in Japan and the Pacific. That Germany should be occupied as an economic whole by the four powers agreed upon at Yalta; that Austria should not be treated as an enemy country. All agreed to by Russia.

But they'd unlawfully attached part of East Prussia and Germany as far west as the Oder to Poland, and had themselves annexed Latvia, Estonia, Lithuania, and a part of East Prussia to Russia, as well as a large area in eastern Poland.

I told Mr. Byrnes just one year ago that we'd stand for justice and would not be bulldozed. We've pursued that policy and they've caved in just as [labor leader John L.] Lewis did in the coal strike. Because they are the same sort of cattle—bullies and nothing else. We only want justice and a just peace. That we'll have and that we'll get. There is no difference in totalitarian states, call them Nazi, fascist or communist—they are all the same. The present dictatorship in Russia is as terrible as the czar's ever was.

By early 1947 the president was on the verge of making up his mind. The process, however, had been much slower than people then or later believed. It took, in fact, a year and a half after the end of the war before he was willing to move against the USSR.

A public pronouncement was occasioned by the British Government's communication to the state department late in February 1947 that it no longer could support the governments of Greece and Turkey. The Truman administration would have to take up the burden, else those countries would pass behind the iron curtain.

There followed a quick series of actions. The cabinet gave immediate approval. The president called a meeting to inform congressional leaders of the need for money, a $400 million appropriation.

During the White House session Secretary Marshall made an uncharacteristically muddled presentation—he was usually first-rate when speaking extempore and could summon historical precedents and put matters in perspective. Undersecretary Acheson interrupted his chief and redirected Marshall's statement in more forceful, so Acheson later said, terms. Acheson may have erred here, as he seems to have called up the Russian menace. Allegedly—the point has never had proof—Senator Vandenberg told the president that the best course with Congress was to "scare hell out of the country." The subsequent speech was carefully put together. When the state department speechwriter, Joseph M. Jones, asked Acheson for general guidance on the speech—how far the proposed assistance should go—Acheson gazed out the window of his office, toward the Washington Monument, and said he thought he knew what Roosevelt would have done in such a situation. FDR would have made a pronouncement covering the world, but asked for an appropriation for Greece and Turkey. When Jones's speech went over to the White House, Elsey seized it and chopped its sentences to make it read better and also accord with the president's pithy style. He may have made it a little more scary.

Even so, congressional opposition proved considerable. One of the arguments was that the Greek government was undemocratic and corrupt, which was true, and that Turkey was not a democracy and had been neutral during most of the recent war, also true. Another assertion was that the aid proposal bypassed the United Nations. To such critics, administration spokesmen could only say that while Greece and Turkey were hardly ideal governments, they were capable of improvement. The original bill gave the UN little attention, perhaps because of Acheson's almost violent feelings against the world organization. It was at about this time that he told Dean Rusk the UN was a monkey house. Vandenberg, however, insisted on public obeisances, which the administration made.

Another congressional argument against aid was that the president's request for funds gave no attention to communism outside Western Europe. Representative Walter H. Judd of Wisconsin, a former medical missionary to China, asked why the United States was opposing Soviet machinations in Greece and Turkey and doing little or nothing for China, which was then in civil war. To this point Acheson offered a weak answer, although it made sense. He said that the United States was trying to use its power where it could; to intervene in Greece and Turkey was one thing, but China was something else. Its size and population were in no way comparable to those of Greece and Turkey: "There have been various statements in the press that this was an ideological crusade. That is not what the president is talking about. He is talking about the fact that where a free world is being coerced to give up its free institutions, we are interested. . . . He did not state, and I think no one would state, that that means wherever this situation occurs, one must react to it in exactly the same way."

The bill for aid to Greece and Turkey passed the Senate by vote of 67 to 23 (April 23), the House by 287 to 107 (May 9), and the president signed it on May 15. To a draft of a press release accompanying his signature Truman added a gentle apostrophe: "We are guardians of a great faith. We believe that freedom offers the best chance of peace and prosperity for all, and our desire for peace cannot be separated from our belief in liberty. We hope that in the years ahead more and more nations will come to know the advantages of freedom and liberty. It is to this end that we have enacted the law I have now signed." For some reason the release did not include this statement.

Such was the first, and in some respects the most important, of Truman's moves in foreign policy that took the country away from its isolationist ways. In passing let it be said again, as Acheson told the speechwriter Jones, and later tried to tell Congressman Judd, that the Truman Doctrine, as it came to be called, was not a doctrine that covered the world. In subsequent years critics of the actions of Truman and his successors made many points on this theme. One of their explanations concerned the way in which Acheson had spoken in the meeting with the congressional leaders, perhaps overstating the dangers of Soviet communism. When the Korean War opened, and especially during the Vietnam War, critics blamed involvement on the Truman Doctrine. Without the doctrine, they said, the United States might have minded its own business. They raised up a host of presidential statements about communism, offered in the 1950s and 1960s by Truman's successors, Republican and Democratic alike, and connected them with the doctrine and drew their awkward conclusion. But there was much evidence to the contrary. As John Lewis Gaddis put it later, "Subservience to Moscow made one a target of containment, not adherence to the doctrines of Marx and Lenin." This had become evident after the defection of Yugoslavia from the Soviet bloc in 1948, which brought aid despite that country's communist government. Truman was trying to restore the European balance of power and had neither the intention nor the capability of policing the world.

The next move, underway within weeks of announcement of the Truman Doctrine, was the European Recovery Act, to which the president attached the name of his secretary of state.

General Marshall deserved a good deal of the credit for the plan's success, because his personal prestige carried it forward. . . . The appointment [of Marshall as Secretary of State] was a success in every way. For one thing it did not take Marshall long to seize control of the department. He told Acheson to straighten out the "chain of command," a task that Acheson undertook with a vengeance. Then, even more important, Marshall began looking into the primary need of foreign policy at the time (the general had had plenty of experience in getting to the center of things), Europe's economic plight. After the hard, cold winter of 1946–1947, Europe was in straits. The winter wheat had died in the ground. Coal production was so low in Britain the electricity was available in London only a few hours a day, and Europe's industry slowed markedly because of lack of coal. Affairs were especially bad in Germany, where in the Western zones industrial production was 27 percent of prewar levels. In 1936, Germany had produced 85 percent of its food; in 1947 the figure was 25 percent. The United Nations Relief and Rehabilitation Administration was coming to an end on March 31, 1947.

Gradually the possibilities for policy in Western Europe began to appear. Congress was in no mood for more emergency plans; everywhere the idea of long-range planning was in the air. But Marshall wanted action. He had just come back from forty-four sessions of a foreign ministers' conference in Moscow in the spring of 1947, the purpose of which was to consider peace treaties for Germany and Austria, but the conference had accomplished little and gave the impression it was tying up the time of Western foreign ministers while Europe's economy plunged. The secretary kept saying to callers and department officials, "Nobody will believe me." He asked the policy planning staff, a new group under Kennan, to draw up a memorandum, some sort of plan or suggestions. Then the undersecretary for economic affairs, William L.

Clayton, who in private life was head of the world's largest cotton merchant firm, Anderson, Clayton and Company, returned from Europe and gave him a memorandum pointing out that Europe did not have the dollars to prime its economic pump. The memorandum became the basis for the Marshall Plan.

It is well known how department officials arranged for Marshall to propose such a plan during a talk at the Harvard commencement on June 5. Truman had little to do with the proposal. Years later Marshall told his biographer, Forrest Pogue, that the arrangements for the speech were so hurried he did not tell the president and later apologized for the failure. After all, though, Truman had approved the whole idea of aid in his speech in March, so nothing was lost. In the talk itself, and subsequent meetings of European leaders, the plan took shape. At the advice of assistants the secretary placed a string in the proposition, that the Europeans must themselves draw up a plan; there could be no more shopping lists. He offered the proposal to all nations "west of the Urals," including the Soviet Union and East European satellites. The British, French, and Russian foreign ministers met in Paris early in June. Molotov refused to take part in a joint proposal, the British and French invited the other nations, the Soviets refused satellite participation, and in September a second Paris conference drew up a plan. Two months later Truman asked Congress for interim aid, telling Leahy privately that his address to a joint session could hurt his administration and party but he was right and could not fail to act. In December the president asked for a first installment of what, when the Marshall Plan ended in 1952, became a $13 billion program. In March 1948 large bipartisan majorities in both Houses appropriated the installment, and Truman on April 3 signed the Recovery Act.

But to relate how the Marshall Plan became reality is hardly to account for the president's part in making the plan possible. He managed it with what a political scientist later ascribed to his successor, Eisenhower, as a "hidden hand." By bringing Marshall into the state department he obtained the reorganization he so wanted. Under Stettinius and Byrnes the department had no chance; its officers were on the outside looking in. Now they took part. Then when the time came to announce a plan Truman credited Marshall—another calculation, for he knew his prestige as president was too fragile to take credit. Clifford had suggested that the president name the program

the Truman Concept or the Truman Plan. "No," said the chief executive. "We have a Republican majority in both Houses. Anything
going up there bearing my name will quiver a couple of times, turn
belly up, and die. Let me think about it a little." A day or two later
the president made his decision: "I've decided to give the whole
thing to General Marshall. The worst Republican on the Hill can
vote for it if we name it after the General."

Last, realizing that any such program needed grassroots support, he did the same thing with it that he had done during the war
with his investigating committee; namely, he brought public opinion behind it. He presided over one of the most calculated manage-
ments of a program ever to come before Congress. At the outset
not everything had been harmonious. Senator Robert A. Taft, Republican of Ohio, said the plan was a Tennessee Valley Authority
for Europe, "global New Dealism." Senator Homer Ferguson, Republican of Michigan, beheld a universal Works Progress Administration (Republicans enjoyed comparisons with the New Deal).
Former president Hoover favored $4 billion, presumably because
the sum was smaller, spread over fifteen months; $3 billion, he said,
should be for his favorite foreign program during and after World
War I: food. Henry Wallace spoke of a "Martial Plan." [Journalist
Walter] Lippmann mildly favored the plan—it was not in opposition to the Soviet Union as was the Truman Doctrine, which he
opposed; it avoided globalism; it did not treat nations as "instruments" of American policy but as independent countries; it allowed
Europeans to save themselves—but he thought a better course
would be for the United States and USSR to leave Europe. Even so,
the president knew how to handle such complaints. Henry Stimson,
the eighty-year-old, rock-ribbed Republican, chaired the Committee for the Marshall Plan to Aid European Recovery, which enlisted
foreign policy associations, church groups, women's clubs, labor
unions, chambers of commerce, and the innumerable groups of the
knife-and-fork circuit—Rotary, Kiwanis, Lions. In speeches and ad-
dresses during the summer, autumn, and early winter of 1947–
1948, prior to passage of the first installment of the program, the
administration struck a popular chord, with arpeggios of flattery.
"Historical records clearly show," Marshall said, "that no people
have ever acted more generously and more unselfishly than the
American people in tendering assistance to alleviate distress and suffering." And again: "Whether we like it or not, we find ourselves,

our nation, in a world position of vast responsibility. We can act for our own good by acting for the world's good."

When the plan came before Congress the Soviet Union helped its passage by conducting a coup in Czechoslovakia, which "sent a shock throughout the civilized world." Everyone thought of Hitler's takeover of Czechoslovakia in 1939. A near crisis atmosphere prevailed when Congress passed the initial appropriation.

It is not easy to assess the result of the plan, save that European recovered. During the plan years local resources accounted for most capital formation and the American contribution was marginal—even though the plan's Washington administrator, the Republican industrialist Paul G. Hoffman, said the plan provided the critical margin. Moreover, and despite the infusion of dollars from the plan, there were clear signs that Europe's economy was faltering in 1949, and it may have taken the Korean War, with its offshore orders from the United States, to provide a "takeoff" for the continent's economy, to use the word of Walt W. Rostow. Too, the worst-off economy in Europe was that of the West German zones, and it looked as if the purpose of the plan was to invigorate the former enemy. The late John Gimbel wrote that the real purpose of Marshall and his assistants, which they had to disguise, was to restore German productivity so Germany again could be the powerhouse of Europe; it was necessary to put the German problem in a European context. (That explanation, of course, is too easy. American officials were gingerly about bolstering Germany's economy. Truman told Forrestal that while he did not believe in the plan of former secretary of the treasury Morgenthau to "pastoralize" Germany, neither did he want Germany rebuilt.) But the end result, and one likes to think it was because of the president's program, was beyond question. At the end of two and a half years, industrial output had increased 40 percent above prewar levels and agricultural 20 percent. The plan constituted a second move after the doctrine (the policies, the president later wrote, with resort to Missouri metaphor, were "two halves of the same walnut"). It helped prevent what had seemed the imminent collapse of Western Europe's economy, provided time in which to work for better relations with the Soviet Union, and marked a notable chapter in acceptance by the American people of what would be the nation's new foreign policy for the foreseeable future. . . .

Announcement of the great change in American foreign policy in 1947–1949 offered the new president opportunity to put his qualities to the test. There remains the need to ask whether he measured his Russian problem with as much precision, as much care, as his fellow citizens could have hoped—bearing in mind the difference between retrospect and action. For as Truman's secretary of state beginning in 1949, Acheson, so fondly related in the introduction to his memoirs, quoting the historian C. V. Wedgwood, "History is lived forwards but it is written in retrospect. We know the end before we consider the beginning and we can never wholly recapture what it was to know the beginning only."

Here a point needs to be made, namely, that in confronting the Soviet Union the president faced an unprecedented situation. The USSR was sui generis. It was unlike any nation any American leader had ever dealt with.

So little was known about what the country really was like at the time. Generally speaking, Western intelligence of its economic and military strength was poor. There seem to have been few Western operatives inside the USSR. What little the West knew was based on captured German aerial maps and interrogation of German and Japanese prisoners returning from the Soviet Union. At the end of the 1940s, with return of most of the prisoners, this information was drying up. A little information was available from flights by unarmed reconnaissance planes just outside territorial waters taking oblique photographs, otherwise from "accidental" overflights; such procedures covered small parts of the USSR, however, and they were dangerous, for once in a while the Soviets shot down planes. Not until 1956, with the first overflights by U-2 planes, could American leaders be fairly sure Soviet defenses were weaker than those of the United States, and not until satellite reconnaissance commencing in 1961 (unlike U-2s, satellites can photograph through cloud cover) could they be certain.

Nor was the nature of the Soviet regime itself any easier to comprehend. The Russian government was an enigma, for almost no reliable information was available. Never had a great government been so secretive, so difficult to understand in its workings, its policies, and its purposes. The Soviets did not allow their nationals to talk with foreigners, and newspaper reporters were reduced to attending receptions and reading the Soviet press, which was strictly party-line, almost byzantine in its revelations.

During Truman's time Westerners pinned their hopes on Stalin, believing him a reasonable autocrat. Stalin displayed none of the bombast of his late antagonist in Germany; on the face of things any comparison seemed not merely improbable but impossible. Quiet, soft-spoken, sometimes even humorous, he captivated Truman at Potsdam. The president believed the Soviets could understand U.S. policies if only he, the president, laid them out to Stalin. There were all the stories, apparently true, of atrocities throughout the 1930s. But then Russia, whether under the tsars or commissars, had never been a place for democratic change, and anyway, as Lenin said, one cannot make an omelet without breaking eggs. The emergency of World War II justified a harsh regime, and the collaboration of 1941–1945 washed away rancors.

Stalin was only the latter-day tsar and surely an improvement over the other tsars; in any event, he was held in check by his advisers. The postwar president told his morning conference, "[I]f only Stalin were concerned on the Russian side . . . everything would be all right." He said he liked Stalin—"the old guy." On this occasion Press Secretary Ross said there probably would be questions in a press conference as to whether he and Stalin should meet, and the president said that at Potsdam he asked Stalin to come to the United States and Stalin replied, "God willing." Clifford interjected, "God—and the Politburo." On June 11, 1948, while campaigning in Eugene, Oregon, Truman said, "I got very well acquainted with Joe Stalin, and I like old Joe! He is a decent fellow. But Joe is a prisoner of the Politburo. He can't do what he wants to. He makes agreements, and if he could he would keep them; but the people who run the government are very specific in saying that he can't keep them."

It is easy to say now how these personal appraisals were so wrong. Terror—sheer Stalinist terror—governed the Soviet Union. Stalin's murders numbered far into the millions, in collectivization of the farms, in the purges of the later 1930s, in the virtually leaderless early military actions of World War II (what with the army's officer corps decimated by the purges), in the postwar repressions. All the while the tyrant of the Kremlin kept much information from getting out, relying on the gullibility of his enemies to keep the rest of his secrets. Within the regime he supervised everything without dissent; Hitler had allowed more discussion, even disagreement. Sometimes the dictator would ask assistants why they appeared nervous or shifty-eyed or furtive. In conferences with Westerners he was observed drawing wolves' heads on a pad of paper. His suspicions, which always had been large, affected everything that passed through the Kremlin offices. In his last years his suspicions went to ridiculous lengths; Nikita S. Khrushchev, in the speech to the Twentieth Party Congress in 1956, drew a portrait of a man who was half crazed, perhaps because of arteriosclerosis—he died of a massive stroke. His advisers were lackeys and could do nothing, say nothing, without his consent. Stalin assigned tasks to the Politburo by dividing it into twos or threes, and he so controlled the group that in 1951 he arranged the execution of one of its members. Nor were the foreign ministers, with whom Westerners dealt and whose humors they often analyzed and divined and held up to glasses or placed on diplomatic litmus paper, any more independent. . . .

Most intriguing of all, in what we now are beginning to learn, is the likelihood that Stalin, who held the Soviet Union in his hand, was intensely fearful of the United States. . . . But Truman did not know this—he knew only the beginning, not the end. He knew only that he was dealing with a man who, commencing in April 1945, challenged American sensibilities time after time, as if willing to take anything to the limit and beyond. In such a time, whatever the illusions that later years erased, the president of the United States needed to announce a foreign policy that was as logical, as coldly rational, as it could be. This is exactly what he did.

Europe After the Second World War

SCALE

Miles 0 — 200 — 400 — 600
Kilometers 0 — 200 — 400 — 600 — 800

Annexed by U.S.S.R.
Annexed by Poland

ATLANTIC OCEAN

ICELAND

IRELAND   Dublin

GREAT BRITAIN   London

NORTH SEA

DENMARK   Copenhagen

NETH.   Berlin
BEL.   Bonn   GERMANY
LUX.   Br. zone   Sov. zone
Cherbourg   Fr. zone   Nuremberg
Paris   Strasbourg   Munich
FRANCE   SWITZ.   Vienna   AUSTRIA
Berne   Geneva
Marseille

SPAIN   Madrid

PORTUGAL   Lisbon

MOROCCO   ALGERIA

MEDITERRANEAN SEA

NORWAY   Oslo

SWEDEN   Stockholm

Archangel   White Sea

FINLAND   Helsinki   Leningrad

BALTIC SEA

ESTONIA   Riga   LATVIA   LITHUANIA

POLAND   Warsaw   Lublin
Stettin   Oder R.   Bug R.
Prague   CZECHOSLOVAKIA
Br. zone   Joint zone
Budapest   HUNGARY
Trieste   YUGOSLAVIA
ITALY   Rome   Belgrade   Danube R.
Sardinia   Tirana   ALBANIA
Corsica
Sicily
TUNISIA   Malta

SOVIET UNION (U.S.S.R.)

Volga R.   Moscow
Stalingrad

Minsk   WHITE RUSSIA
Kiev   Dnieper R.   UKRAINE   Curzon Line

Yalta   BLACK SEA

RUMANIA   Bucharest
BULGARIA   Sofia
GREECE   Athens   Piraeus   The Dardanelles   Istanbul   Ankara   TURKEY
Crete

Aral Sea

CASPIAN SEA   Baku   AZER-BAIJAN   Teheran
Tabriz   IRAN
SYRIA   LEBANON   Cyprus
IRAQ   Baghdad
CAUCASUS

Carolyn Eisenberg

DIVIDING GERMANY

As virtually all historians of the Cold War have acknowledged, the disposition of defeated Germany loomed from the outset as one of the most nettlesome, and most fundamental, issues separating the Soviet Union and the Western powers. Differences over Germany proved a major source of East-West tension throughout the entire postwar era; indeed, divided Germany came to symbolize the broader Cold War division of Europe. In this selection from her prizewinning book, *Drawing the Line* (1996), Carolyn Eisenberg argues that there was nothing inevitable about the Soviet-American rupture over Germany. Decrying "the cloud of inevitability that hangs so heavily over the Cold War," she urges students of history to regain a sense of contingency about the events that led to the division of Germany. That division derived from human decisions rather than from impersonal structural forces. And the Americans and their British partners, Eisenberg contends, not the Soviets, bear the primary responsibility for Germany's partition. The Anglo-American partners initiated all the actions that eventually led both to formal separation and to the subsequent creation of an independent West German state. Those steps, which carried momentous consequences for the peoples of Europe, and the world, were driven by the Anglo-American fixation with West Germany's centrality to the revival and reintegration of Western Europe. Tragic consequences flowed from the American decision to divide Germany, Eisenberg concludes, most notably the abandonment of East Germany and much of Eastern Europe to the Soviets and the increased militarization of Europe.

Carolyn Eisenberg has written a series of essays and reviews, in addition to *Drawing the Line: The American Decision to Divide Germany, 1944-1949* (1996), from which the selection below is drawn. The book won the Stuart Bernath prize of the Society for Historians of American Foreign Relations. Eisenberg is a professor of history of Hofstra University.

He was in the lead jeep when they first spotted the Russians, stretched along the east bank of the Elbe River. His commanding officer saw the sun glinting off the soldiers' medals and remembered hearing that the Red Army wore their decorations in combat. Certain now that these were Soviet troops and not Germans, the elated Americans shot up two green flares and shouted their greetings into the stiff wind that was blowing across the water. It was 11:30 in the morning, April 25, 1945.

On the other side of the world, in San Francisco, the delegates to the founding meeting of the United Nations were asleep in their hotels. For these Allied representatives this was to be a historic day, the occasion for establishing a new international organization dedicated to the preservation of peace. Yet on the eve of their conclave, the Second World War was a continuing reality. Inside Germany the obstinate Wehrmacht was battling on, as the massive armies of Generals Zhukov and Eisenhower closed in from east and west.

The man standing in the first jeep was Private Joseph Polowsky of Chicago, a rifleman with G Company, 273rd Infantry. Third Platoon, Sixty-ninth Division, First Army. Polowsky had been awarded a Bronze Star in the Battle of the Bulge and was part of a unit that had fought its way across Germany. One day earlier the men had reached Trebsen, a town twenty miles west of the Elbe. There, G Company had been ordered to dispatch a patrol in the direction of the river to obtain more precise information about the location of the Red Army. The soldiers were under instructions not to attempt an actual linkup, lest there be accidental casualties.

But the emotions of the moment had proved overwhelming. In the final stage of the most devastating war in human history, the prospect of actually meeting the Russian troops and helping sever the German army was irresistible. On the morning of the 25th the group's leader, Lieutenant Alfred "Buck" Kotzebue, chose to ignore headquarters' restriction and to push ahead to the Elbe. Later the same day, two other patrol leaders from the Sixty-ninth Division would also ignore their instructions, as their troops surged forward in search of the Red Army.

Kotzebue's men were the first to make contact. Joe Polowsky had been placed in front so he could talk to the Russians. Because nobody in the unit knew their language, the lieutenant was counting on Polowsky's German to permit communication.

As they pulled up to the Elbe the Americans were perplexed about how to get across. The closest bridge had been obliterated in an earlier battle and the river, which was swollen by the spring rain, was flowing swiftly. Suddenly Kotzebue spotted some small boats chained to the shore. Unable to unfasten them by hand, he balanced a grenade on the knot of chains, pulled the pin, and took cover. The explosion released one of the sailboats, and six of the men eagerly climbed in. Using makeshift oars, they paddled through the heavy currents and reached the eastern bank.

An appalling spectacle met their eyes as they tried to disembark. Extending along both sides of the ruined bridge were hundreds of corpses of German civilians. These old men, women, and children had been fleeing the Red Army in horse-drawn carts. The previous night the Russians had seen the light of their encampment, and mistaking the people for German soldiers had bombarded the location with their artillery. Now the bodies were "piled up like cordwood" along the water.

In order to greet the Soviet soldiers, the Americans "literally waded knee-deep through the bodies of the German refugees." Private Polowsky later recalled being overcome by the scene, unable to remove his gaze from the body of a young girl who was lying on the ground, clutching her doll with one hand and her fallen mother with the other.

Despite the surrounding horror, there was a feeling of exhilaration as the Americans recognized that their rendezvous spelled the defeat of the Third Reich. Visibly moved, Kotzebue turned to his translator proposing that we "make a resolution with these Russians here," that "this would be an important day in the lives of the two countries." Polowsky recollected that the suggestion was "very informal, but it was a solemn moment. There were tears in the eyes of most of us. . . . We embraced. We swore never to forget."

The Russians quickly produced some bottles of vodka along with German wine and beer. In a tumultuous outpouring of excitement, hope, and grief, the six soldiers from G Company joined the men from the Red Army in repeated toasts and pledges. Standing beside the bodies of the slain civilians, they promised that they would remember the destruction and forever honor the memory of the Elbe. With impassioned words flowing from many lips, Private Polowsky found his work unexpectedly arduous and affecting.

Company G had encountered the Russians in the town of Strehla, sixteen miles south of Torgau. Because there were no reporters present, this first linkup received little publicity. Four and one half hours later a second American patrol, headed by Lieutenant Robertson, found the Red Army at Torgau. Hundreds of reporters were nearby, and it was this meeting that was immediately immortalized in the Allied press by photographs of the first handshake.

The euphoria at Strehla was replicated at Torgau. Bill Robertson later remembered that

> We three Americans were standing with the Russians on the river bank laughing, shouting, pounding each other on the back, shaking hands with everyone. Frank, George and I were shouting in English, our hosts in Russian. Neither understood the other's words, but the commonality of feeling was unmistakable. We were all soldiers, comrades in arms. We had vanquished a common enemy. The war was over, peace was near. All of us would live for another hour, another day.

Andy Rooney, reporter for the army's *Stars and Stripes,* described "a mad scene of jubilation on the east and west banks of the Elbe at Torgau as infantrymen of Lieutenant Courtney H. Hodges, First U.S. Army, swapped K rations for a vodka with soldiers of Marshal Kornian's Ukrainian army, congratulating each other, despite the language barrier on the link-up." Later the men from the Sixty-ninth Division sat in warm sunshine on the banks of the Elbe, with the enemy guns finally silent, passing around bottles with their new Russian friends and watching the soldiers of the Red Army dance and sing. Reflecting on this panorama, Rooney wrote, "You get the feeling of exuberance, a great new world opening up."

Between them the two Allied armies had traversed a distance of 2,200 miles. The Russian forces had begun at Stalingrad on the Volga, the Americans at Normandy. When they came together in the heart of Germany, they had split the remainder of the German army through the center of "a shrinking corridor" from the North Sea to the plains of northern Italy.

Wherever they stood on the Elbe that day, to the Americans and Russians who were there, April 25 was a glorious moment of triumph and brotherhood. For some, like Joseph Polowsky, it was a transforming experience, an entry into history, a perception of human possibility and obligation. . . .

At the time of Joe Polowsky's death [in 1983], there were few who treasured the symbolism of the Elbe. That sudden explosion of fraternal feeling as the Allied armies joined in Germany had been virtually buried in historic memory. Yet in April 1945, the import of the occasion had been evident not only to the soldiers who were there, but to millions of people around the world.

In a period darkened by vast atrocities and unimaginable suffering, the linking of American and Soviet troops was a source of inspiration, signifying the potential for human cooperation across barriers of language, nationality, and social systems. Amidst the ruins of the European Continent the urgency of international friendship, trust, and mutual accommodation required little explanation. And as battered veterans wept and danced and told their stories, the preciousness of peace was never more apparent.

Under the influence of the Cold War, historical studies of the Grand Alliance have generally emphasized the sources of future discord. The Western powers and the Soviet Union had been hostile to each other before the Second World War. The partnership had been dictated by absolute necessity. The Soviet Union was fighting for its life and needed all the help it could get. The United States and Britain saw the Red Army as the last hope for stopping Hitler. Despite a surface collaboration, each of the principals continued to nourish private resentments, ideologies, and plans. Even at the height of their cooperation, Roosevelt, Stalin, and Churchill had quarreled over many issues.

All of these elements seem more important in hindsight than they did at the time. When the war ended, the compelling fact was that the United States, the United Kingdom, and the Soviet Union had worked together successfully to defeat Germany. Faced with a common peril, they had submerged differences of experience and ideology. Whatever the discomforts of the Alliance, bonds of sympathy and appreciation had been forged among the participants, and the publics of all three nations had come to value the connection.

Like the dramatic imagery of the Elbe encounter, these hopeful developments were nearly erased from historical consciousness. But in disregarding this part of the past, the meaning of subsequent events is also lost. What is forgotten is how unwelcome and unexpected the U.S.-Soviet rupture really was. From our present standpoint we are apt to see the Cold War as an automatic by-product of the divergent patterns of society and governance, an inevitable resumption of hostilities once the specter of fascism had been exorcised. During the Second World War, however, there were many wise people on both sides of the Atlantic who were convinced that such divergences could be managed peacefully. This assessment flowed directly from the knowledge, born of the Grand Alliance, that heterogeneous societies—even Marxist and capitalist ones—could compromise when survival required it.

By recalling these original perceptions, we can penetrate the cloud of inevitability that hangs so heavily over the Cold War, and observe that the East–West conflict was the product of human decisions. In 1945 other aspirations had existed and other outcomes had seemed possible. To understand why the Great Powers failed to establish a durable peace, it is necessary to focus on the choices that were made, the reasons for their adoption, and the identity of the choosers. Though this is no longer the fashion, the search for Cold War origins must entail the exploration of responsibility. . . .

Forty years of Cold War . . . ended abruptly on November 9, 1989, when euphoric Germans from east and west breached the wall in Berlin. Their reunion, oddly reminiscent of an earlier rendezvous when the two joyous Allied armies joined at the Elbe, terminated an exceptionally dangerous and tragic period of international relations.

To an American audience, the denouement in Germany held an obvious meaning: The Russians had split the country, and they had lost. For a generation, the Berlin Wall had been the prime symbol of the Cold War era. It exemplified the Soviet habit of foisting communism on unwilling people and imprisoning them forever. Although erected in 1961, twelve years after the establishment of two separate German states, it was the tangible proof of the Soviet Union's culpability.

Despite their manifold violations of human freedom, the Soviets were not the architects of the German settlement. It was the Americans and their British partners who had opted for partition with the associated congealment of the continental division. In contrast to their British confederates, U.S. policy makers had made their decision slowly and reluctantly, but it was America's wealth and power that assured its realization.

Though long forgotten, the Americans and British had initiated all the formal steps toward separation. In violation of the quadripartite framework established at Yalta and Potsdam, they had opted to fuse their two zones economically (December 1946), to incorporate western Germany in the Marshall Plan (July 1947), to implement a separate currency reform (June 1948), and to convene a Parliamentary Council for the establishment of a West German state (September 1948). In each instance, there was some equivalent move in the eastern zone. Yet the pattern of U.S.-British action and Soviet response was a consistent one.

As in a divorce where the party filing papers is not necessarily the one who caused the rupture, formal situations are not always illuminating. Indeed at the time they adopted these measures, the Americans and British maintained that the Soviets had created the schism through their unofficial obstruction of German unity. Such claims nurtured the impression of both their publics that Germany was divided because the Soviet Union had closed off the east.

From the beginning of its occupation in April 1945, the Soviet authorities had imposed a repressive regime, which significantly curtailed German liberties. However, at the point when the Americans and British began their formal moves toward partition, the eastern zone was still a relatively open place—certainly in comparison to what it subsequently became. Not surprisingly, the greatest latitude existed in the quadripartite city of Berlin where, under the protection of the Allied Kommandatura [control commission], people and goods were circulating freely and political parties were competing fiercely for public support. Because Berlin was inside the Soviet zone, this ferment and diversity spilled over to the surrounding areas, limiting the Russians' ability to control the sentiments and activities of the populace.

While the relationship among the four zones was less fluid than the situation in Berlin, there was controlled trade and travel with an associated transmission of books, newspapers, and ideas. Political conditions inside the eastern zone tightened appreciably after March 1946, when the Soviets forced the merger between the Communist and Social Democratic parties, and granted the new Socialist Unity Party (SED) predominant power over administrative agencies. Even then, two bourgeois parties—the Christian Democrats (CDU) and the Liberal Democrats (LDP)—were allowed to operate independently with their own press and regular public meetings. Though frequently harassed, these anticommunist groups participated actively in provincial elections and polled a strong vote during the fall of that year.

The same mixed pattern obtained in the economic sphere, where the Soviets pursued an inconsistent, opportunistic policy. In late 1945 they had pushed through a radical land reform measure, which divided all estates over one hundred hectares, but the resulting parcels were widely distributed into the private hands of landless settlers and poor farmers. In the industrial field, they had authorized the Länder [provinces] to sequester "ownerless property" as well as the property of the German government, the Nazi organizations, and the "leading members and influential followers" of the Nazi Party. Yet they were slow to transfer ownership to the state. During the summer of 1946 the eastern provinces held referenda on the disposition of the sequestered facilities, thus paving the way for substantial socialization. However, some portion of these confiscated enterprises were returned or resold to private individuals. In conjunction with those properties that had not qualified for sequestration, this meant that much of the eastern industry was still under private ownership.

Between 1947 and 1949 Soviet policy accelerated in a dictatorial direction. By the end of the period, their alleged commitment to political and social pluralism had given way to one-party control and state direction of economic life. However, in distinguishing cause-and-effect, the chronology remains pertinent. In the summer of 1947, when the Americans and British reached a clear decision to divide Germany, the presence of these trends had not yet obliterated the alternative voices, political organizations, and social institutions in the east.

Furthermore, while the American and British officials deplored the internal trends in the Soviet zone, this was never their primary focus. Among U.S. representatives in Germany it was widely assumed that if a satisfactory formula for reunification could be found that troublesome conditions in the east might still be ameliorated. However, during a succession of foreign ministers' meetings—commencing in April 1946 and culminating in November 1947—the leaders of both governments decided that such a formula was impossible. When they referred to Soviet intransigence and obstructionism, they had chiefly in mind the Soviet Union's conditions for amalgamating the zones.

To a remarkable extent, these Soviet conditions remained unchanged from the time of Yalta and were devoid of Marxist content. Especially noteworthy was the Soviet negotiating position at the Moscow Council of Foreign Ministers in March–April 1947. This was the first such meeting that was devoted exclusively to a consideration of German and Austrian problems, and it was by universal agreement the most important policy discussion since the war's end. Because the conclave occurred against the background of the Truman Doctrine speech and an overall deterioration of East–West relations, it would not have been surprising if the Soviet Union had been uncooperative.

As presented by Foreign Minister Molotov, the Russian package was designed to meet pragmatic security and material requirements. In speeches grown stale with repetition, Molotov stressed the necessity for reparations and reaffirmed the figure of 10 billion dollars, which he insisted should come from current production rather than capital equipment. He also recycled demands for four-power control of the Ruhr and a vigorous policy of "democratization"—by which he denoted land reform, denazification, decartelization, the rapid reconstruction of trade unions and other social initiatives. In the biggest change of Soviet policy, he accepted the concept of a freely elected German provisional government, which he expected to be centralized along the lines of the Weimar constitution.

During the official sessions, Molotov promised that if the Soviet terms were met, his government would accept an upward revision of the German Level of Industry and would facilitate the rapid reintegration of the zones. Off the record, the Russians intimated to their Western colleagues that many of their planks could be modified if reparations demands were satisfied.

Whatever the merits of the Soviet program, it did not differ appreciably from that previously advanced by liberals in the Roosevelt administration, whose ideas had been partly embodied in the Yalta reparations clauses, the German provisions of Potsdam, and the Joint Chiefs of Staff Directive 1067. Such convergence was admittedly of slight comfort to the less reform-minded members of the Truman team who viewed these documents skeptically. Their displeasure notwithstanding, the Soviet Union was still exhibiting a surface willingness to accept the norms of parliamentary democracy and to open a wide door for capitalism in the eastern zone.

During the Moscow meetings, U.S. officials recognized that the Russians were desirous of German unification, even though some versions would not be acceptable. The Soviets would not, for example, forfeit reparations removal from their zone in order to reintegrate the country. However, the Soviets' appetite for a bargain was apparent for a reason that was scarcely mysterious. As prescribed by Yalta, the western zones of Germany included the majority of the land, people, and resources of the country. The Ruhr alone contained sufficient coal, steel, and chemicals to make West Germany an economic and political power in its own right. Should the country be split, not only would the Soviet Union lose access to the wealthiest portion; it ran the risk that West Germany could, in association with the Western nations, become a grave military threat.

In the two tense years that followed the Moscow deliberations, the Americans and British never lost sight of the Soviet wish to reconnect the zones. Once the Marshall Plan was launched, with its presumption of West German participation, their policy was shaped by a fear that the desperate Soviets might offer a deal that could not be rejected. It was this anxiety that Ambassador Walter Bedell Smith was voicing, when he wrote his friend Eisenhower in December 1947:

> The difficulty under which we labor is that in spite of our announced position, we really do not want nor intend to accept German unification in any terms that the Russians might agree to, even though they seemed to meet most of our requirements.

In the wake of the Berlin blockade, Smith himself would become more receptive to unification. However, even in the darkest days of that crisis—when the success of the airlift was in doubt and a third World War seemed to threaten—the U.S. government was skittish about negotiations, perceiving a Soviet ambush that could forestall the German partition.

As they implemented the division of the country, the Americans and British were not simply ratifying an already existing situation. The conditions of the eastern zone remained unsettled and the Soviet bargaining position showed numerous signs of flexibility. In the gathering momentum for a separate West German state, there was continuing evidence that unification could be achieved.

Why did U.S. officials prefer schism? At the end of the Second World War, American policy had been different. The prevailing view then, even among administration conservatives, was that Germany should be kept together and supervised by the Great

Powers. During 1946–47, as this attitude was reevaluated, one pervasive element was the mounting fear of Soviet aggression. Washington policy makers were strongly affected by the reports from George Kennan and others, who perceived a Soviet plan to take over Western Europe. As applied to Germany, that analysis presumed the Soviet Union would use any centralized machinery to subvert democratic institutions in the western zones. Thus even if unification was attainable, it would be too dangerous.

Significantly, the leaders of U.S. Military Government in Germany did not share Kennan's assessment. In hundreds of cables and oral reports, they highlighted the weakness of the Communist Party in western Germany, the ineffectiveness of the Soviets in reversing that situation, the fragility of the SED's grip in the east, and the probability that unification would extend democratic influences beyond the Elbe. These observers also believed the Russians were economically desperate, and would forfeit political advantages in order to garner reparations.

If Washington officials listened more to Kennan than their representatives in Germany, this was because his gloomy prognostications fit their policy preferences. The core of realism in their position was the appreciation of a genuine clash of interests between even the minimum Soviet program for reparations and security, and their own aspiration for West European recovery and integration. Though it had initially seemed possible to reconcile the two agendas, difficulties in procuring coal, steel, and chemicals from the Ruhr, and restoring the German market for West European goods had reduced that prospect. As the western zones stagnated, each Russian demand—for reparations deliveries, for quadripartite controls in the Ruhr, for a breakup of the large German combines, for denazification of management, for a politicized labor movement—became harder to tolerate. Ultimately, it became an intellectual fine point whether these Russian claims reflected sincere anxieties about German militarism or nefarious schemes for taking over the country. To U.S. officials what mattered was the Soviet interference with their plans for German rehabilitation.

After mid-1947 there was even less room for argument as Soviet rhetoric and behavior became significantly more provocative. Within Europe, the formation of the Comintern was accompanied by a summons to Western communist parties to engage in disruption and sabotage, and by mounting repression in Hungary, Rumania, and Poland. Inside Germany itself, the western Community Party (KPD) was mobilizing working-class resistance to the Marshall Plan, while the Soviet military authorities were accelerating the trend to one-party rule in the east. Taken in aggregate, these developments seemed to confirm the analysis of those American officials who viewed the Soviets as unscrupulous partners, whose only genuine goal was world revolution. When these transgressions were capped by a Russian decision to blockade Berlin, the brief against the Soviet Union hardened into doctrine.

Yet even in this latter phase, there was a willful narrowness in American thinking. If Soviet behavior was getting worse, it was also true that they were being locked out of western Germany and denied the benefits of their World War II victory. The likelihood that these situations were connected, that Soviet belligerence was partly the result of feeling cheated and threatened, were topics that could not be probed. Only on the political fringes would a dissident like Henry Wallace wonder if a German compromise could still reverse the most dangerous developments in Western and Eastern Europe. Within mainstream circles, such an inquiry was anathema.

During 1948–49, as in the earlier period, the American disposition to adopt the most pessimistic view of Soviet intentions was sustained by external considerations. Of special weight were the cleavages that had opened in the Western camp during the London conference, as the United States pushed the pace of West Germany's economic and political restoration. With neighbors questioning the rapid dismantling of controls, and German politicians bridling at the terms of governance, any prospect of Russian reinvolvement was unappealing.

The Berlin blockade also played a major role in fixing Washington's attitude, not only for the obvious reason that it demonstrated Russian malevolence but because it revealed the uses of Cold War polarization. Mindful of fissures among the Western principals, the Soviets had begun the blockade hoping to widen them, and thereby arrest the movement toward partition. Yet with the inception of the airlift, U.S. policy makers were surprised to discover that the East–West confrontation was enabling them to solve previously intractable problems. Under the shadow of the blockade they were able to forge agreements on the international organization for the Ruhr, the reduction of economic controls in western Germany, and the structure and powers of the new West German state.

While there was a rational underpinning for the rigid anti-Sovietism, the indulgence in hyperbole produced some irrational effects. At crucial moments, American officials were unable to make hardheaded assessments of diplomatic opportunities. One such occasion was the Moscow Conference of Foreign Ministers, when General Clay urged his American colleagues to authorize a technical study of current production reparations in order to determine whether there was some level of allocations that could be harmonized with a German recovery program. This modest but sensible idea was buried by the ideologues in the U.S. delegation, for whom the practical arithmetic was eclipsed by the diabolical nature of the Soviets.

Eighteen months later, a similar dynamic was at work when a chastened George Kennan offered Plan A as a possible solution to the Berlin crisis. By this time, Kennan had drastically modified his earlier views and had become profoundly disturbed by the impending division of Europe. To arrest this development in Germany, he had crafted a proposal that provided for a single provisional government and the scaling back of the political and military presence of the occupying authorities. Because the plan was stacked with one-sided clauses, such as the provision for a united Germany to participate in the Marshall Plan, Kennan was doubtful that the Soviets would accept it. Yet were they acquiescent, they would be surrendering their exclusive position in the east in exchange for a very limited role in the west. Remarkably, Kennan's superiors were loathe to explore the matter, preferring not to know whether the Soviet Union would accept the strict conditions.

This willed ignorance and reluctance to explore negotiating possibilities was a recurrent feature of the American stand in Germany. While partially stimulated by the ostensible advantages of polarization, it also derived from a perception of Soviet vulnerability. For all their alarms about Russian aggression, U.S. policy makers saw the Soviets as weak both economically and militarily. This judgment allowed them to make careless calculations, to disregard the Soviet interests with a sense of impunity, and to sacrifice potentially favorable bargains with the expectation of a complete collapse down the road.

The road was very long, and there is reason to wonder if ordinary citizens would have chosen it. In retrospect, it is shocking to consider how inaccurately the U.S. government communicated its German policy to constituents. For the first two years after the war, little was said about the effort to rebuild the country. As far as most Americans knew, the main goal was to punish Nazis and reform the society.

After mid-1947, the focus shifted to the containment of Soviet aggression. With the inception of the Berlin blockade, President Truman articulated a simple story that featured the Russians, trampling the wartime agreements in their ruthless grab for the former German capital. The president did not explain that the United States had abandoned Yalta and Potsdam, that it was pushing the formation of a West German state against the misgivings of many Europeans, and that the Soviets had launched the blockade to prevent partition.

In offering this distorted account, Truman was partly responding to the pressures of confrontation and the need for a short, intelligible description that would rally public support. Yet since his experience at Potsdam, the president had never involved himself in the German problem, and it is doubtful that he understood its complexities. Though informed of the London decisions, he did not seem aware that his subordinates were propelling separation, nor did he apprehend the gravity of the Soviet response.

The importance of German policy, notwithstanding, momentous decisions were made without the significant participation of any elected officials. Even Senator Vandenberg, the most informed of Washington legislators, was startled when Secretary Acheson came before the Foreign Relations Committee in 1949 and outlined the State Department's approach. Until that point, neither Vandenberg nor his colleagues on the committee had realized how determined the State Department was to create a separate West German state, regardless of Soviet terms.

This abdication of political leadership framed the public's obliviousness to the issues. Without accountable officials, able and willing to outline the existing options, there was little opportunity for democratic debate. Instead, policy was established by the national security bureaucracies, with their strong penchant for secrecy. Lacking pertinent information, citizens were relegated to the sidelines, where they could cheer for the airlift.

There are some grounds for claiming that the public interest was well served, even in the absence of informed consent. U.S. policymakers aimed to protect the nation's security by salvaging free market economies in Western Europe. For this purpose the exclusion of the Russians from the western portion of Germany seemed increasingly attractive. Once the severance had occurred, West Germany played the projected role, reviving quickly and providing goods and markets to its neighbors. The success of the Marshall Plan sustained American prosperity and offered a margin of military safety through the stabilization of Western Europe.

One price of these accomplishments was that East Germany was abandoned to the Russians, along with the rest of Eastern Europe. Ironically, it was George Kennan—the earliest and most vigorous proponent of "containment"—who became most disturbed by this consequence. For years, he had lamented the Soviet infringements of eastern rights and called upon his government to disassociate itself. But at the point of partition, Kennan apprehended how much more repressive the regimes could become and discarded his own counsel.

Another charge for the division of Germany was the militarizing of Europe. As illustrated by the Berlin blockade, the splitting of the country meant that the United States and the Soviet Union would become mortal enemies, whose urgent interests could engender armed conflict. U.S. policymakers reckoned that their monopoly of nuclear weapons and ability to join with Western Europe in a buildup of conventional forces would deter Soviet advances.

However, the very reliance on military power made the international environment more menacing. Not only did it insure that the Soviets would cling to every scrap of territory they had gained; it guaranteed a costly arms race and endowed even remote places on the globe with a strategic significance they might not otherwise have held. Later many would wonder why young Americans were dying in Korea and South Vietnam, but the logic of a military rivalry lent reason to these encounters.

Among the small circle of Americans who set policy for Germany there was little attempt to weigh alternatives. What finally gave shape to their deliberations was a conception of national security that took the expansion of West European free trade as an absolute requirement for the United States. Though this reflected the aspirations of the large internationally oriented corporations and banks, it was less clearly in line with the predilections of the public, for whom issues of East European freedom and the maintenance of peace held greater salience.

From the perspective of the mid-1990s, with Soviet communism so severely discredited, there is a temptation to again lay at their feet the blame for every international transgression. This disposition has been quite naturally strengthened by the opening of archives, which offer new manifestations of Eastern bloc despotism.

Though the atmosphere is unpropitious, there is still good reason for historical fairness. The oppressive internal policies of the Soviet Union that were gradually imposed upon the population of East Germany were not the source of the postwar schism. In the aftermath of victory, what produced that unwanted result was an ambitious American agenda, which was juxtaposed on a European continent that was more impoverished, strife-ridden, and unruly than anyone in Washington had envisioned. In conjunction with America's preponderance of military and economic power, this yielded high-risk policies, whose most painful consequences were mainly borne by others.

Had American officials been more flexible and sought a compromise solution in occupied Germany, it is possible that the Soviets would have blocked or overturned it. But this is something we cannot know since the United States selected a different course. In the wreckage of the Cold War, America has yet to acknowledge responsibility for the structures that it built.

Robert A. Garson

THE LIMITS OF AMERICAN POWER IN EASTERN EUROPE

Even before war's end, Eastern Europe, like Germany, had emerged as a major source of Soviet-American confrontation. In the following selection, British scholar Robert A. Garson depicts American policy toward that region as far more realistic than many specialists have acknowledged. Although United States diplomats at first tended to exaggerate America's ability to shape the political structures of Eastern European

Robert A. Garson, "American Foreign Policy and the Limits of Power: Eastern Europe, 1946–50," *Journal of Contemporary History*, 21 (July 1986), 347–354, 357–365. Reprinted by permission of the author.

societies, they adjusted quickly when faced with firm Soviet resistance. Garson argues that the Truman administration recognized, at least by 1946, that its power was sharply circumscribed in what was fast becoming a Soviet sphere of influence—and acted accordingly. The United States actually came to identify political advantages in the Kremlin's rather heavy-handed behavior in Eastern Europe. The Soviet record there, Garson observes, ironically helped the United States to mobilize support at home and abroad for its far more important initiatives in Western Europe. The author also credits American policymakers with shrewdly recognizing that independent-minded Yugoslavia, which began receiving U.S. aid by the late 1940s, formed an Achilles', heel for the Soviet Union.

A senior lecturer in American Studies at Keele University in Great Britain, Robert A. Garson has written *The Democratic Party and the Politics of Sectionalism, 1941–1948* (1974) and *The United States and China: A Troubled Affair* (1994). He is a co-author of *The Uncertain Power: A Political History of the United States since 1929* (1990).

The rapidity of unfolding events abroad in the wake of the surrender of Germany and Japan in 1945 forced the United States to reconsider its position in international affairs with particular and arguably unaccustomed urgency. Given the military position of the Allied armies in 1945 and the uncertain intentions of the Soviets, the United States found itself involved in areas of the world which less than a decade earlier had ranked fairly low on the agenda of diplomatic priorities. Many historians have argued that America's new involvement was premature and unnecessarily ambitious. The very titles and sub-titles of so many histories of this period, such as *The Rise of Globalism, Pax Americana, Architects of Illusion, The National Security State* and *Struggle for the World* reveal the assumptions of this school. These slogans may be apt descriptions of America's involvement in the countries of the third world. However, it is important to recognize that in its first direct confrontation with the Soviet Union, namely in Eastern Europe, the United States came to grips fairly quickly with the limits of its own power and even reneged on many previous commitments. American policy in Eastern Europe, particularly after the formulation of the Truman Doctrine and the European Recovery Plan, revealed a sophisticated and considered appreciation of its capabilities and weaknesses. Furthermore, the administration of Harry S. Truman realized that its earlier and largely unfruitful contest with the Soviets over Eastern Europe could be turned to advantage in its quest to win public support for its policy of economic and military aid to Western Europe. Indeed, by the time the conflict in Korea had broken out, Washington had made a realistic appraisal of its influence in Eastern Europe, had converted its earlier impotence in that area into an effective rallying call for its maturing ideological and foreign economic policies, and had even managed to establish closer ties with one country, Yugoslavia, thereby opening up the prospect of revealing a crucial Achilles heel in Soviet power.

The decision to retrench its ambitions in Eastern Europe only came after the shock of failure, however. For, in their initial confrontation with the Soviets during and just after the second world war, the Americans tended to exaggerate their ability to shape the political structure of Eastern Europe. Franklin Roosevelt had always believed that he could temper Josef Stalin's ambitions towards his neighbours. The President was confident that he could placate Stalin by establishing a strong collective security organization and by reassuring him of his understanding of Russia's desire to have sympathetic regimes on its borders. Yet his private soothings were not consistent with his public declarations in favour of self-determination. Nor, indeed, was his optimism shared by his advisers and diplomats. They shared Roosevelt's desire to limit Soviet interference in the affairs of Eastern Europe, but they believed this could only be achieved by developing a public and structured commitment to political democracy. So when Harry S. Truman acceded to the presidency, he felt obliged to continue his predecessor's public commitments and to push for a modicum of self-determination in Eastern Europe. He accepted the State Department's view that, subordinate as it was to the Soviet command, American representation on the tripartite Control Commissions in Hungary, Romania and Bulgaria should be exploited as far as possible to embarrass the Soviets into tolerating some kind of political pluralism in those countries. Furthermore, he hoped to get the communists to relax their political controls in other parts of Eastern Europe by holding out the bait of economic aid. Above all, and this was particularly true for Byrnes, policy-makers believed they could soften the Kremlin's external designs by creating and maintaining a special interest in the Soviet orbit. So the administration's efforts to secure free elections in Poland and, after Potsdam, to broaden the governments of Romania and Bulgaria, were inspired not by the narrower urge to increase the area's receptivity to free trade but by the desire to demonstrate its ability to make Stalin consider and acknowledge America's authority. If the Soviets could be curbed in Eastern Europe, then the United States would be strengthened in its ability to protect Western Europe from internal political convulsion or from external pressures. In short, in the months that followed the end of the hostilities, Truman believed that the future of Eastern Europe was integral to the shape of the post-war settlement. The United States would take a firm stand there to test the insistency of Moscow's power and to demonstrate its wider concern for political democracy and unilateral trade. The administration generally felt that the Soviets' authoritarian power was fragile and inherently ephemeral. Russia's economic strength had been sapped by the horrendous destruction of war. Its ability to impose regimes on unwilling nations was doomed, Americans believed, because a populace's natural desire for political freedom would inevitably surface. As soon as Truman had acceded to the presidency, Averell Harriman had counselled that the Russians were weak, but "will take control of everything they can by bluffing." He hoped the United States would demonstrate the Soviets' weakness by contesting and exposing it in Eastern Europe. He believed that once the Soviet Union "had control of bordering areas, it would attempt to penetrate the next adjacent countries, and he thought the issue ought to be fought out in so far as we could with the Soviet Union in the present bordering areas." The Soviets' dominion in the occupied zones of Eastern Europe was still thought to be tenuous and precarious; careful but firm diplomacy would expose their deceptive power.

However, it soon became clear that the Soviets would continue to tighten their controls over the governments of Eastern Europe. The administration realized that it did not have the capacity to restrain the communists. Even greater priority was to be given to the reconstruction of Western Europe and to countries that sought to align themselves with the United States. So President Truman and his advisers began to resign themselves to the fact that they would be unable to shape significantly developments in areas still under Russian occupation. In February 1946 Byrnes, contrary to the advice of Burton Berry, the US Representative in Bucharest, decided to recognize the communist-dominated government of Romania despite the fact that only cosmetic alterations had been carried out there. Byrnes acknowledged that the United States had little remaining power in Romania, and anyway hoped that diplomatic recognition would expedite a peace treaty and the concomitant withdrawal of the Red Army. Clark Clifford, Truman's Special Counsel, advised Truman after detailed and thorough soundings from various government sources to "confine Soviet influence to its present area" and so reduce his efforts to obtain self-determination in Eastern Europe.

Yet despite the growing preoccupation with affairs in Western Europe and particularly in Germany, the administration did not entirely give up its attempts to realize the promise of the Yalta Declaration on liberated Europe. It continued to believe, or at least to try to believe, that the Soviets' strength was overextended and illusory and so could be undermined. In his influential "long telegram" George Kennan, the chargé d'affaires in Moscow, had reminded Washington that the "success of the Soviet system as a form of internal power is not yet finally proven . . . Soviet system will now be subjected, by virtue of recent territorial expansions, to a series of additional strains which once proved a severe tax on Tsardom." So the United States sought to find a policy that would enable it to exploit this belief in the frailty of Soviet power and at the same time to divert its diplomatic attentions to the consolidation of Western Europe. It did not publicly or manifestly renege on its commitment to democracy in Eastern Europe, but it did subordinate its efforts in the satellites to its Western European policy and so reduced its campaign to roll back Russian influence. In many ways the United States confirmed the division of Europe through this very process of defining its interests and priorities on the Continent more precisely. By recognizing its diminished authority in the East, it underscored the irreconcilability of the two superpowers.

Thus, during the year preceding the launching of the European Recovery Programme, the United States continued to oppose Soviet hegemony in Eastern Europe, although it did not expect to change political conditions there. The administration adjusted itself to the view that the political and economic structure of Eastern Europe was not inextricably connected to the security of the West. It also no longer regarded its diplomatic achievements there as an accurate indicator of America's general ability to determine the shape of the post-war world. Essentially, the United States posed a modified challenge in the year prior to the announcement of the Marshall Plan for two reasons. First, the administration was aware of the need to rally public support for its programme of aid to Britain and Western Europe and believed it could further its campaign by drawing people's attention to the consequences that followed from the loss of initiative and influence. The "iron curtain" would be held up as a reminder of the fate that awaited societies that could not be aided. Second, the administration accepted Kennan's diagnosis of Soviet strength which, Kennan believed, could flourish only by the ruthless exercise of military power. If, therefore, the military capability of the Soviet Union could somehow be circumscribed in the satellite countries, then Soviet power could still be checked. And there was always a nagging fear that the Russian armies of occupation could threaten the stability of their Western European and Middle Eastern neighbours.

The first reason for the administration's reluctance to relinquish completely its advocacy of greater independence in Eastern Europe lay in its domestic political strategy. It was convinced that the public would be more easily aroused to pay for the containment of communism if it were reminded of its practical social impact. So as the United States proceeded to give up gradually its attempt to stop communist consolidation in Eastern Europe, it simultaneously publicized its very inability to influence events in areas under Russian control. Experts on Soviet affairs generally believed that confrontation and ideological warfare were inherent characteristics of the Soviet system and so the United States had no choice but to imitate this posture. An emphasis on the ideological contrasts would generate an additional premium by providing a focus and a clarity for American foreign policy as a whole. In March 1946 Kennan had advised Byrnes that "there can be no more dangerous tendency in American public opinion than one which places on our government an obligation to accomplish the impossible by gestures of goodwill and conciliation toward a political entity constitutionally incapable of being conciliated." Such antipathy to a rapprochement had a profound impact on America's dealings with Eastern Europe. Truman and Secretary Byrnes acknowledged their limited ability to alter developments there, but recognized the need to combine their sense of resignation with a political rhetoric that accentuated the irreconcilable differences between the two blocs. Thus the image of the "iron curtain," developed by Winston Churchill at Fulton, Missouri, in March 1946, became an indispensable metaphor in America's containment policy. Similarly, when the President enunciated the Truman Doctrine in March 1947, he specifically cited the recent histories of Poland, Romania, and Bulgaria in his brief for assistance to Greece and Turkey. "Every nation," he posited, "must choose between alternative ways of life." He promised a concerted effort to thwart the "second way of life" that "relies upon terror and oppression, a controlled press and radio, fixed elections and the suppression of personal freedoms." The United States would not aim to draw back the iron curtain but it would hold it up as a sobering example to other nations that sought to maintain or nurture representative government.

The Truman administration also took considerable pains to reduce the military muscle of the Soviet Union in Eastern Europe, particularly in the former Axis satellites. Although America's ability to shape military developments there was slight, it could still play a role in the negotiations for peace treaties with Hungary, Romania and Bulgaria. It did not possess any special material interests in these former enemy states, but it did hope that a reduced and controlled military establishment there might inhibit the possibility of a Soviet intervention in neighbouring countries and, perhaps, even reduce Russia's grip on its own dependants. Defence experts and representatives on the spot firmly believed that the Soviets would use their presence in Eastern Europe to establish bases in the Dardanelles and the Mediterranean. Maynard Barnes, US Representative in Sofia, warned that Russia was determined "to fashion a South Slav Union dominated by it to emasculate Turkey and Greece and to place Russia squarely on the eastern Mediterranean and Adriatic." The Joint Chiefs of Staff affirmed in July 1946 that "in seeking to establish puppet regimes in the Balkans, Turkey and Iran, the Soviets are projecting corridors to the Adriatic . . . and Indian Ocean." Accordingly, in the negotiations over treaties with Hungary, Bulgaria and Romania, America aimed to limit their reparations payments to Russia, to secure a withdrawal of the Red Army, and to establish equal international rights in civil aviation. The United States did not expect to attain its objectives as the Soviets would merely wish to "confirm the advantages which they have already obtained." But it was not prepared to relinquish its efforts to reduce the satellites' dependency on Russia. For if it could do nothing to diminish Russia's control, it could still use the negotiations over military levels to highlight the differences between East and West. Byrnes told Georges Bidault, the French Foreign Minister, that if deadlock arose in the course of the negotiations, he would suggest that "the meetings be thrown open to the public so that world opinion can see just what the situation is and just where stumbling blocks lie." Washington recognized it had little room for manoeuvre in Eastern Europe, but it would not give up its claims. Russia, it believed, could only maintain its authority by force, and a continuing interest in Eastern European affairs might expose the essential frailty of the Kremlin's hegemony. "If we remain firm in our beliefs," commented Barnes in Sofia, "and we live up to the trust of others in us by a 'hard' policy in this part of the world, somewhere from the Baltic to the Aegean, that vulnerable spot will be uncovered and then the fire of regained freedom will spread from one sea to the other."

However, Washington did not rely on discovering the location of "that vulnerable spot." For after the formulation of the Truman Doctrine, the defence establishment fully recognized the limitations of America's power in Eastern Europe and made no serious attempts in its planning to realize the goals of the Yalta Declaration. In April 1947 the Joint Chiefs of Staff recommended that the United States should cease to provide economic aid to countries under Russian dominion "until every vestige of Soviet control has been removed." Unity of purpose, they believed, could only be attained in Western Europe if all nations, including France and Germany, could be made to understand their interdependence. This interdependence could, they argued, best be achieved by emphasizing the danger of "the emergence of a principal world power to the east of them, ideologically opposed to all their traditional way of life, whose ultimate aim is world conquest." Thus, by 1947, the armed services had not only resigned themselves to Soviet domination of Eastern Europe but had also come to recognize that this very domination could serve to assist them in their plans to consolidate America's position in Western Europe, the Far East and Latin America. In fact, when the Joint Chiefs' Strategic Survey Committee drew up a list, in order of priority, of countries that were thought to be important to the national security of the United States, not one Eastern European state was even mentioned.

Despite occasional and sporadic attempts to secure political reform in Eastern Europe by rhetorical proclamation or the conditional grant of financial credits, the administration came close to viewing communist methods in Eastern Europe as a useful tool in its confrontation with Russia. It somehow had to make the best of a hopeless situation. The repression in Eastern Europe could be used to goad Western European governments into closer cooperation with each other and with the United States. The communists' tactics might also provoke an indigenous challenge to their power. Many officials in Washington still believed that the Russians might sow the seeds of their own destruction. In November 1947, George Kennan's Policy Planning Staff anticipated the communist coup in Czechoslovakia by three months, but it did not view the prospect in any way as a danger to the West. A Policy Planning Staff paper predicted the formation of "underground anti-communist political forces in the Soviet satellite area." It echoed the familiar refrain that "it is unlikely that approximately one hundred million Russians will succeed in holding down permanently . . . some ninety millions of Europeans with a higher cultural level and with long experience in resistance to foreign rule." American power, therefore, was redundant in any attempt to open up Eastern Europe. Internal contradictions and strain would eventually erode the Russian grip. The United States should continue to restrain itself in its efforts to roll back the communists' control. The prospect of internal revolution in Eastern Europe was not wholly welcome anyway. For if Russian domination began to crumble, "the Kremlin may then feel itself seriously threatened internally and may resort to desperate measures." The United States, therefore, had a kind of perverse interest in continued Russian predominance in the East. For if there were insurgency in the Soviet sphere, the Kremlin could be tempted to counter in the West "and go so far as to engage our interests directly."

So when in 1947 and 1948 Moscow tightened its control over Eastern European affairs even further, the United States adopted a dual strategy. It declined to challenge the Kremlin directly, while it tailored its ostensible outrage to America's allies at home and abroad. It seemed more anxious to keep the Soviet hegemonic system in the limelight than to change that system. The administration had concluded that it could not expedite a political reorientation in Eastern Europe as the Soviets were determined to create a unified political bloc in this sphere. Various events, such as the manipulation of elections in Poland, the forced abdication of King Michael in Romania, political trials in Romania and Bulgaria, the creation of the Cominform in September 1947, and the ousting of non-communist members of the Czech cabinet in February 1948, all pointed to the fact that the Soviet Union was no longer concerned with preserving even a cosmetic front of representative government in order to save face with the West. So Washington toned down its direct opposition to the communists' tightening grasp. It fully recognized its impotence to influence events in the East but still hoped that it could employ that impotence and resignation in its diplomatic armoury. But Washington's occasional outbursts over Russian policy were basically a ruse for justifying its own policies of consolidation. For example, the administration generally welcomed the Eastern bloc's walk-out at the Paris conference on European aid since it provided a further fillip to its own diagnosis of the dangers to Europe as a whole. As early as May 1947 the Policy Planning Staff had suggested that the recovery programme should be designed "in such a form that the Russian satellite countries would either exclude themselves by unwillingness to accept the proposed conditions or agree to abandon the exclusive orientation of their economies." So despite their public agitation, policy-makers realized they could not and should not seek to establish Western interests in the Soviet sphere. . . .

Although the United States was most concerned about the effects of its export policies in Western Europe, it did recognize that there were certain instances where radical changes in the pattern of trade could produce change in the Russian satellites. After Tito's expulsion from the Cominform in June 1948, American policy-makers realized that the rift between Tito and Stalin could be maintained by gradually realigning Yugoslavia's economic interests with those of the ECA countries. Nevertheless, expectations were cautious and modest, and officials were able to discriminate between the short-term economic possibilities of trade with Yugoslavia and the long-term prospect of political change. They were particularly cognizant of the fact that their ability to exacerbate tension between Stalin and Tito would be shaped almost entirely by Tito's posture in the dispute. They eschewed dramatic initiatives, particularly at the beginning of the schism, as these had seldom paid off. America followed the example of its European allies, who were sceptical of the West's ability to exploit the quarrel. Ernest Bevin, for example, felt Stalin and Tito should be left to "quarrel among themselves," as any Western influence might rebound against Tito. However, once it became clear that there would be no reconciliation between Moscow and Belgrade, the United States slackened its commercial restrictions and joined with other ECA members in trying to redirect Yugoslavia's trade.

The United States had no illusions about any ability to use its economic power to subvert communism in Yugoslavia. Cavendish Cannon, U.S. Ambassador, advised Dean Acheson that Tito was firmly entrenched, as he had carried the army, the police and the party with him on his chosen course. He described Tito as having "the strongest position of any rebel since Henry VIII." He advised that it should serve Western interests "to permit Tito to maintain himself as orthodox but prosperous communist." This kind of reformism would prove to be a thorn in the flesh for the Kremlin and would show that communism could thrive without being aligned with Moscow. Truman agreed with this analysis. In February 1949 he authorized a major relaxation of controls on exports to Yugoslavia. The President's aim was essentially modest. Nobody believed that Yugoslavia could be integrated with the West, or, indeed, that progress toward state socialism could be stopped. The provision of export licenses would merely enable Tito to purchase from the West essential goods and materials not obtainable as a result of the Soviet embargo. This diversion of Yugoslavia's trade from east to west was "an important European Recovery Programme objective," and had the added attraction of strengthening Tito in his policy of resistance.

After February 1949, therefore, the United States stepped up its aid to Tito and encouraged an expansion in trade. It gave its blessing to an $800-million trade agreement with Britain and in July 1949 the International Bank for Reconstruction and Development informed Yugoslavia that it would seriously consider a loan of $25 million. In the following month, Dean Acheson defended the decision to authorize the export of a blooming mill for the production of processed steels. Plant of this kind was on the so-called "1-A list," which was an inventory of items that were normally automatically banned for export to Eastern Europe. The military establishment had strongly objected to the sale of the $3.2 million mill, but Acheson argued that "the maintenance of the Tito-

Kremlin split should continue to be an important objective of our current foreign policy. I do not believe there can be any dispute on this point." He believed that if Tito failed to develop industry in his country, he would be toppled and as a result "Yugoslavia would again come under Soviet domination." The United States, therefore, had every incentive to sustain the Tito regime, despite the fact that until 1948 relations had been so strained. Policy-makers still believed that Russia's hegemony in Eastern Europe would rebound, and ultimately contribute to a weakening of the Soviet State. So the status quo did have its political compensations. Charles E. Bohlen, an expert on Soviet affairs and in October 1949 Minister to France, believed "we should go the limit. The Tito heresy was the most important recent development, striking at the very roots of Kremlin domination, and may prove to be the deciding factor in the cold war."

As the decade drew to a close, the United States had made a fairly accurate assessment of its capabilities in Eastern Europe. No major initiative to reduce Soviet authority was taken after Byrnes had left the State Department. The administration was more absorbed in launching the European Recovery Programme successfully and in ironing out difficulties resulting from the formation of NATO. Yet there still existed an influential circle that maintained a belief in the ultimate disintegration of Soviet power. George Kennan's Policy Planning Staff (PPS) was particularly concerned to ensure that foreign policy took cognizance of this prophecy. . . .

It must be emphasized that such views were generally expressions of wishful thinking. On the whole, America recognized its limited capabilities in Eastern Europe. Even so, it could not shrug off its belief in the weakness of the Soviet system. Its policy towards the Soviet orbit combined its political realism and its enduring hunch about the durability of communist regimes. Washington held out no hope for an accommodation, particularly when, after 1947, Moscow emphasized the doctrine of the "two camps." This argued that socialism and capitalism were inherently competitive and that differences could not be reconciled. This mutual feeling of irreconcilability had encouraged further consolidation within the Soviet bloc, and it would be futile to try and dismember it. In this respect, American policy had come closer to the views of the Western European powers which had wanted to use the *Gleichschaltung* in the East as an incentive for further economic co-operation. The

Truman administration was quite aware that Eastern Europe had become indispensable to the Soviets. Its best hope was to convert its impotence in the East into some kind of asset, however slight this might be. The National Security Council (NSC) reported to Truman at the end of 1949 that, "Were we to set as our inevitable goal the replacement of totalitarianism by democracy, an overwhelming portion of the task would fall on us, and we would find ourselves directly engaging the Kremlin's prestige and provoking strong Soviet reaction. . . . At best, we would find ourselves deeply enmeshed in the Eastern European situation and saddled with an indefinitely continuing burden of political, economic and military responsibility for the survival of the uncertain regimes which we had placed in power." The NSC was confident, however, that Soviet power would eventually be eroded by internal contradictions and tensions. The Russians had a "comparatively shallow hold," and "the traditional conflicts of the area . . . always outweighed the cohesive influences at work." American policy, therefore, should aim not to challenge the Soviets directly, but to expedite in an unintrusive way the nascent and frustrated dissidence in Eastern Europe. The methods most favoured for this purpose were propaganda, official visits, tourism and broadcasting. Activities of this kind would keep alive the prospect of heresy and would help also to focus attention on the ideological differences between East and West. In a policy statement on Czechoslovakia, the State Department stressed its desire "to strengthen the spirit of hope and resistance" by broadcasting America's continued interest in democracy for that country. In Poland, too, the United States would continue to publicize the consequences of Soviet domination. Yet it was careful to avoid open encouragement of outright rebellion in Poland. For a revolt could force the Russians to wield a heavier hand, and perhaps even encourage it to incorporate its satellites into the Soviet Union. "Our purpose," the State Department declared, "is not to excite the masses to open rebellion, which would be disastrous and futile at this time, but rather to strengthen hope and discourage apathy."

So with the exception of the trade embargo, the United States restricted its efforts to influence events in Eastern Europe after the formation of the Cominform. In the field of diplomacy, it confined itself to periodic meetings of foreign service officers posted in Eastern Europe to discuss possible sanctions against the satellites. Attempts were also made in the United Nations General

Assembly to censure Bulgaria, Romania and Hungary for violations of the peace treaties, particularly with regard to human rights. The use of the United Nations as a forum of criticism was a device to keep developments in the satellites in the public eye and to demonstrate to other nations America's continuing identification of Western co-operation with political libertarianism. One other recourse deserves brief mention. Propaganda, particularly through the Voice of America and the United States Information Service, was used as an integral part of the ideological armoury. These agencies sought principally to publicize the benefits of Western democracy and capitalism and to give encouragement to dissidence in the satellite areas. Indeed, by 1950, government officials had become convinced that propaganda was the most effective way of encouraging disunity within the Soviet orbit. The Soviets' proselytisms, according to the CIA, aimed to subvert the emergence of a moral force in smaller nations. The United States should, therefore, aim to identify its national interests "with the hopes and fears of mass opinion." In fact, whenever officials in Eastern Europe resorted to the confiscation of American newspapers and pamphlets or the jamming of transmitters, the Americans took it as a sign of their effectiveness. There was an additional incentive for the use of ideological inculcation. The intellectual effort involved in disseminating the Western view would also play a "part in alerting the American people and the western world to the true intentions of Soviet directed communism." In short, the highlighting of repression in Eastern Europe would inject an adhesive element in the attempts to develop a Western European unity on economic and defence issues. This particular effect was appreciated by Britain in the planning of its propaganda. R. M. Hankey of the Foreign Office wrote: "We want the other European powers to be frightened into the fold, not terrified into scattering."

Thus, by the time the Korean war broke out, the Truman administration had developed a policy for Eastern Europe that fully appreciated Russia's determination to hold on to that area and its own inability to affect developments there in any direct way. No major challenges were made to Russian authority behind the "iron curtain." American policy had concentrated on guaranteeing Western Europe and Eastern Asia from communism, and events in Eastern Europe were treated as secondary problems. But Truman, who had always fully appreciated the difficulties of mobilizing public opinion in the prosecution of an expensive cold war, cited the fate of the Eastern European countries to rally support for such enterprises as the European Recovery Programme, the Berlin airlift, food shipments to Italy, economic assistance to China and the Point Four Programme. By drawing specific attention to events in Eastern Europe, Truman also hoped to frighten socialist supporters in Western Europe away from their presumed orientation towards the Soviet Union. In February 1948, Truman used the opportunity of the Czech coup to get Congress to expedite passage of the European Recovery Programme and to restore selective service. His policy towards the Soviet orbit and the rhetoric that legitimated it, therefore, did not hold out the promise of reducing Russian influence or restoring *anciens régimes*. Truman tried to convince the public that the expansion of American power and interests in other parts of the globe since 1945 had been fully justified by events in Eastern Europe. In a public address in June 1950, just before the outbreak of hostilities in Korea, Truman told his audience that the Soviets had "turned the school-children of Eastern Germany into the same kind of political robots that marched into hopeless battle for Hitler." But such developments were not without their compensations, as Truman pointed out. "The result of these tactics," the President added, "has been to spur the free nations on to greater cooperation and more rigorous efforts for the improvement and the defence of their own institutions."

American policy towards the Soviet satellites, in short, revealed after 1947 a combination of resignation and optimism. The administration had resigned itself to Russia's continuing domination of its neighbours for the foreseeable future. Its economic ambitions in the Soviet orbit were insignificant and it did not envisage any major role for the Cominform powers in the development of Western Europe. Because of the dispensability of Eastern Europe, it changed its view that all nations were interdependent and learned to tolerate concessions of authority. Just after the war, the United States had virtually manufactured an interest in the areas occupied by the Red Army in its pursuit of a uniform international order. But its escalation of interests had done nothing to hinder the Russians' territorial and economic ambitions; indeed, it may well have hardened the determination of Stalin to extend his influence. So America's growing commitment to the reconstruction and defence of Western Europe was paralleled by a decline in its active interventions in the East. But the United States' acknowledgement of the limits of its power was accompanied by a confident optimism. Policy-makers were still convinced that the Soviet system rested on fragile foundations and that these foundations would crumble in time. However, it was not within the power or even the province of the United States to nurture this dissolution. It could not be an instigator in the expected communist reformation. Change would occur, but it would have to be generated from within. When an indigenous challenge did come, the United States would support it, but as the example of Yugoslavia demonstrates, it would do so with caution and restraint. Meanwhile, Americans would hold up the "iron curtain" to the rest of the world in the hope of strengthening its determination to resist communism. And in that sense the existence of the "iron curtain" ironically became an indispensable instrument in America's quest for allies overseas.

Frank Costigliola

DEMONIZING THE SOVIETS: GEORGE F. KENNAN'S LONG TELEGRAM

On February 22, 1946, the young chargé d'affairs at the American Embassy in Moscow, George F. Kennan, sent the State Department his famous "long telegram." Destined to become one of the pivotal documents of the early Cold War, Kennan's hard-hitting cable laid out the case for pursuing a presumably realistic policy of containment in order to check the dangerously expansionistic tendencies of Soviet Russia. At a time when American officialdom was seeking guidance in dealing with the inconsistent and ofttimes perplexing policies of the Soviet state, Kennan offered a simple, clearcut—and reductive—explanation of the Kremlin's foreign policy. As Frank Costigliola suggests in the next selection, Kennan made containment seem the only sensible, healthy, and

Frank Costigliola, "'Unceasing Urge for Penetration': Gender, Pathology, and Emotion in George Kennan's Formation of the Cold War," *Journal of American History*, 83 (March 1997), pp. 1309–1313, 1328–1339. Reprinted with permission.

"manly" response to the Soviet threat. The American diplomat did so, in large part, Costigliola points out, through the power of his emotive and highly gendered prose. Kennan offered what amounted to an emotional sermon, one that depicted the Soviet Union as a demonic force bent on destroying the United States and the American way of life. For all his vaunted realism, as the author of this essay argues, Kennan's Cold War discourse actually derived from a complex combination of his conflicted feelings about the Soviet government, the Russian people, American society, and his own career. Costigliola's nuanced analysis of the interconnection between personal dynamics and foreign policy recommendations offers a novel and challenging perspective on the early Cold War.

The author of *Awkward Dominion: American Political, Economic, and Cultural Relations with Europe, 1919–1933* (1984) and *The Cold Alliance* (1992), on United States-French relations, Frank Costigliola teaches history at the University of Connecticut.

In the *New York Times Book Review* of April 7, 1996, Fareed Zakaria, managing editor of *Foreign Affairs,* reviewed the latest book by George F. Kennan, the ninety-two-year-old former diplomat and author of the containment doctrine. Zakaria began his review by praising the "clarity" and the "gripping, declarative prose" of Kennan's "famous long telegram from Moscow in 1946." In that 5,540-word telegram, Kennan laid out the argument for deemphasizing negotiations with Moscow on issues arising from World War II and for instead emphasizing the containment of the Soviet Union. Ever since Kennan's cable reached the State Department a half century ago, officials and scholars have been pointing to Kennan's prose—without, however, examining why his language appeared so clear and so gripping or how his emotions and rhetorical strategies infused his writings, particularly the long telegram (LT), with such persuasive force. A close reading of Kennan's writings demonstrates that the language is neither transparent nor value-free, and that Kennan's figures of speech—which scholars have quoted as "colorful language" but have not fully analyzed—emotionalize and condition the interpretation of his ostensibly realistic prose.

Kennan wrote the LT on February 22, 1946, after two decades of deep, conflicted feelings about the Soviet people and their government. For much of that period, he longed to immerse himself in Russian society even as he felt alienated from United

States society. Perhaps his deepest aspiration was to use what he saw as the primitive vitality of Russian culture to revitalize the United States. The exuberance and sensuality that Kennan and other United States diplomats such as William C. Bullitt and Charles E. Bohlen had enjoyed in Moscow in 1933–1934 sharpened the bitterness with which they approached United States-Soviet relations at the onset of the Cold War. Kennan expressed his intense feelings in his writing, often in metaphors of gender and pathology. Because these emotion-laden tropes remained camouflaged by Kennan's expertise on Soviet affairs and his claim to realism, they offered a particularly effective rhetorical strategy for demonizing the leadership of the Soviet Union in a supposedly dispassionate analysis.

In the LT, Kennan portrayed the Soviet government as a rapist exerting "insistent, unceasing pressure for penetration and command" over Western societies. A few months later, he compared the Soviet people to "a woman who had been romantically in love with her husband and who had suddenly seen his true colors revealed. . . . There was no question of a divorce. They decided to stay together for the sake of the children. But the honeymoon was definitely over." The analogy fit a favorite narrative of Kennan in which the Russian people figured as feminine (and often an object of desire), the Soviet government appeared as a cruel masculine authority, and he stood forth as the unrequited but true lover of the Russian people.

Kennan also represented the Soviet leadership as mentally ill, suffering "a psychosis which permeates and determines [the] behavior of [the] entire Soviet ruling caste." The discourse of psychological pathology privileged Kennan and his listeners—they had the authoritative gaze of physicians—while it positioned the Soviet Union as a mental patient without a legitimate subjectivity. If the Soviet government could not reason normally, why try to cooperate with it? Moreover, the discourse of psychology helped remove the issue of relations with Moscow from the realm of popular judgment—where some Americans favored cooperation with the Soviets, while others believed that a war might be necessary—and placed that issue instead in the realm of experts, such as Kennan, who favored the isolation and containment of Moscow. Underscoring the need for specialized knowledge, Kennan told public audiences that the problem of the Soviet Union "is a frightfully complicated, involved thing; it is very dangerous to try to describe. Russia is not a clear personality. . . . Russia is at least a dual personality and sometimes I think quadruple and more."

Kennan and his writings have been much studied, but insufficiently analyzed, by historians. . . .

No historian has examined Kennan's quasi-mystical hope of becoming—through his understanding of Russia and his near-expatriate view of America—a link enabling Russian society and American society to help each other. This essay foregrounds this concern, building on [Walter] Hixson's discussion of Kennan's emotionalism, [Anders] Stephanson's critique of Kennan's Soviet expertise, and [John Lamberton] Harper's psychological suppositions, by examining the meanings revealed and created by what Kennan called his "florid showmanship in prose." Kennan's language, particularly his tropes of gender and pathology, created an emotionalized context in which his exaggerated depictions of the "Soviet threat" appeared rational and credible.

On the second page of his memoirs, Kennan acknowledged that he lived, "right on to middle age, in a world that was peculiarly and intimately my own. . . . I habitually read special meanings into things, scenes, and places—qualities of wonder, beauty, promise, or horror." For Kennan, who found "the great land and life of Russia, more interesting . . . than any other in the world," who found Russian "a natural language, in which words sounded the way they ought to sound," and who expressed "doubt that there could be anyone in the Western world who [had] deeper feelings" than he for the Russian people, Russia did hold a personal "wonder" and "beauty." Although historians have documented Kennan's "horror" of the Soviet government, they have largely missed his belief that Russia also held "promise," sometimes as a model, sometimes as threat.

Throughout his career, Kennan criticized what he saw as the excessive individualism and commercialism of United States society. He repeatedly came back to the idea that Russia—as inspiration or menace—might spur the United States to correct these deficiencies. In 1933–1934, he "hope[d] that somewhere in that Russian world—in the freshness and spontaneity of its human relationships, in its childishly blunt reaction to the problems of civilization, in the unfathomable warmth and beauty of its language—things could be found which could help us in solving the problems of our own culture." By 1938, he concluded that the brutality of the Soviet government and the meager prospects for cultural interchange "left no exciting answers to be sought in Russia." He feared that his inability to use the example of Russia to reform America "placed a definite ceiling . . . to my professional aspirations, to my conception of the potentialities of Soviet-American relations." A great irony in Kennan's life is that in 1946–1947 the demand in the United States for an easily understood explanation of Soviet behavior and for a policy to deal with that behavior would lift the "ceiling" from Kennan's career and give him another chance to present Russia, this time in the form of the "Soviet threat," as a prod to domestic American reform.

When Kennan wrote the LT, in February 1946, Americans were searching for a clear-cut, simple explanation of Soviet foreign policy. Joseph Stalin's government, however, displayed a confusing mixture of caution and self-aggrandizement. The Soviets angered the United States by their continued occupation of northern Iran and Manchuria, by their pressure on Turkey for base rights in the Dardanelles, and by their defense of Soviet spies caught in Canada. Yet they evacuated northern Norway and the Danish island of Bornholm in the Baltic Sea, discouraged revolution in Western Europe, offered no leadership to Communist revolutionaries in Southeast Asia, and played to both sides in the Chinese civil war; further, they went on to allow free elections in Hungary, Czechoslovakia, and Finland. What was the pattern in these events? Americans wondered. Was it possible and desirable to extend wartime cooperation into the postwar era? There was "great confusion" in Washington, observed Dwight D. Eisenhower. The British ambassador reported that American leaders suffered "uneasy bewilderment," "fear of the unknown," and "baffled dismay."

American officials also debated whether to make the concessions necessary for a possible deal with Moscow. In December 1945, Secretary of State James F. Byrnes made a preliminary agreement with Stalin on control of the atomic bomb, only to have the accord killed by President Harry S. Truman and Republican senator Arthur Vandenberg. Soviet ambivalence continued. On January 25, 1946, Stalin met with Igor Kurchatov, head of the Soviet atomic bomb project, and told him to spare no expense in quickly building a bomb. Four days later, Byrnes reported to the cabinet that although the Soviets still wanted "to discuss stability and peace with the United States alone" without Britain, and although "they were always eager to do so . . . he had discontinued the practice of having private meetings with the Russians."

Kennan's long telegram helped the Truman administration arrive at a reductive but clear picture of Soviet policy. The emotive force of this document helped delegitimate what Kennan called "intimate collaboration" with Moscow, making containment, a policy that already had strong support in the Truman administration, seem the only realistic, healthy, and manly alternative. At a time when the United States priority was already shifting away from dealing with Moscow and toward building a viable "free world," the LT convinced many that the Soviet government was a monstrous force, fanatically committed to destroying the United States and the American way of life. . . .

Kennan's personal resentment at the Soviet government's isolation of its citizens led him to personalize foreign policy disputes. In August 1944, Stalin refused to order the Red Army to help the Warsaw uprising against the Germans because he wanted to cripple any indigenous Polish resistance to Soviet domination. Although brutal, this decision reflected the geopolitics of a specific area, where the Soviets were determined to establish a controlled, "friendly" government despite the Poles' historic hatred of Russia. Kennan, however, characterized the Soviet action more broadly, as a "gauntlet thrown down, in a spirit of malicious glee, before the Western powers." "Malicious glee" suggested that Soviet policy toward Poland derived not from security concerns, but from unreasonable, almost fiendish hostility—that is, from a pathological personality. The connotation of masculine combat in "gauntlet" illustrated Kennan's use of gendered language to convey intense feelings.

In conventional language usage, the assumptions of masculine superiority and of a basic polarity between masculine and feminine, along with the powerful emotions evoked by gender, make the rhetorical strategy of mapping gendered differences onto other differences, such as issues of foreign policy, highly effective. This gendering works to emotionalize and polarize issues. Kennan's strong emotions, his ambition to be persuasive, and the sensuality that he and his friends had experienced in the Soviet Union—all made gendered language a particularly important rhetorical strategy.

As Soviet-American relations deteriorated in 1944–1946, Kennan's emotive rhetoric helped delegitimate the wartime policy of striving to cooperate with the Soviets. Bitter at Soviet restrictions on his access to the Russian people and to officials, Kennan disparaged and discouraged the ties that others might develop with Soviet leaders. He depicted those Americans seeking postwar cooperation with the Soviets as prone to "gushing assumptions of chumminess." The phrase called up an image of gullible United States officials, almost inevitably men, emasculating themselves and their nation with uncontrolled flows of homosocial feeling. Although Kennan's realism prescribed the containment of both the Soviet Union and such "gushing assumptions of chumminess," Kennan himself, at least once, delighted in such chumminess.

Kennan recounted the episode in the diary of his June 1945 trip across Siberia. This document, which Kennan gave to Harriman, offers a fascinating glimpse into the complexity of Kennan's feelings about Soviet authority and the way those feelings interacted with his opposition to cooperation with the Soviets. Kennan found it easy to share the official prerogatives of a new acquaintance, Leonid Borodulin, "a burly young party secretary from Novosibirsk, obviously a person of considerable competence and power." He described their night out on the town: "For one lovely evening I was, to all intents and purposes, a member of the Soviet governing elite. We visited several theaters, barging in through side doors, staring down anyone who questioned our arrival, and installing ourselves without ceremony in the government box." Comfortable with Borodulin's peremptoriness, Kennan unselfconsciously related how "we forced an unshaven and somewhat bewildered station master to show us the place from top to bottom." On subsequent days, "B[orodulin] and I got fed up with the uncertainty, and he decided to turn up the heat"; "again B[orodulin] and I snatched the best room." The men bonded by sharing privilege and by diminishing the women whom they encountered: some "terrible . . . Isadora Duncan dancers" and a circus lady who put her head in a lion's mouth. "After having a good second look at the lady [we] agreed—to our great mutual satisfaction—that we were lost in admiration for the courage of the lion." Perhaps influenced by this homosocial bonding, Kennan in his trip diary sensualized the Russian people as positively masculine as well as feminine: they were "a virile, fertile people." For Kennan—who had long favored privilege and authority for the talented elite and who had respected the "strong-nerved, lean" commissars of 1933—Stalin's rule grated not just because it was so brutal but also because it excluded him and separated him from the Soviet people.

Kennan applied his observations in Siberia to the policy issue of a possible United States reconstruction loan to Moscow. American and Soviet advocates of such a loan believed it could ease the harshness of Soviet rebuilding, establish a postwar exchange of Soviet raw materials for United States manufactures, and facilitate political cooperation. Affirming that the suffering Russian people deserved such foreign help, Kennan also alluded wistfully to the benefits that Americans could derive from contact with them. He coded the Russian people as an implicitly masculine, potentially positive influence on the feminized West. The Russians were "appealing people, purged by hardship of so much that is vulgar and inane in the softer civilizations, organized and prepared . . . for the building of a decent, rational society."

After revisiting his frustrated dream, Kennan suddenly claimed the discourse of realism. "But the fact is: there is no way of helping the Russian people." The assertion of objectivity notwithstanding, Kennan's discourse remained emotional. Writing shortly after the revelation of the Nazi death camps, he described the Kremlin as "a regime of unparalleled ruthlessness and jealousy," which "has those people completely in its hand." Kennan concluded that the United States—and he himself—had to seek distance from, rather than contact with, the Soviet Union: "The benevolent foreigner . . . cannot help the Russian people; he can only help the Kremlin. And conversely, he cannot harm the Kremlin; he can only harm the Russian people."

Kennan did his best to distance the United States from the Soviet Union. On a variety of issues he advised the State Department against informing, consulting with, inquiring from, or otherwise engaging with the Soviets. Shortly before the February 1945 Yalta conference, he wrote Bohlen that the United States should adopt a spheres-of-influence policy, writing off Eastern Europe and abandoning efforts at cooperation. Characteristically, Kennan loaded and polarized the issue of cooperation by employing gendered/sexualized language. He contrasted the "political manliness" of those who would isolate the Soviets with the emotionalism and implied femininity and/or homosexuality of those who "yearn" for "intimate collaboration" with the Soviets. Kennan urged aloofness from what he regarded as an immoral Soviet domination of Poland. Presidential adviser Harry Hopkins concluded from a talk with Kennan: "Then you think it's just sin, and we should be agin it." "That's just about right," Kennan replied. At the December 1945 Allied foreign ministers conference, when Secretary of State Byrnes stood on a public balcony and shook hands with a Soviet leader, sparking cheers from the Moscow crowd below, Kennan became "furious," an embassy official observed, "because such gestures masked the true nature of Soviet-American relations." By the time Kennan wrote the LT, his concept of isolating the Soviets had expanded into containing the Soviets.

Although bitterness did not alone lead Kennan to advocate isolating and containing the Soviet Union, such emotion made it difficult for him to see cooperation or close contact with Stalin's government as anything but debased "collaboration." In the LT, Kennan channeled his complex feelings about the Soviet government, the Russian people, American society, and his own career into an emotional sermon that helped shape the meaning of the Cold War. As he recalled, "I am a person who rouses himself to intellectual activity only when he is stung. The more outraged I become at the preposterousness of the things other people say, the better I do." Although Kennan reported in his memoir that he had written the LT in a state of outrage, this memory misses part of the documentary record. With United States sentiment already concerned about Stalin's election speech of February 9, 1946, State Department colleagues Harrison Freeman "Doc" Matthews and Elbridge Durbrow advised Kennan that the department would welcome a major "interpretive analysis" from him.

In his memoirs Kennan cites, not this telegram, but one originating in the Treasury Department. Treasury officials had, in Kennan's words, clung "ferociously" to "naive . . . hopes . . . for postwar collaboration with Russia." The Treasury had cabled asking why the Soviet government was refusing to join the International Monetary Fund (IMF) and the World Bank. By characterizing this query as an "anguished cry of bewilderment," Kennan depicted those who still hoped for cooperation with Moscow as overemotional and infantile. In Kennan's polarity, the "preposterousness" of the Treasury viewpoint accentuated the righteousness of his response, the LT. He wrote in his memoirs: "Here was a case where nothing but the whole truth would do. They had asked for it. Now, by God, they would have it."

The "whole truth" of the LT actually invoked a fantastic reality in which leaders of the Soviet Union appeared as an inhuman force, without morality, beyond the appeal of reason, unable to appreciate objective fact or truth, and compelled to destroy almost every decent aspect of life in the West. Echoing his painful experience with Stalin's crackdown in the late 1930s, Kennan asserted that the "most disquieting feature of diplomacy in Moscow" was the isolation from Soviet policy makers, whom one cannot "see and cannot influence."

At the end of the LT, Kennan assured his readers that the Soviet Union did not want war, was weaker than the United States, and could be contained without war if the United States and the West took the necessary steps. Yet it was his emotionalized picture of the Soviet threat and his militarized language that grabbed the attention of readers. Kennan described the Soviet Union as "impervious to [the] logic of reason and . . . highly sensitive to [the] logic of force." The United States should determine how to apply such logic of force with "political general staff work . . . approached with [the] same thoroughness and care as [the] solution of [a] major strategic problem in war." To Kennan's later consternation, many people concluded that containment required a massive military buildup.

Kennan's reliance on the discourse of pathological psychology to describe Soviet leaders dramatized his argument that the United States could not expect, and should not try, to have mutually understanding relations with Moscow. Kennan described Soviet leaders as "afflicted" with acute insecurity and "mentally too dependent to question [their] self-hypnotism." He urged Americans to observe the Soviet Union with the attitude "with which [a] doctor studies [an] unruly and unreasonable individual." In a sentence that was itself tortured, he portrayed Soviet leaders as mentally confined by the Marxist dogma that justified "the dictatorship without which they did not know how to rule," the "cruelties they did not dare not to inflict." Morally as well as mentally crippled, the Soviet leadership had "in the name of Marxism . . . sacrificed every single ethical value." Extending the imagery of pathology and dehumanization, he likened "world communism" to a "malignant parasite."

Kennan wrote of the Kremlin's inability to reason on the basis of reality, objectivity, or truth. For Kennan, whose 1951 appraisal of American diplomacy came to be known as the "realist" critique, "real" was a word to be flourished with confidence. In the West, he wrote in the LT, "objective fact about human society is . . . the measure against which [our] outlook is constantly being tested and reformed." In contrast, he argued, the Soviet Union "is seemingly inaccessible to considerations of reality in its basic reactions." With "disrespect . . . for objective truth, indeed . . . disbelief in its existence," Soviet leaders regarded truth as only "a grab bag from which individual items are selected arbitrarily and tendentiously to bolster an outlook already preconceived." One item from the "grab bag" was the complaint by Stalin and others that the Soviet Union again stood encircled by antagonistic powers. Although Kennan dismissed this notion as "not based on any objective analysis," Harriman acknowledged that the Anglo-American monopoly of the atomic bomb was giving the Soviets considerable worry. For Kennan, however, Soviet anxieties stemmed from the "Kremlin's neurotic view of world affairs."

Other rhetorical strategies, including the near absence in the text of recognizable people and the intensive use of the passive voice, helped construct this drama of polarization. The 5,540 words of the LT included the names of only two persons: Lenin, who was mentioned once in passing, and Stalin, who was quoted once and mentioned twice. The principal agents in the LT were not people, but abstract noun phrases, such as the "steady advance of uneasy Russian nationalism," the "instinctive urges of Russian rulers," and the "official propaganda machine." The monster of the LT was so scary and such an unlikely negotiating partner because it was not a person who, however cruel and ambitious, was nevertheless human and able to compromise, but a soulless "machine" or "force."

In one of the most widely quoted sentences of the LT, Kennan wrote: "In summary, we have here a political force committed fanatically to the belief that with [the] U.S. there can be no permanent *modus vivendi,* that it is desirable and necessary that the internal harmony of our society be disrupted, our traditional way of life be destroyed, the international authority of our state be broken, if Soviet power is to be secure." Because the agent here was an abstract "political force" and because much of the sentence was in the passive voice and the archaic subjunctive, it was difficult to challenge its underlying premises by asking whether the leaders of the Soviet Union had such designs, how capable they were of achieving them, and how Kennan came to know of them. The prospects for American resistance appeared particularly grim because the reader could glean little idea of how the United States would "be disrupted" and "be destroyed." The LT had many sentences with similar construction: "Poor will be set against rich, black against white, young against old. . . ." "No effort will be spared to discredit and combat. . . ." The repetition of passive sentences—all with an archaic tone and all conveying the message of unlimited action by an evil force—suggested a religious text or a fairy tale. Such "realism" one had to accept largely on faith.

The tropes of gender in the LT were more nuanced than the representations of pathology. Throughout the document, the Soviet leadership, whether portrayed as a machine, a force, or as persons, engaged in the driving, aggressive behavior conventionally associated with masculinity. Kennan underscored this association in the LT by repeating the word "penetration" five times in reference to the Soviets' insistent, unwanted intrusion. The Soviet leadership appeared as monstrously masculine. Kennan represented the Communist objective as splitting open Western societies that were already too divided. "Efforts will be made . . . to disrupt national self confidence . . . to stimulate all forms of disunity."

Juxtaposed to this image of the Soviet government as a masculine rapist was Kennan's representation of the West as dangerously accessible through "a wide variety of national associations or bodies which can be dominated or influenced by such [Communist] penetration." Kennan listed such potentially subversive elements: "labor unions, youth leagues, women's organizations, racial societies, religious societies . . . liberal magazines."

Kennan proposed that the West respond to the monstrous hypermasculinity of the Soviet Union by itself acting more masculine. He urged that the United States "tighten" up, achieve greater "cohesion, firmness and vigor," and approach the Soviet Union with the conventionally masculine virtues of "courage, detachment, objectivity, and . . . determination not to be emotionally provoked or unseated." The United States should play the "doctor" and calm the "hysterical anti-Sovietism" of those who expected or who wanted a war with Moscow. In the LT, implicitly gendered language helped construct an attention-grabbing morality tale.

Despite the organization of the LT in five sections, the most significant turn of argument appears midway through the last part, where Kennan moved from demonizing the Soviet Union to prescribing how the United States and the West should respond to this threat. Although scholars have long noted Kennan's reassurance that Soviet power could be held back without a war, they have not noted the significance of the very next sentence, in which Kennan shifted focus from the Soviet threat to the West's internal divisions, while linking these two problems. Characteristically, he signaled this move, and the leap of logic that it required, with the word "really." He wrote that the Soviets' "success will really depend on [the] degree of cohesion, firmness and vigor which [the] Western World can muster."

The most decisive arena lay, not in foreign lands, but in the United States: "Every courageous and incisive measure to solve [the] internal problems of our own society . . . is a diplomatic victory over Moscow worth a thousand diplomatic notes and joint communiqués." Kennan concluded the LT with five suggestions on "how to deal with Russia": appraise the problem with objectivity rather than emotion, launch a government program to educate the public, guide Western Europe, abstain from Soviet methods, and "solve [the] internal problems of our own society" with "improve[d] self-confidence, discipline, morale and community spirit." Four of these suggestions involved actions to be taken at home, the fifth touched on Western Europe, and none directly involved the Soviet Union. Although genuinely alarmed at the Soviet Union's expansion, Kennan also exaggerated this danger in order to focus the attention of the American citizenry. For him the Communist threat was a "point at which domestic and foreign policies meet."

The LT's message about domestic problems reflected a long-held ambition. In 1933–1934, Kennan had hoped to use the "freshness" of Russian society somehow to revitalize American society. In 1938, he had advocated restricted suffrage and authoritarian government to counter what he saw as the nation's self-indulgence, political corruption, and crass commercialism. In the conclusion of the 1947 "X" article, Kennan depicted the deterioration in United States–Soviet relations as a fair trial of America's "national quality. . . . The issue of Soviet-American relations is in essence a test of the over-all worth of the United States." He expressed "gratitude" that the "implacable challenge" of the Kremlin forced Americans to "pull themselves together." Although he would soon deplore the excesses of the Cold War, Kennan at first welcomed that cataclysm.

The LT and the "X" essay, formal presentations in which Kennan bid for influence as an expert in Soviet affairs, did not convey the depth of his feelings. In December 1946, midway between the writing of the two documents, he lectured to American military officers at the National War College. The talk, "The Background of Current Russian Diplomatic Moves," was a more freewheeling effort to link the Soviet challenge to American domestic problems. This lecture reveals Kennan's identification with the Russian people, his longing for intimacy with them, his ability to have them ventriloquize his concerns, and his tendency to slip into conjecture and even fantasy when explaining what was "really" going on in Russia:

> The Soviet attack on us was based on a shrewd and pitiless analysis of our own national faults. . . . The Russian people are powerfully inclined to admire us. They wish in their heart of hearts that they could be proved wrong in their skepticism about us and that we would really turn out in the end to have the answers which they so desperately need. If they have been ready to destroy us, it was in reality for our failure to eradicate the weaknesses of our own society, for our failure to be what they thought we should be, to bring out the best they felt was in us.
>
> The Russians . . . have never been a menace to us except as we have been a menace to ourselves. But being forced to see this country for many years through Russian eyes has left me with a conviction that we cannot escape a final settlement with these failings which the Russians have detected in our society and which have enabled them, an economically weak and politically backward nation, to come so close to disrupting our society. . . . The real threat to our society, the threat which has lain behind the Soviet armies, behind the *Daily Worker,* and behind the aberrations of confused American left-wingers, will not be overcome until we have learned to view

ourselves realistically and to purge ourselves of some of our prejudices, our hypocrisies, and our lack of civic discipline.

Asserting that he could "see" the United States "through
Russian eyes," Kennan projected into the Russians' "heart of
hearts" his own agenda for reforming the United States. He
claimed for the Russian people nearly supernatural insight into
America's "national faults." Further, the Russian people, like an
angel that was both avenging and guardian, wanted to "destroy us
for our failure to eradicate the weaknesses of our own society."
Kennan constructed the Russians as not just a threat but also a
moral force. In terms of the historiographical debate over whether
the United States faced an implacable foe in the Cold War, Kennan, at least the nominal author of containment, offered a stunning assessment: "the Russians, I can assure you, have never been a
menace to us except as we have been a menace to ourselves." In
this speech Kennan for a moment attained fusion with the Russian
people. His fantasy, however, depended on the widening fissure
between the United States and Soviet governments.

The LT was seized upon by United States officials, some
of whom were already warning of the "Soviet threat" but with less effective rhetoric. A State Department colleague observed that
Matthews, who had encouraged Kennan to write the LT, "engineered" distribution of the text to United States officials in Washington and around the world. Understanding that Kennan's language
was intrinsic to his message, the usually parsimonious department reproduced the entire document, explaining that it was "not subject to
condensation." The copies went out on March 5, 1946, coincidentally the day of Winston Churchill's Iron Curtain speech. An observer found United States diplomats in Europe "very excited" by
the LT's "new line." With masculine-inflected language, Henry Norweb, the United States ambassador to Cuba, lauded Kennan's "masterpiece of 'thinking things out' " his "realism devoid of hysteria,"
and his "courageous approach to a problem."

Another promoter of the LT was Navy Secretary James Forrestal, who had been trying to persuade others of the Soviet threat.
Forrestal's biographers noted that he found in Kennan's analysis
the "authoritative explanation he had been seeking." Forrestal
sent copies to Truman, the cabinet, newspapers, and people in

Congress and in business, and he made the LT required reading for navy officers. With this sudden acclaim, Kennan became a "transformed person," according to a colleague. Brought back from Moscow in April 1946, he gave some thirty department-sponsored lectures across the United States, seeking to "instill into our public appreciation for basic realities"—"realities" that echoed the LT. With Forrestal's backing, Kennan became deputy commander and a teacher at the National War College in August 1946 and the first director of the State Department's Policy Planning Staff in 1947.

Although the LT alone did not cause the shift in United States policy toward the Soviets, the cable helped restrict debate. With its simplified, emotional, and yet authoritative explanation of Soviet behavior, the LT encouraged United States officials to bypass the vexing problems of understanding and accommodating the Soviets. Citing the LT, Bohlen, then special assistant to the secretary of state and a chief adviser on relations with the Soviet Union, recommended that rather than agonizing over the possibility of cooperating with the Soviets, the United States government should "take as accepted" the imperative of containing them. When Byrnes sent Kennan statements defining policy toward such countries as India, China, and Iraq, the latter reworked the documents to emphasize—and to exaggerate—the dangers of what he called "Soviet penetration." Enthusiastic about this "coordination" and "discipline" of policy, Kennan worked to globalize Washington's anti-Soviet stance.

The pervasiveness of emotion, sensuality, and personal aspiration in shaping Kennan's attitudes and policies toward the Soviet Union suggests that historians need to deepen the debate about the origins of the Cold War and to widen diplomatic history by exploring the connections between the personal and public lives of foreign policymakers. While Kennan's "florid showmanship in prose" makes a close reading of his language particularly rewarding, we should also examine the language of other historical subjects. We can gain a fuller understanding of both text and context if we understand that the text, such as the LT, often creates its own context by the use of allusive language that conditions—although it does not determine—how we interpret the text. This is especially the case with tropes of gender and pathology, which mobilize powerful emotions because they touch on the body, on personal fears and fantasies, and on unquestioned beliefs that take as "natural" relationships that are socially constructed.

The language of the LT fostered feelings that delegitimated co-operation with the Soviets. Emotions reframed the question from whether the United States and the Soviet Union could reach compromises that would safeguard the vital interests of both nations, to whether it was realistic and manly to deal with a regime fanatically committed to destroying the United States and everything else decent. Kennan's rhetorical strategies in the LT worked so effectively because the Truman administration was looking for a clarifying statement and because Kennan—with the authority of his expertise and his ostensible realism—was able to appeal to emotions in the name of reason.

But precisely to what extent, one may ask, did Kennan's emotions determine his policies? To what extent did the LT contribute to the Cold War? What is the causal connection between Kennan's representation of United States-Soviet relations—that is, his production and circulation of emotion-evoking images and symbols— and the origins of the Cold War? Such questions arise from the premise that there must be single, clear, unequivocal causes for policies and actions, and that one can attribute those causes to the conscious decision of unitary agents. A belief in these apparently clear lines of causation can lead to the overconfident assumption that a historical analysis is akin to a scientific explanation. We often thus talk of "proving" narratives about how and why things happened. My approach, however, begins with the observation that causes of historical events and situations, such as the Cold War, tend to be complex and diffuse; that not all aspects of such causes are attributable to single agents or conscious intention; and that the connotations of figurative language have real, although never absolute, causal effect. On broad issues, such as the origins of the Cold War, we generally cannot measure historical causation as precisely as we may claim. The intent of this essay, rather, is to deepen the historiographical discussion by contributing to the many histories of the Cold War an analysis of the implications for policy of personal desire and expression. In the debate over the relative weight of internal and external determinants of foreign policy, this essay underscores the importance of two relatively neglected internal factors: emotions, which in Kennan's case suffused his views of the Soviet Union, and a domestic agenda, which for Kennan intertwined with his foreign policy recommendations.

The Cold War developed in a way that Kennan soon deplored. In trying to contain the Soviet Union, the United States did suffer a cataclysm, but the resulting unity produced McCarthyism and the national security state rather than Kennan's earlier ideal of a benevolent but authoritarian regime. Little more than a decade after he succeeded with the militarized metaphors of the LT, Kennan failed to persuade Western leaders to demilitarize the confrontation in central Europe. Kennan's handicaps in the disengagement debate included not just the entrenchment of Cold War polices and his retirement from government but also the masculine bias in foreign policy discourses. Urging negotiation with the Soviets, Kennan could not answer in kind the critics who de-masculinized and thereby delegitimated his plan as "obvious nonsense," suitable for "scared mothers and fuzzy liberals," and as a policy of "supine impotence" inviting Soviet "penetration." Kennan's attempts in the LT and in the "X" essay to stimulate domestic change also failed. Most of Kennan's readers missed his prescriptions for reform, and those who noticed dismissed them. Cold War architect Dean Acheson judged that Kennan's "recommendations . . . to look to our own social and economic health . . . were of no help.". In postwar years Kennan continued to call, in vain, for "a very extensive measure of social control over . . . our national life."

Perhaps most sadly for himself, Kennan failed to control his explosive emotions about the Soviet Union. His ambassadorship to Moscow in 1952, the culmination of his diplomatic career, blew up after a few months because of his public denunciation of Soviet policies isolating him from the Russian people. Astonished at Kennan's "frame of mind," British diplomats observed that his "lack of self control is extraordinary." Although we may fault the professionalism of a diplomat who allowed Soviet insults to hurt so much, we should also sympathize with the frustration of a man who beheld the Russian people as "a beautiful lady guarded by a jealous lover."

Thomas J. McCormick

ECONOMIC CRISIS AND AMERICAN MILITARIZATION

An early proponent of revisionism, Thomas J. McCormick seeks to reformulate that interpretation in his book *America's Half-Century* (1995). Drawing on world-systems theory, he stresses the primacy of economic forces in international relations. American Cold War policies cannot be understood without reference to the larger structural crisis that plagued postwar capitalism. As the world's leading capitalist power, contends McCormick, the United States sought to create a unitary, integrated world-system—or a system of hegemony. The United States succeeded initially in repairing the structural imbalances caused by world depression and world war, but by 1949–1950 American policy faced a new crisis. The persisting dollar gap, the Soviet detonation of an atomic bomb, and the victory of the Chinese communists, according to McCormick, combined to create one of the most momentous crises of the entire postwar era. The Truman administration responded with what McCormick calls "the militarization option," a policy direction that culminated with the adoption of National Security Council Paper 68 (NSC-68) in early 1950.

Thomas J. McCormick is a professor of history at the University of Wisconsin, Madison. He has also written *China Market: America's Quest for Informal Empire, 1893–1901* (1967) and coedited *America in Vietnam: A Documentary History* (1985).

On a gloomy, grey, Friday afternoon, February 21, 1947, the British embassy delivered a "blue piece of paper"—an extraordinarily important note—to American Under Secretary of State Dean Acheson. It announced Britain's intentions to end its military and financial support of the Greek monarchy and the Turkish government within the ensuing thirty days. The announcement climaxed seven days that had seen Britain end its three-decade control of Palestine and its centuries-old dominion over India. Three days after receiving the "blue note" and following a weekend of frenetic State Department activity, Acheson mused aloud to a journalist friend on their way to lunch at the Metropolitan Club: "There are only two powers left. The British are finished, they are through. And the trouble is that this hits us too soon, before we are ready for it. We are having a lot of trouble getting money out of Congress."

Ready or not, the denouement of British imperium in the eastern Mediterranean would provoke a rapid and decisive American initiative to fill the void. Its most dramatic manifestation would be the Truman Doctrine. Neither British action nor American reaction, however, was as important as the larger context in which both took place. The crisis of British disengagement was but part of a much larger structural crisis in postwar capitalism, exacerbated by a challenge from the Soviet empire. And the Truman Doctrine was but a stop-gap response to that larger crisis, both less important and less enduring than the revolutionary responses embodied in the Marshall Plan of 1948 and the North Atlantic Treaty Organization in 1949. Even those measures, for all their startling innovativeness, would not remedy capitalism's troubles. Renewed structural crisis and renewed Russian challenge in late 1949 and early 1950 would dictate an even more revolutionary turn in American foreign policy. Its ultimate expression would be National Security Council document paper #68, NSC-68. Its consequence would be a new kind of cold war, one both more militaristic and more Third World oriented.

From the last fiscal quarter of 1946 through the first fiscal quarter of 1950 the world-system labored with a crisis born of paradox and steeped in irony. World capitalism seemed to require a hegemonic center (at that point, the United States) to insure that the various parts of the system would act in ways that would produce the greatest health of the whole. Because the preponderant economic power of the United States, upon which its hegemony largely rested, so overwhelmed the devastated European economies that commercial imbalance among major trading parts threatened the well-being of the whole, American economic supremacy nearly undermined its hegemonic function. The shorthand expression of this postwar paradox was graphic as well as cryptic; it was called the dollar gap crisis. . . .

A contemporary television sports program talks about "the thrill of victory and the agony of defeat." From August 1949 until April 1950, American leaders endured the psychic fragmentation of experiencing both feelings at once. On one hand, the United States had weathered the initial structural crisis in world capitalism and responded effectively with the ideological, economic, political, and military innovations of the Truman Doctrine, the Marshall Plan, and NATO. But, like some cosmic dialectic, history repeated and embroidered itself with renewed and deepened crisis in late 1949 and early 1950. The world-system seemed once more threatened from within, this time by the calamitous consequences of the American "reverse course" policy in Japan and by the continued bottlenecks and dollar shortages that plagued the European Recovery Program [ERP] (At the same time, this internal crisis was exacerbated from without by Russian acquisition of the atomic bomb and by the triumph of the Chinese communists in the Chinese civil war.)

The near catastrophe of America's Japan policy was more immediately frightening than any other facet of the renewed crisis. Since 1948, the United States had reversed its earlier course of decentralizing and democratizing Japanese economic life. American occupation authorities had ceased efforts to break up large-scale monopoly capital (the *Zaibatsu*) and were exploring strategies of reindustrialization instead. This "reverse course" reflected a number of factors. The U.S. Congress was anxious to make the Japanese occupation self-supporting, able to sustain itself without American subsidies; and the ERP burden of $17 billion only made Congress more eager to put Japan on a pay-as-you-go footing. In addition, American occupation authorities were fearful that earlier attempts at economic decentralization had strengthened the political hand of Japanese communists and socialists. While Japanese radicals preferred nationalization of private industry, they saw competitive capitalism as more acceptable than monopoly capital, because it diminished the power of traditional industrial oligarchs. Finally, the obvious collapse of the Chinese nationalists and the likely triumph of the Chinese communists had killed any notion of China's acting as a regional surrogate for the United States. Only Japan seemed a likely role model to demonstrate to the rest of Asia the advantages of a procapitalist, prointegrationist model of economic development. To play the role effectively, however, Japanese industry had to be organized on the same principles as that in North America and the OEEC [Organization for European Economic Cooperation] countries: large-scale, specialized production for the world market that would reap the higher profits of comparative advantage and economies of scale.

Following the blueprint laid out by Joseph Dodge, a prominent banker and consultant, the American government instituted the Dodge Plan in late 1948 and early 1949. It aimed at reviving Japanese industrial productivity, making export goods competitive in world markets, and putting the economy on a self-sustaining basis. While clearly similar to ERP goals for Europe, the Dodge Plan differed in one fundamental way. European reindustrialization was geared as much to the enlargement of an integrated domestic market as it was to giving European nations a greater share of the world market. Japan's reindustrialization was focused more single-mindedly on production for export, and not until 1960 would the Japanese home market receive equivalent stress. This difference had profound implications for Japanese social and economic policy. Specifically, Japanese workers tended to be viewed largely as cost-factors rather than potential consumers, and this put a greater premium on keeping wage bills as low as possible so Japanese exports could underprice competitors.

Reflecting this difference, the Dodge Plan was even more wedded to austerity measures than was the Marshall Plan. The latter had financed itself from the pocketbooks of both American taxpayers and European workers. The former attempted to finance itself almost entirely out of labor's decreased share of national income. Accordingly, the Dodge Plan called for severe cuts in social services, a sharp reduction of government employees, repression of the more militant labor unions, Draconian measures to outlaw and suppress strikes, reduction of wages to subsistence levels at which three-quarters of income went for food, and a balanced budget to halt inflation and enhance Japan's competitive position in world trade. Intense resistance by Japanese trade unions did soften American policy somewhat, but by and large the Dodge Plan was enacted as envisioned.

Its consequences, however, were far from anticipated. Industrial productivity did increase perceptibly, but buyers for those products did not materialize. The austerity program forcibly repressed domestic demand while various factors continued to inhibit foreign demand. Civil war and revolution severely limited Japan's traditional markets in China, Southeast Asia, and Northeast Asia. Moreover, protective tariffs still restricted access to North America and Europe, and the Americans retained an insuperable advantage in the high-profit product lines that Japan was determined to enter. By late 1949 and early 1950, Japan's trade deficit with the United States (its counterpart of Europe's dollar gap) was rising as fast as the strength of the yen was falling. More than a few Japanese and American observers feared that Japan stood on the precipice of economic catastrophe, in a situation akin to a business teetering on the brink of bankruptcy. One of earth's four great industrial cores was in danger of becoming a dysfunctional part of the world-system and a drag on the whole.

Compounding that systemic problem were parallel shortcomings in the European core. The Marshall Plan at midpassage had hardly closed the dollar gap. Europe still financed a third of its American imports out of grant dollars, while private profits were slow to generate the dollars to take up the slack. Indeed, dollar scarcity in Britain was so severe that even the United States had to accept the necessity of a sharp devaluation of the pound from $4.03 to $2.80 in September 1949. Since the ERP was set to expire in 1952 and Congress was unlikely to extend it, there remained real fear that the persistent dollar gap would yet wreak havoc on American exports and European recovery. Secretary of State Acheson summed up the situation in early 1950: "Put in its simplest terms, the problem is this: as ERP is reduced, and after its termination in 1952, how can Europe and other areas of the world obtain the dollars necessary to pay for a high level of U.S. exports, which is essential both to their own basic needs, and to the well-being of the American economy. This is the problem of the 'dollar gap' in world trade."

Part of Europe's continuing difficulties were supply-side problems of nagging bottlenecks in European productivity. Still, these seemed soluble problems and productivity, for both factory and farm, had generally increased. The greater problem seemed on the demand side. As George Kennan put it in August 1949, "*It is one thing to produce; it is another thing to sell.*" (Emphasis added.) As in Japan, austerity measures had dampened domestic demand, the Cold War had restricted access to the "socialist" markets, and congressional protectionism and a serious American recession in early 1949 had caused the major capitalist market to contract. Nor did the anticipated alternatives materialize as easily as hoped. European integrationism lagged as the ECA [Economic Cooperation Administration] focused on the more immediate problem of production snarls, so inter-European trade and the common market movement were stymied until the European Payments Union helped free the course of commerce in 1950.

To make matters worse, the periphery failed to fill the void. Production of primary commodities in Europe's traditional spheres of influence was static and inadequate. Parts of the periphery, especially in Asia, were beset by wars of national liberation against Western colonialism or by civil wars to see who would rule at home once the imperialists were gone. Even relatively tranquil territories were often more interested in developing domestic manufacturing than in increasing raw material production for their core customers. Because primary commodity production grew so slowly in relation to Europe's demand, Europe paid higher prices for its raw materials than did the United States; and the added costs undercut Europe's ability to compete with America in the world market. It also meant that because Europe's periphery made so little money out of its low-volume exports, it lacked the means to pay for significant amounts of European imports. In short, the revival of European industrial productivity had far less positive impact than expected because it was not accompanied by a parallel and complementary revival of primary commodity productivity in the periphery. The Third World (as it was soon to be called) needed to play its role (assigned it by the core powers) as efficient supplier of low-cost raw materials and as efficient supplemental market for finished products from the core.

This renewed crisis within the world-system was deepened by critical developments in the external world, in both the Russian and the Chinese empire. In two trip-hammer blows that shook the self-confidence of the capitalist world, Russia acquired the atomic bomb and China went communist. The first event broke the half-decade atomic monopoly enjoyed by the United States and provoked a heated debate among American leaders about its implications. Some feared that by 1954, when Russia might have a meaningful weapons stockpile and a delivery system, the USSR would be a serious threat to world peace. Under Secretary of State Robert Lovett, for example, warned, "We are now in a mortal combat. . . . It is not a cold war. It is a hot war." Others disdained that worst-case scenario and were inclined to regard the Russians as inherently cautious and disinclined to take high risks. George Kennan argued that the Soviet A-bomb added "no new fundamental element to the picture," and he saw "little justification for the impression that the 'cold war' . . . has suddenly taken some turn to our disadvantage." Still under his influence, the Policy Planning Staff of the State Department concluded there was little likelihood of a Russian attack on either the United States or its allies, even after 1954.

Both groups, however, agreed that Russian atomic diplomacy might be dangerous even if Russian atomic weaponry was not. However secure some Americans might feel, Europe and Japan were less likely to be sanguine about Russian intentions. Sharing a physical proximity to the USSR, they were apt to be more concerned about the coupling of the Red Army with the atomic bomb. Likewise, both might have been uncertain that America would risk atomic attack on its homeland to defend them against the Russian empire. They might question the credibility of the American military shield to protect the system. Such fears of the Soviets and doubts about the Americans might easily have led other core capitalist powers to waver in their deference to American hegemony and might have tempted them to play the Russian card in ways that would undermine the new world order for which America had fought World War II.

At the same time, the Chinese communists completed their triumph in the civil war as the last substantial nationalist forces fled the mainland to Taiwan. Communist victory heightened the possibility that China would exit the capitalist world-system, and that prospect seemed more certain with the signing of the Sino-Soviet pact of February 1950, creating a bilateral defense commitment, a settlement of historic territorial issues, and a modest Russian economic aid program. This Chinese departure prompted a famous State Department white paper to defend the administration from charges of culpability by "Pacific rim Republicans," but it also stirred an important debate within the executive branch on the nature and importance of the "loss" of China.

Asian specialists among career bureaucrats tended to think that China was not a Russian puppet, notwithstanding the 1950 treaty, and believed that preconditions existed for splitting the two apart and enticing China back into the world-system. Moreover, they dismissed the notion of foreign adventurism by China and assumed that, once Taiwan was captured, China would devote itself to internal affairs and the task of building a new China. Only if provoked would China intervene in Northeast or Southeast Asia. Global thinkers among more highly-placed "ins-and-outers" assumed otherwise: that China already was part of a monolithic external area (international communism) hostile to the American world order and that China would quickly try to export its revolution eastward into Korea and southward into French Indochina.

In one crucial sense, the internal debate was a moot one that made it immaterial which group was right and which was wrong. Whether China was expansionist or not, a Russian lackey or not, the communist revolution had usurped almost all of Northeast Asia from the world-system (North China, Manchuria, North Korea). That area historically had been Japan's most important market and source of raw materials. Given the near bankruptcy of Japan by early 1950, there was real fear among American leaders that beleaguered Japan might be forced to strike a bargain with China. If that occurred, it might spell the beginning of a Japanese drift away from integration with the American-dominated international system and toward an autarkic, regional arrangement with the Asian mainland. Such a direction taken by Japan might well undermine the very goals for which the United States had fought the Pacific war.

From 1947 to early 1950, the American foreign policy elite had persisted in its hegemonic pursuit of a unitary, integrated world-system. Confronted with Russian opposition, European reluctance, and popular ambivalence at home, American leaders had addressed the structural imbalance in world capitalism that was the chief legacy of world depression and world war. The Truman Doctrine tried to ease Britain's dollar gap while creating the ideological justification for isolating Russia outside of the world-system. It also provided part of the raison d'être for the Marshall Plan and the more ambitious project of European reconstruction and the integration of a reindustrialized Germany into what they hoped would soon be a common market. In turn, NATO provided the political-military-psychic glue to keep Europe together and in the world-system even when the tenure of the Marshall Plan had elapsed. Then, at the height of the American triumph—with NATO secured, West Germany established, and Russian opposition in the

Berlin blockade crushed—some hidden hand seemed to pull the plug. The failure of the Dodge Plan in Japan, the shortcomings of the Marshall Plan in Europe, the Russian termination of America's atomic bomb monopoly, and the loss of China to the world-system—all combined to produce yet another crisis, this one of a magnitude that would not be seen again for thirty years. In short, by late 1949 and early 1950, American policymakers faced the awesome task of getting European and Japanese reindustrialization and reconstruction back on track while keeping Europe from playing the Russian card and Japan from playing the China card. Their response would be a staggering reorientation of American foreign policy that would determine its shape and direction for the next twenty-three years.

The Truman administration confronted three alternative ways to respond to this tripartite crisis of the dollar gap, the Russian A-bomb, and the Chinese revolution. One option was to acknowledge the altered equation of world power and to negotiate with the Soviet Union over nuclear arms, German policy, and the status of China. Save for a small group of careerists in the State Department, headed by George Kennan, that was not an option afforded serious consideration by American leaders. *Any* negotiations with Russia, whatever their results, seemed likely to endow that country with a certain legitimacy and co-equal "super-power" status. Such a move seemed tantamount to an end of containment and a readmission of Russia to the world-system, which in turn would mean a diminution of American hegemony.

Such developments could only erode free world deference to American-style internationalism and facilitate separate arrangements by Europe and Japan with the Russian-dominated external world that seemed now to stretch from the Elbe to the Amur. Moreover, any concrete results of Russo-American negotiations could only make such consequences more probable. For example, mutual agreement to forego development of the H-bomb ("the super") could only diminish America's role as nuclear umbrella and military shield for the world-system. Neutralization of a reunified Germany could only impair the American policy of integrationism and raise the specter that any future shift to the left in German politics would also produce a shift to the east in German foreign policy. Recognition of the People's Republic of China would legitimize any Japanese tendency toward accommodation with mainland Asia.

The second American option was to do more of what it had been doing: concentrate on the internal problem central to the world-system, namely the dollar gap crisis, and elaborate upon the tested tools of economic diplomacy epitomized by the ERP. What that meant in the long haul was a lowering of American tariff walls to make it easier for Europe and Japan to earn dollars directly by selling in the American market or indirectly by having their customers in the periphery earn dollars by exporting primary commodities to the United States. In the interim, what that suggested was an extension of the ERP beyond its 1952 cut-off date and a parallel "Marshall Plan for Asia," a temporary plug to the dollar gap until the demand-stimulus of the American market could effect a permanent seal. This option was initially favored by the Policy Planning Staff of the State Department and endorsed by representatives of international business and chief executives of both the AFL and the CIO.

Two factors, however, made the choice impracticable in the early 1950s. Domestically, foreign aid legislation and tariff liberalization faced insurmountable opposition from a hostile Congress influenced by interest groups seeking to protect domestic jobs and markets, by fiscal conservatives trying to balance the budget, by Pacific regionalists persuaded of a European bias in American economic diplomacy, and by middle-class taxpayers unwilling to subsidize foreign consumption at the expense of their own. But even if that domestic opposition could be overcome, an extension of pre-1950 economic diplomacy could not address other considerations raised by the 1949–50 crisis. It could not assuage the fears of those who anticipated a real Russian military threat to the world-system after the mid-1950s. It could not reassure Europe and Japan of the reliability of the American military shield and thus reinforce their acceptance of American hegemony. It could not discipline unstable parts of the periphery to end their revolutions, forego forced industrialization, and accept their subordinate place in the world economic division of labor.

The third alternative was to opt for massive militarization. Concretely, that came to mean the development of the H-bomb; the quadrupling of the military budget, from $14 billion in 1950 to $53 billion in 1952; the expansion of conventional forces, including six permanent divisions in central Europe; the doubling of the air force to ninety-five groups with new strategic bases in Morocco, Libya, Saudia Arabia, and Spain; the transformation of NATO from a political to a military alliance and the addition to NATO of Turkey and Greece; the rebuilding of a German army and its integration into NATO forces; and finally, the substitution of military aid for economic-technical assistance and the merger of both forms in one program in the Mutual Security Act of 1951.

That militarized option was, in economic terms, less ideal than the option of expanded economic diplomacy. There were some well-grounded fears that governmental military purchases might become a substitute for the export of surplus domestic production and thus diminish the demand for multilateral trade and programs that fostered it. Indeed, foreign aid bills did face even tougher sledding and administration efforts to ratify the International Trade Organization (ITO) charter for trade liberalization never made it out of congressional committee. More importantly, massive military spending raised the possibility—again made real over time—that government subsidization of profits would siphon away funds for technical research and capital investment from the civilian goods sector, leaving it less innovative and undercapitalized and thus less competitive in the world economy. Finally, American rearmament would necessitate at least a measure of the same from Europe, a sign to Congress that American taxpayers would not shoulder the whole burden of militarization. While that burden was modest for most European economies, it was heavy for Great Britain, attempting to maintain its military contributions to NATO, the Commonwealth, the Near East, and the Korean War as well. Certainly, that factor helped cause the sterling crisis of 1951–52 and led to a general loss of British foreign markets to German competition.

Countervailing economic advantages, political imperatives, and diplomatic goals combined, however, to outweigh those material shortcomings of the militarization option. Many of the economic calculations were positive. Military spending, in the short term, would salvage the troubled aviation industry and might generate recovery from the American recession of 1949–50. In the medium term, it could maintain full productivity and employment until multilateralism was in place and world trade revived. It might prove more a technological stimulus than a deterrent, especially in electronics and the new sphere of atomic power. Moreover, military aid and military subcontracts to foreign corporations would provide a way to launder foreign aid dollars—that is, to maintain the financial tranfusion to address the dollar gap, but to do it in the name of national security rather than economic internationalism. Not only did those military aid dollars release European and Japanese capital to develop civilian technology and production, they helped make the periphery a better market for their products. In effect, American military spending, with its insatiate demand for raw materials, fueled a world-wide triangular trade in which the periphery exported raw materials to the United States, which in turn exported capital goods and food to Europe and Japan, which exported finished consumer goods to the periphery.

Politically, the militarization choice seemed the only one that could override domestic resistance on the right. Relatively quiescent since 1948, those right-wing elements revived in the congressional election of 1950, which produced a freshman senatorial class headed by Richard Nixon. Tacitly supported and used by mainstream Republicans, the politics of this element took an ominous turn in the McCarthyism and "Red Scare" witch hunts of alleged communists and fellow-travellers in government and in education, the media, and entertainment. However disreputable, McCarthyites and their sympathizers gained credibility from the administration's own internal security programs, from labor union purges of their left-wing opposition, and from business blacklisting of dissidents. That credibility made them a potent source of opposition to administration foreign policy.

Influenced by Pacific regionalists in their midst, many conservatives questioned the "Asia last" policy of the administration (to quote the Republican platform of 1952), echoing General Douglas MacArthur's belief that Europe was "a dying system" and that America's future lay in the western rimlands of the Pacific basin. Not only did the right-wing opposition question policy, it questioned policymakers themselves. Drawing on a constituency of midwestern small businessmen, Sun Belt nouveau riche oil men and land developers, and some Americans of Irish, German, and East European backgrounds, that opposition harbored a steady antagonism to the eastern, Yankee, Protestant patricians that they perceived as making policy. ("Fordham's revenge on Harvard" was used as a characterization of McCarthyism.) In that political context, only the alternative of militarization could keep the rightist opposition inside a Cold War consensus. Only an option couched in anticommunism and national security concerns could demonstrate to political critics that the administration's ideology was as pure as Caesar's wife. What had been expedient in selling the Truman Doctrine and the Marshall Plan in 1947 and 1948 now became an ironic imperative in the early 1950s.

Finally, and most importantly, the militarization choice did address three policy considerations not wholly confronted by economic diplomacy: national security, European integrationism, and Third World development. Its stress on American and European rearmament appealed to those, in and out of government, who took a Russian military threat seriously or who simply thought it prudent, in a nuclear age, to operate on the basis of a worst-case scenario. Its reaffirmation of America's role as military protector of the world-system—especially by the building of the H-bomb and an increased conventional presence in Europe—would reassure other core powers of the reliability and efficacy of that protection and keep them oriented to the American goal of integrated production and a common market for Europe itself. Indeed, the American effort to rearm Germany was a powerful incentive to European economic cooperation; it provided the most likely means to subsume German freedom of action—including the freedom to do military mischief—within a matrix of economic interdependence. And the stress on military capabilities might provide an important tool to facilitate the systematic development of Third World extractive economies, so they might function more effectively as markets and raw material providers for European and Japanese recovery. Since much of the periphery, especially the Asian rimlands, was destabilized by war and revolution, military pacification and forced stabilization seemed likely prerequisites to rapid and predictable economic growth. So an updated "big stick" became a potential weapon for coercing parts of the periphery to accept the American rules for the international game.

The National Security Council adopted the militarization option in early 1950, and President Truman examined and approved in principle its position document (NSC-68) in April. One of the most pivotal policy documents in American history, NSC-68 began with an historical preamble that sketched the decline of British paramountcy, the twice-attempted German challenge, the disintegration of European empires, and the Cold War competition for hegemony between the United States and the Soviet Union. Picturing the latter as a revolutionary, fanatical power, driven toward domination of the Eurasian land mass and ultimately the world, the document argued that only superior military force could deter it. Formulated chiefly by Secretary of State Acheson and the new Policy Planning Staff chief, Paul Nitze, this characterization of the Soviet Union evoked sharp protests from within that same department by Russian experts and careerists, notably George Kennan and Charles Bohlen. They counterargued that Russian foreign policy was motivated more by limited geopolitical and geoeconomic goals than by limitless revolutionary zeal. Consequently they urged that NSC-68 either be modified or junked altogether and that ERP-style economic diplomacy be reaffirmed.

While acknowledging possible hyperbole in the policy document, both Nitze and Acheson insisted that the militarization alternative was the only one that could be sold to Congress as well as the Bureau of the Budget and the General Accounting Office. Moreover, it was the only choice that dealt with all the exigencies and long-term concerns generated by the crisis of 1949–50. Whatever the merits of the respective arguments, Kennan and Bohlen were out-gunned. Possessing no power base outside the ranks of State Department bureaucracy, they were no match for their in-and-outer opponents, who not only held positions of greater influence within the government but were plugged into outside sources of power in the Democratic party and the world of corporate business and law.

In its final form, NSC-68 called not only for massive military spending but for significant tax increases to fund it, a reduction of social welfare programs and all services not related to military needs, a civil defense program, tighter loyalty programs for internal security, greater media efforts to build a public opinion consensus for Cold War policies, and psychological warfare and propaganda to encourage popular uprisings in Eastern Europe and Russia itself. The last rested on the possibility that a quantum jump in the arms race might distort the Soviet-bloc economies so badly, and so delay consumer gratification of its subjects, that it might spark internal upheaval.

No precise dollar tag was assigned by NSC-68 to the militarization policy, but guesses by staff people ranged from $37 to $50

billion per year—triple the amount originally requested by the Pentagon for 1950. How to get that kind of money from a fiscally conservative Congress, even in the name of anticommunism, presented
no small task for the administration. What was required was an international emergency, and since November 1949, Secretary Acheson had been predicting that one would occur sometime in 1950 in
the Asian rimlands—in Korea, Vietnam, Taiwan, or all three. Two
months after the President examined NSC-68, that crisis happened.
Acheson was to say later, "Korea came along and saved us."

John Lewis Gaddis

TWO VERY DIFFERENT EMPIRES

During the latter phases of the Cold War, some commentators suggested
that the American and Soviet spheres of influence were roughly comparable, even morally equivalent. John Lewis Gaddis strongly disputes
that notion. In the following selection, drawn from his latest book, *We
Now Know: Rethinking Cold War History* (1997), Gaddis emphasizes
that profound differences obtained between the American and Soviet
spheres of influence in Europe. Whereas the Soviet empire was built on
armed might, political terror, and authoritarian rule, its American counterpart allowed freedom and political pluralism to flourish. The Soviet
empire was imposed on its subjects in Eastern Europe, Gaddis argues;
the Western Europeans, in sharp contrast, accepted and even *invited*
American hegemony. This essay, and the longer study from which it is excerpted, draws upon recently declassified documents from the former
Soviet Union, Eastern Europe, China, and elsewhere to bolster a neo-
traditional interpretation of the Cold War and its origins.

John Lewis Gaddis is a professor of history at Yale University. His numerous books include *The United States and the Origins of the Cold War*
(1972); *Strategies of Containment* (1982); *The Long Peace* (1987); and
The United States and the End of the Cold War (1992).

By 1947, it was clear that cooperation to build a new order among
the nations that had vanquished the old one was not going to be

26-36, 51-53

possible. There followed the most remarkable *polarization* of politics in modern history. It was as if a gigantic magnet had somehow come into existence, compelling most states, often even movements and individuals within states, to align themselves along fields of force thrown out from either Washington or Moscow. Remaining uncommitted, in a postwar international system that seemed so compulsively to require commitment, would be no easy matter. The United States and the Soviet Union were now as close as any great powers have ever been to controlling—as Tocqueville had foreseen Americans and Russians someday would—"the destinies of half the world."

Theorists of international relations have insisted that in seeking to understand such a system we need pay little attention to the "units" that make it up. Because states exist within an anarchic environment, survival has to be their common objective; power is the means by which all of them—regardless of their internal makeup—seek to ensure it. Nations therefore behave like featureless billiard balls: their collisions are significant, but their character is not. Tocqueville's distinction between authoritarian and democratic traditions in the Russian-American relationship, from this perspective, would be quite irrelevant.

The historian must point out, though, that however "great" the United States and the Soviet Union were during the Cold War, the "power" they obtained and wielded was rarely comparable. If these were billiard balls, they were not of the same size or weight or mass. Nor did the spheres of influence Washington and Moscow dominated resemble one another, whether from a military, economic, ideological, or moral perspective—a fact that has become obvious now that one of them no longer exists. Apples and oranges might be the better metaphor: at least it would allow for asymmetry, irregularity, and the possibility of internal rot.

But even this model has its deficiencies, because it leaves little room for the role of third parties—to say nothing of fourth, fifth, and nth parties—in shaping the Soviet-American relationship. It makes a big difference if great powers have to extend their authority against, rather than in concert with, the wishes of those subjected to it. The choice is between resistance and collaboration, and it falls to those incorporated within spheres of influence, not to those who impose them, ultimately to make it. If we are to grasp the nature of the post-World War II international system, then we will need an analytical framework capable of accounting for the rise and fall of great powers; but also one that incorporates variations in the nature of power and the influence it produces, as well as the limitations on power that permit peripheries to make a difference, even when things are being run from very powerful centers.

Such a framework exists, I think, in a more ancient method of governance than either democracy or authoritarianism: it is *empire*. I mean, by this term, a situation in which a single state shapes the behavior of others, whether directly or indirectly, partially or completely, by means that can range from the outright use of force through intimidation, dependency, inducements, and even inspiration. Leaders of both the United States and the Soviet Union would have bristled at having the appellation "imperial" affixed to what they were doing after 1945. But one need not send out ships, seize territories, and hoist flags to construct an empire: "informal" empires are considerably older than, and continued to exist alongside, the more "formal" ones Europeans imposed on so much of the rest of the world from the fifteenth through the nineteenth centuries. During the Cold War years Washington and Moscow took on much of the character, if never quite the charm, of old imperial capitals like London, Paris, and Vienna. And surely American and Soviet influence, throughout most of the second half of the twentieth century, was at least as ubiquitous as that of any earlier empire the world had ever seen.

Ubiquity never ensured unchallenged authority, though, and that fact provides yet another reason for applying an imperial analogy to Cold War history. For contrary to popular impressions, empires have always involved a two-way flow of influence. Imperializers have never simply acted upon the imperialized; the imperialized have also had a surprising amount of influence over the imperializers. The Cold War was no exception to this pattern, and an awareness of it too will help us to see how that rivalry emerged, evolved, and eventually ended in the way that it did.

Let us begin with the structure of the Soviet empire, for the simple reason that it was, much more than the American, deliberately designed. It has long been clear that, in addition to having had an authoritarian vision, Stalin also had an imperial one, which he proceeded to implement in at least as single-minded a way. No comparably influential builder of empire came close to wielding power for so long, or with such striking results, on the Western side.

It was, of course, a matter of some awkwardness that Stalin came out of a revolutionary movement that had vowed to smash, not just tsarist imperialism, but all forms of imperialism throughout the world. The Soviet leader constructed his own logic, though, and throughout his career he devoted a surprising amount of attention to showing how a revolution and an empire might coexist. Bolsheviks could never be imperialists, Stalin acknowledged in one of his earliest public pronouncements on this subject, made in April 1917. But surely in a *revolutionary* Russia nine-tenths of the non-Russian nationalities would not *want* their independence. Few among those minorities found Stalin's reasoning persuasive after the Bolsheviks did seize power later that year, however, and one of the first problems Lenin's new government faced was a disintegration of the old Russian empire not unlike what happened to the Soviet Union after communist authority finally collapsed in 1991.

Whether because of Lenin's own opposition to imperialism or, just as plausibly, because of Soviet Russia's weakness at the time, Finns, Estonians, Latvians, Lithuanians, Poles, and Moldavians were allowed to depart. Others who tried to do so—Ukrainians, Belorussians, Caucasians, Central Asians—were not so fortunate, and in 1922 Stalin proposed incorporating these remaining (and reacquired) nationalities into the Russian republic, only to have Lenin as one of his last acts override this recommendation and establish the multi-ethnic Union of Soviet Socialist Republics. After Lenin died and Stalin took his place it quickly became clear, though, that whatever its founding principles the USSR was to be no federation of equals. Rather, it would function as an updated form of empire even more tightly centralized than that of the Russian tsars.

Lenin and Stalin differed most significantly, not over authoritarianism or even terror, but on the legitimacy of Great Russian nationalism. The founder of Bolshevism had warned with characteristic pungency of "that truly Russian man, the Great-Russian chauvinist," and of the dangers of sinking into a "sea of chauvinistic Great-Russian filth, like flies in milk." Such temptations, he insisted, might ruin the prospects of revolution spreading elsewhere in the world. But Stalin—the implied target of Lenin's invective—was himself a Great Russian nationalist, with all the intensity transplanted nationals can sometimes attain. "The leaders of the revolutionary workers of all countries are avidly studying the most instructive history of the working class of Russia, its past, the past of Russia," he would write in a revealing private letter in 1930, shortly after consolidating his position as Lenin's successor. "All this instills (cannot but instill!) in the hearts of the Russian workers a feeling of revolutionary national pride, capable of moving mountains and working miracles."

The "Stalin constitution" of 1936, which formally specified the right of non-Russian nationalities to secede from the Soviet Union, coincided with the great purges and an officially sanctioned upsurge in Russian nationalism that would persist as a prominent feature of Stalin's regime until his death. It was as if the great authoritarian had set out to validate his own flawed prediction of 1917 by creating a set of circumstances in which non-Russian nationalities would not even *think* of seceding, even though the hypothetical authority to do so remained. The pattern resembled that of the purge trials themselves: one maintained a framework of legality—even, within the non-Russian republics, a toleration of local languages and cultures considerably greater than under the tsars. But Stalin then went to extraordinary lengths to deter anyone from exercising these rights or promoting those cultures in such a way as to challenge his own rule. He appears to have concluded, from his own study of the Russian past, that it was not "reactionary" to seek territorial expansion. His principal ideological innovation may well have been to impose the ambitions of the old princes of Muscovy, especially their determination to "gather in" and dominate all of the lands that surrounded them, upon the anti-imperial spirit of proletarian internationalism that had emanated from, if not actually inspired, the Bolshevik Revolution.

Stalin's fusion of Marxist internationalism with tsarist imperialism could only reinforce his tendency, in place well before World War II, to equate the advance of world revolution with the expanding influence of the Soviet state. He applied that linkage quite impartially: a major benefit of the 1939 pact with Hitler had been that it regained territories lost as a result of the Bolshevik Revolution and the World War I settlement. But Stalin's conflation of imperialism with ideology also explains the importance he attached, following the German attack in 1941, to having his new Anglo-American allies confirm these arrangements. He had similar goals in East Asia when he insisted on bringing the Soviet Union back to the position Russia had occupied in Manchuria prior to the Russo-Japanese War: this he finally achieved at the 1945 Yalta Conference in return for promising to enter the war against Japan. "My task as minister of foreign affairs was to expand the borders of our Fatherland," Molotov recalled proudly many years later. "And it seems that Stalin and I coped with this task quite well."

From the West's standpoint, the critical question was how far Moscow's influence would extend *beyond* whatever Soviet frontiers turned out to be at the end of the war. Stalin had suggested to Milovan Djilas that the Soviet Union would impose its own social system as far as its armies could reach, but he was also very cautious. Keenly aware of the military power the United States and its allies had accumulated, Stalin was determined to do nothing that might involve the USSR in another devastating war until it had recovered sufficiently to be certain of winning it. "I do not wish to begin the Third World War over the Trieste question," he explained to disappointed Yugoslavs, whom he ordered to evacuate that territory in June 1945. Five years later, he would justify his decision not to intervene in the Korean War on the grounds that "the Second World War ended not long ago, and we are not ready for the Third World War." Just how far the expansion of Soviet influence would proceed depended, therefore, upon a careful balancing of opportunities against risks. "[We] were on the offensive," Molotov acknowledged:

> They [presumably the West] certainly hardened their line against us, but we had to consolidate our conquests. We made our own socialist Germany out of our part of Germany, and restored order in Czechoslovakia, Poland, Hungary, and Yugoslavia, where the situations were fluid. To squeeze out capitalist order. This was the cold war.

But, "of course," Molotov added, "you had to know when to stop. I believe in this respect Stalin kept well within the limits."

Who or what was it, though, that set the limits? Did Stalin have a fixed list of countries he thought it necessary to dominate? Was he prepared to stop in the face of resistance within those countries to "squeezing out the capitalist order"? Or would expansion cease only when confronted with opposition from the remaining capitalist states, so that further advances risked war at a time when the Soviet Union was ill-prepared for it?

Stalin had been very precise about where he wanted Soviet boundaries changed; he was much less so on how far Moscow's sphere of influence was to extend. He insisted on having "friendly" countries around the periphery of the USSR, but he failed to specify how many would have to meet this standard. He called during the war for dismembering Germany, but by the end of it was denying that he had ever done so: that country would be temporarily divided, he told leading German communists in June 1945, and they themselves would eventually bring about its reunification. He never gave up on the idea of an eventual world revolution, but he expected this to result—as his comments to the Germans suggested—from an expansion of influence emanating from the Soviet Union itself. "[F]or the Kremlin," a well-placed spymaster recalled, "the mission of communism was primarily to consolidate the might of the Soviet state. Only military strength and domination of the countries on our borders could ensure us a superpower role."

But Stalin provided no indication—surely because he himself did not know—of how rapidly, or under what circumstances, this process would take place. He was certainly prepared to stop in the face of resistance from the West: at no point was he willing to challenge the Americans or even the British where they made their interests clear. Churchill acknowledged his scrupulous adherence to the famous 1944 "percentages" agreement confirming British authority in Greece, and Yugoslav sources have revealed Stalin's warnings that the United States and Great Britain would never allow their lines of communication in the Mediterranean to be broken. He quickly backed down when confronted with Anglo-American objections to his ambitions in Iran in the spring of 1946, as he did later that year after demanding Soviet bases in the Turkish Straits. This pattern of advance followed by retreat had shown up in the purges of the 1930s, which Stalin halted when the external threat from Germany became too great to ignore, and it would reappear with the Berlin Blockade and the Korean War, both situations in which the Soviet Union would show great caution after provoking an unexpectedly strong American response.

What all of this suggests, though, is not that Stalin had limited ambitions, only that he had no timetable for achieving them. Molotov retrospectively confirmed this: "Our ideology stands for offensive operations when possible, and if not, we wait." Given this combination of appetite with aversion to risk, one cannot help but wonder what would have happened had the West tried containment earlier. To the extent that it bears partial responsibility for the coming of the Cold War, the historian Vojtech Mastny has argued, that responsibility lies in its failure to do just that.

Where Western resistance was unlikely, as in Eastern Europe, Stalin would in time attempt to replicate the regime he had already established inside the Soviet Union. Authority extended out from Moscow by way of government and party structures whose officials had been selected for their obedience, then down within each of these countries through the management of the economy, social and political institutions, intellectuals, even family relationships. The differentiation of public and private spheres that exists in most societies disappeared as all aspects of life were fused with, and then subordinated to, the interests of the Soviet Union as Stalin himself had determined them. Those who could not or would not go along encountered the same sequence of intimidation, terror, and ultimately even purges, show trials, and executions that his real and imagined domestic opponents had gone through during the 1930s. "Stalin's understanding of friendship with other countries was that the Soviet Union would lead and they would follow," Khrushchev recalled. "[He] waged the struggle against the enemies of the people there in the same way that he did in the Soviet Union. He had one demand: absolute subordination."

Stalin's policy, then, was one of imperial expansion and consolidation differing from that of earlier empires only in the determination with which he pursued it, in the instruments of coercion with which he maintained it, and in the ostensibly anti-imperial justifications he put forward in support of it. It is a testimony to his skill, if not to his morality, that he was able to achieve so many of his imperial ambitions at a time when the tides of history were running against the idea of imperial domination—as colonial offices in London, Paris, Lisbon, and The Hague were finding out—and when his own country was recovering from one of the most brutal invasions in recorded history. The fact that Stalin was able to *expand* his empire when others were contracting and while the Soviet Union was as weak as it was requires explanation. Why did opposition to this process, within and outside Europe, take so long to develop?

One reason was that the colossal sacrifices the Soviet Union had made during the war against the Axis had, in effect, "purified" its reputation: the USSR and its leader had "earned" the right to throw their weight around, or so it seemed. Western governments found it difficult to switch quickly from viewing the Soviet Union as a glorious wartime ally to portraying it as a new and dangerous adversary. President Harry S. Truman and his future Secretary of State Dean Acheson—neither of them sympathetic in the slightest to communism—nonetheless tended to give the Soviet Union the benefit of the doubt well into the early postwar era. A similar pattern developed within the United States occupation zone in Germany, where General Lucius D. Clay worked out a cooperative relationship with his Soviet counterparts and resisted demands to "get tough" with the Russians, even after they had become commonplace in Washington.

Resistance to Stalin's imperialism also developed slowly because Marxism-Leninism at the time had such widespread appeal. It is difficult now to recapture the admiration revolutionaries outside the Soviet Union felt for that country before they came to know it well. "[Communism] was the most rational and most intoxicating, all-embracing ideology for me and for those in my disunited and desperate land who so desired to skip over centuries of slavery and backwardness and to bypass reality itself," Djilas recalled, in a comment that could have been echoed throughout much of what came to be called the "third world." Because the Bolsheviks themselves had overcome one empire and had made a career of condemning others, it would take decades for people who were struggling to overthrow British, French, Dutch, or Portuguese colonialism to see that there could also be such a thing as Soviet imperialism. European communists— notably the Yugoslavs—saw this much earlier, but even to most of them it had not been apparent at the end of the war.

Still another explanation for the initial lack of resistance to Soviet expansionism was the fact that its repressive character did not become immediately apparent to all who were subjected to it. With regimes on the left taking power in Eastern and Central

Europe, groups long denied advancement could now expect it. For many who remembered the 1930s, autarchy within a Soviet bloc could seem preferable to exposure once again to international capitalism, with its periodic cycles of boom and bust. Nor did Moscow impose harsh controls everywhere at the same time. Simple administrative incompetence may partially account for this: one Russian historian has pointed out that "[d]isorganization, mismanagement and rivalry among many branches of the gigantic Stalinist state in Eastern Europe were enormous." But it is also possible, at least in some areas, that Stalin did not expect to *need* tight controls; that he anticipated no serious challenge and perhaps even spontaneous support. Why did he promise free elections after the war? Maybe he thought the communists would win them.

One has the impression that Stalin and the Eastern Europeans got to know one another only gradually. The Kremlin leader was slow to recognize that Soviet authority would not be welcomed everywhere beyond Soviet borders; but as he did come to see this he became all the more determined to impose it everywhere. The Eastern Europeans were slow to recognize how confining incorporation within a Soviet sphere was going to be; but as they did come to see this they became all the more determined to resist it, even if only by withholding, in a passive but sullen manner, the consent any regime needs to establish itself by means other than coercion. Stalin's efforts to consolidate his empire therefore made it at once more repressive and less secure. Meanwhile, an alternative vision of postwar Europe was emerging from the other great empire that established itself in the wake of World War II, that of the United States, and this too gave Stalin grounds for concern.

The first point worth noting, when comparing the American empire to its Soviet counterpart, is a striking reversal in the sequence of events. Stalin's determination to create his empire preceded by some years the conditions that made it possible: he had first to consolidate power at home and then defeat Nazi Germany, while at the same time seeing to it that his allies in that enterprise did not thwart his long-term objectives. With the United States, it was the other way around: the conditions for establishing an empire were in place long before there was any clear intention on the part of its leaders to do so. Even then, they required the support of a skeptical electorate, something that could never quite be taken for granted.

The United States had been poised for global hegemony at the end of World War I. Its military forces played a decisive role in bringing that conflict to an end. Its economic predominance was such that it could control both the manner and the rate of European recovery. Its ideology commanded enormous respect, as Woodrow Wilson found when he arrived on the Continent late in 1918 to a series of rapturous public receptions. The Versailles Treaty fell well short of Wilson's principles, to be sure, but the League of Nations followed closely his own design, providing an explicit legal basis for an international order that was to have drawn, as much as anything else, upon the example of the American constitution itself. If there was ever a point at which the world seemed receptive to an expansion of United States influence, this was it.

Americans themselves, however, were not receptive. The Senate's rejection of membership in the League reflected the public's distinct lack of enthusiasm for international peace keeping responsibilities. Despite the interests certain business, labor, and agricultural groups had in seeking overseas markets and investment opportunities, most Americans saw few benefits to be derived from integrating their economy with that of the rest of the world. Efforts to rehabilitate Europe during the 1920s, therefore, could only take the form of private initiatives, quietly coordinated with the government. Protective tariffs hung on well into the 1930s—having actually increased with the onset of the Great Depression—and exports as a percentage of gross national product remained low in comparison to other nations, averaging only 4.2 per cent between 1921 and 1940. Investments abroad had doubled between 1914 and 1919 while foreign investment in the United States had been cut in half; but this shift was hardly sufficient to overcome old instincts within the majority of the public who held no investments at all that it was better to stand apart from, rather than to attempt to dominate, international politics outside of the Western hemisphere.

This isolationist consensus broke down only as Americans began to realize that a potentially hostile power was once again threatening Europe: even their own hemisphere, it appeared, might not escape the consequences this time around. After September 1939, the Roosevelt administration moved as quickly as public and Congressional opinion would allow to aid Great Britain and France by means short of war; it also chose to challenge the Japanese over their occupation of China and later French Indochina, thereby setting in motion a sequence of events that would lead to the attack on Pearl Harbor. Historians ever since have puzzled over this: why, after two decades of relative inactivity on the world scene, did the United States suddenly become hyperactive? Might the administration have realized that it would never generate public support for the empire American elites had long desired without a clear and present danger to national security, and did it not then proceed to generate one? Can one not understand the origins and evolution of the Cold War in similar terms?

There are several problems with such interpretations, one of which is that they confuse contingency with conspiracy. Even if Roosevelt had hoped to maneuver the Japanese into "firing the first shot," he could not have known that Hitler would seize this opportunity to declare war and thereby make possible American military intervention in Europe. The Pacific, where the United States would have deployed most of its strength in the absence of Hitler's declaration, would hardly have been the platform from which to mount a bid for global hegemony. These explanations also allow little room for the autonomy of others: they assume that Hitler and the Japanese militarists acted *only* in response to what the United States did, and that other possible motives for their behavior—personal, bureaucratic, cultural, ideological, geopolitical—were insignificant. Finally, these arguments fail to meet the test of proximate versus distant causation. The historian Marc Bloch once pointed out that one could, in principle, account for a climber's fall from a precipice by invoking physics and geology: had it not been for the law of gravity and the existence of the mountain, the accident surely could not have occurred. But would it follow that all who ascend mountains must plummet from them? Just because Roosevelt *wanted* the United States to enter the war and to become a world power afterwards does not mean that his actions alone made these things happen.

A better explanation for the collapse of isolationism is a simpler one: it had to do with a resurgence of authoritarianism. Americans had begun to suspect, late in the nineteenth century, that the internal behavior of states determined their external behavior; certainly it is easy to see how the actions of Germany, Italy, and Japan during the 1930s could have caused this view to surface once again, much as it had in relations with tsarist Russia and imperial Germany during World War I. Once that happened, the Americans, not given to making subtle distinctions, began to oppose authoritarianism everywhere, and that could account for their sudden willingness to take on several authoritarians at once in 1941. But that interpretation, too, is not entirely adequate. It fails to explain how the United States could have coexisted as comfortably as it did with authoritarianism in the past—especially in Latin America—and as it would continue to do for some time to come. It certainly does not account for the American willingness during the war to embrace, as an ally, the greatest authoritarian of this century, Stalin himself.

The best explanation for the decline of isolationism and the rise of the American empire, I suspect, has to do with a distinction Americans tended to make—perhaps they were more subtle than one might think—between what we might call benign and malignant authoritarianism. Regimes like those of Somoza in Nicaragua or Trujillo in the Dominican Republic might be unsavory, but they fell into the benign category because they posed no serious threat to United States interests and in some cases even promoted them. Regimes like those of Nazi Germany and imperial Japan, because of their military capabilities, were quite another matter. Stalin's authoritarianism had appeared malignant when linked to that of Hitler, as it was between 1939 and 1941; but when directed against Hitler, it could come to appear quite benign. What it would look like once Germany had been defeated remained to be seen.

With all this, the possibility that even malignant authoritarianism might harm the United States remained hypothetical until 7 December 1941, when it suddenly became very real. Americans are only now, after more than half a century, getting over the shock: they became so accustomed to a Pearl Harbor mentality—to the idea that there really are deadly enemies out there—that they find it a strange new world, instead of an old familiar one, now that there are not. Pearl Harbor was, then, the defining event for the American empire, because it was only at this point that the most plausible potential justification for the United States becoming and remaining a global power as far as the American people were concerned—an endangered national security—became an actual one.

Isolationism had thrived right up to this moment; but once it became apparent that isolationism could leave the nation open to military attack, it suffered a blow from which it never recovered. The critical date was not 1945, or 1947, but 1941.

It did not automatically follow, though, that the Soviet Union would inherit the title of "first enemy" once Germany and Japan had been defeated. A sense of vulnerability preceded the identification of a source of threat in the thinking of American strategists: innovations in military technology—long-range bombers, the prospect of even longer-range missiles—created visions of future Pearl Harbors before it had become clear from where such an attack might come. Neither in the military nor the political-economic planning that went on in Washington during the war was there consistent concern with the USSR as a potential future adversary. The threat, rather, appeared to arise from war itself, whoever might cause it, and the most likely candidates were thought to be resurgent enemies from World War II.

The preferred solution was to maintain preponderant power for the United States, which meant a substantial peacetime military establishment and a string of bases around the world from which to resist aggression if it should ever occur. But equally important, a revived international community would seek to remove the fundamental causes of war through the United Nations, a less ambitious version of Wilson's League, and through new economic institutions like the International Monetary Fund and the World Bank, whose task it would be to prevent another global depression and thereby ensure prosperity. The Americans and the British assumed that the Soviet Union would want to participate in these multilateral efforts to achieve military and economic security. The Cold War developed when it became clear that Stalin either could not or would not accept this framework.

Did the Americans attempt to impose their vision of the postwar world upon the USSR? No doubt it looked that way from Moscow: both the Roosevelt and Truman administrations stressed political self-determination and economic integration with sufficient persistence to arouse Stalin's suspicions—easily aroused, in any event—as to their ultimate intentions. But what the Soviet leader saw as a challenge to his hegemony the Americans meant as an effort to salvage multilateralism. At no point prior to 1947 did the United States and its Western European allies abandon the hope that the Russians might eventually come around; and indeed negotiations aimed at bringing them around would continue at the foreign ministers' level, without much hope of success, through the end of that year. The American attitude was less that of expecting to impose a system than one of puzzlement as to why its merits were not universally self-evident. It differed significantly, therefore, from Stalin's point of view, which allowed for the possibility that socialists in other countries might come to see the advantages of Marxism-Leninism as practiced in the Soviet Union, but never capitalists. They were there, in the end, to be overthrown, not convinced. . . .

It would become fashionable to argue, in the wake of American military intervention in Vietnam, the Soviet invasions of Czechoslovakia and Afghanistan, and growing fears of nuclear confrontation that developed during the early 1980s, that there were no significant differences in the spheres of influence Washington and Moscow had constructed in Europe after World War II: these had been, it was claimed, "morally equivalent," denying autonomy quite impartially to all who lived under them. Students of history must make their own judgments about morality, but even a cursory examination of the historical record will show that these imperial structures could hardly have been more different in their origins, their composition, their tolerance of diversity, and as it turned out their durability. It is important to specify just what these differences were.

First, and most important, the Soviet empire reflected the priorities and the practices of a single individual—a latter-day tsar, in every sense of the word. Just as it would have been impossible to separate the Soviet Union's internal structure from the influence of the man who ran it, so too the Soviet sphere of influence in Eastern Europe took on the characteristics of Stalin himself. The process was not immediate: Stalin did allow a certain amount of spontaneity in the political, economic, and intellectual life of that region for a time after the war, just as he had done inside the Soviet Union itself after he had consolidated his position as Lenin's successor in 1929. But when confronted with even the prospect of dissent, to say nothing of challenges to his authority, Stalin's instinct was to smother spontaneity with a thoroughness unprecedented in the modern age. This is what the purges had accomplished inside the USSR during the mid-1930s, and Eastern Europe underwent a similar process after 1947. There was thus a direct linkage from Stalin's earliest thinking on the nationalities question prior to the Bolshevik Revolution through to his management of empire after World War II: the right of self-determination was fine as long as no one sought to practice it.

The American empire was very different: one would have expected this from a country with no tradition of authoritarian leadership whose constitutional structure had long ago enshrined the practices of negotiation, compromise, and the balancing of interests. What is striking about the sphere of influence the United States established in Europe is that its existence and fundamental design reflected as frequently pressures that came *from those incorporated within it* as from the Americans themselves. Washington officials were not at all convinced, at the end of World War II, that their interests would require protecting half the European continent: instead they looked toward a revival of a balance among the Europeans themselves to provide postwar geopolitical stability. Even the Marshall Plan, an unprecedented extension of American assistance, had been conceived with this "third force" principle in mind. It was the Europeans themselves who demanded more: who insisted that their security required a military shield as well as an economic jumpstart.

One empire arose, therefore, by invitation, the other by imposition. *Europeans* made this distinction, very much as they had done during the war when they welcomed armies liberating them from the west but feared those that came from the east. They did so because they saw clearly at the time—even if a subsequent generation would not always see—how different American and Soviet empires were likely to be. It is true that the *extent* of the American empire quickly exceeded that of its Soviet counterpart, but this was because *resistance* to expanding American influence was never as great. The American empire may well have become larger, paradoxically, because the American *appetite* for empire was less that of the USSR. The United States had shown, throughout most of its history, that it could survive and even prosper without extending its domination as far as the eye could see. The logic of Lenin's ideological internationalism, as modified by Stalin's Great Russian nationalism and personal paranoia, was that the Soviet Union could not.

The early Cold War in Europe, therefore, cannot be understood by looking at the policies of either the United States or the Soviet Union in isolation. What evolved on the continent was an interactive system in which the actions of each side affected not only the other but also the Europeans; their responses, in turn, shaped further decisions in Washington and Moscow. It quickly became clear—largely because of differences in the domestic institutions of each superpower—that an American empire would accommodate far greater diversity than would one run by the Soviet Union: as a consequence most Europeans accepted and even invited American hegemony, fearing deeply what that of the Russians might entail.

Two paths diverged at the end of World War II. And that, to paraphrase an American poet, really did make all the difference.

Melvyn P. Leffler

THE PRIMACY OF SECURITY IN SOVIET FOREIGN POLICY

In this essay, Melvyn P. Leffler examines Soviet foreign policy in light of some of the most important new scholarship based upon formerly closed Soviet and Eastern European archival records. Although he focuses on many of the same books and articles that John Lewis Gaddis builds upon in the previous selection, Leffler reaches some strikingly different conclusions. Those works, he contends, do not support the traditional view of an inveterately expansionistic Soviet Russia, or the related notion of a Cold War pattern of Soviet action/American response. Rather, recent scholarly literature, according to Leffler, tends to emphasize Stalin's indecisiveness and the absence of any master plan for territorial conquest in Soviet policymaking. Recent scholarship also makes clear the primacy of security considerations to the Soviet leadership, the significant, though secondary, role played by ideology, and the frequently independent-minded behavior of the Kremlin's supposed client states. This essay demonstrates that it will

Melvyn P. Leffler, "Inside Enemy Archives: The Cold War Reopened," *Foreign Affairs*, 75 (July/August 1996), pp. 120–126, 128–129, 131–135. Reprinted by permission of *Foreign Affairs*, Copyright 1996 by the Council on Foreign Relations.

take more than new documents to resolve longstanding debates about the origins and nature of the Cold War.

Only three or four years ago, historians of the Cold War worked without knowing what was in Soviet archives. They relied heavily on Western records, inferring the motivations and goals of Soviet foreign policy. But the Russians and their former Warsaw Pact allies have begun to open their records for research. The Chinese, too, have opened selected materials, especially ones that illuminate the duplicity and depravity of the men in the Kremlin. Regime changes and liberalization in many countries have made former officials more reflective and more willing to write about their years in power.

Pondering the archival documents, memoirs, and new assessments, one asks how they might affect debate about the origins and evolution of the Cold War. They reveal a Soviet system as revolting as its worst critics charged long ago. Some scholars go further, asserting that the archives confirm not only the genocidal actions and fundamental brutality of the regime but also its ideological underpinnings and hegemonic aspirations. The highly publicized 1994 television documentary *Messengers from Moscow* resuscitated the old claim that Stalin planned to conquer the globe for Marxism-Leninism, declaring that interviews and documents prove the Soviet leader sent hundreds of agents abroad after 1945 to foment revolution. The historian Steven Merritt Miner cautions readers to be wary of the memoirs and sensitive to the selectivity of the newly released documents, but announces, "Ideology is once again central [to the study of the Soviets' conduct of the Cold War], after having been played down by scholars for two decades." John Lewis Gaddis, the leading U.S. expert on the Cold War, maintains that America's containment policy was indispensable in thwarting the march of the Soviet behemoth, and keeping America itself a beacon of hope to a world menaced by Stalinist totalitarianism. Other scholars share Gaddis' view that the new evidence affirms the most traditional interpretations of Cold War events.

A close reading of the books and articles based on the archival materials suggests more nuanced conclusions. The Cold War was not a simple case of Soviet expansionism and American reaction. Realpolitik held sway in the Kremlin. Ideology played an important role in shaping their perceptions, but Soviet leaders were not focused on promoting worldwide revolution. They were concerned mostly with configurations of power, with protecting their country's immediate periphery, ensuring its security, and preserving their rule. Governing a land devastated by two world wars, they feared a resurgence of German and Japanese strength. They felt threatened by a United States that alone among the combatants emerged from the war wealthier and armed with the atomic bomb. Soviet officials did not have preconceived plans to make Eastern Europe communist, to support the Chinese communists, or to wage war in Korea. Soviet clients, moreover, could and did act in pursuit of their own interests, sometimes goading the Kremlin into involvements it did not want.

Although Soviet actions were more contingent than previously thought, probably nothing the United States could have done would have allayed Soviet suspicions in the early years of the Cold War. Nevertheless, U.S. words and deeds greatly heightened ambient anxieties and subsequently contributed to the arms race and the expansion of the Cold War into the Third World. Rather than congratulate themselves on the Cold War's outcome, Americans must confront the negative as well as the positive consequences of U.S. actions and inquire much more searchingly into the implications of their nation's foreign policies.

At the center of the Cold War was the struggle for Germany. Although Soviet military authorities worked with their German comrades to establish a police state in the Soviet-occupied zone, the Kremlin did not have a master plan for Germany. Soviet policies, Norman Naimark concludes after studying documents from East Germany and the Soviet Union, "were often driven by concrete events in the zone, rather than by preconceived plans or ideological imperatives." The Soviets had nothing comparable to Joint Chiefs of Staff memo 1067, the American blueprint for the occupation of Germany. They wanted to gather support for the communist-led Socialist Unity Party through moderate economic policies, coalition-building, and backing for unification. But the need for reparations and for uranium from the mines of southern Saxony, and Red Army troops' looting and mass rape in the zone, undercut Soviet mobilization of support for German communists.

Stalin could not decide whether he wanted a unified Germany run by the German communists, a demilitarized, neutral Germany along the lines of the Weimer Republic, or a sovietized eastern zone amenable to the Kremlin's every whim. His ambivalence was reflected in the contradictory actions in the Russian zone by officials of the Soviet military administration, the secret police, the Foreign Ministry, and reparations teams that were seizing factories for relocation to the Soviet Union. Much like Jan Gross, the author of a remarkable book on the Soviet occupation of Poland, Naimark concludes that Soviet officers in eastern Germany "bolshevized the zone not because there was a plan to do so, but because that was the only way they knew how to organize society."

Nor does it appear that Stalin had a definite design for the economies and societies of Eastern Europe. Although he told the Yugoslav communist leader Milovan Djilas that great powers spread their economic system wherever they occupy territory, he stressed to Stanislaw Mikolajczyk, the leader of the Polish Peasant Party, that communism fit Poland like a saddle fit a cow. Historians have not located concrete plans for turning Poland, Hungary, Romania, or other East European states into command economies or communist dictatorships. Stalin may have been chary of acting too quickly; especially when relations with the West were still unclear. When, as late as 1947, Hungarian communists approached Foreign Minister Vyacheslav M. Molotov about Soviet plans in Hungary, they were unable to ascertain precisely what the Kremlin had in mind.

Some historians believe Stalin subordinated Hungary to Poland, but the new scholarship points up the fluidity even in Poland in the early postwar months and years. Polish Communist Party documents from late 1944 and early 1945 are full of an internal debate over the best strategy for mobilizing support. There was tremendous unrest in the countryside. Soviet troops were still battling the Germans. Polish Home Army units inside Poland and other militantly nationalist groups, some linked to the conservative government-in-exile in London, also fought the Germans but intermittently turned their guns on Polish communists and Red Army forces. The Soviet-installed communist government in Lublin mounted a campaign of arrests, killings, and deportation of opposition members. This operation backfired in late 1944, when some 80,000 armed nationalist partisans roamed the country, killing about 800 Communist Party members and 300 Russian soldiers. The Lublin government then reversed course and sought to establish a coalition with Mikolajczyk, the popular leader of the Peasant Party.

Mikolajczyk was convinced that he had room to maneuver—that Stalin, fed up with his incompetent and unpopular clients, was not wedded to a communist regime in Poland. If he assured Stalin that he would accommodate Soviet security needs, Mikolajczyk thought, the Kremlin might accept his leadership. But after Mikolajczyk and his party mobilized a great deal of political support in the countryside in late 1945 and early 1946, the Polish communists resumed the campaign against their political opponents. During 1947 and 1948 the Peasant Party was crushed and the communists consolidated control of the country.

The new literature on Poland assigns more agency to the local communists and somewhat less to Stalin, whom it depicts as obsessed with Soviet security and lacking a plan for Poland's internal configuration. Much the same picture emerges in China, where Stalin initially had no intention of helping the Chinese Communist Party win the civil war and gain power. In *Cold War and Revolution,* the Norwegian historian Odd Arne Westad cites Chinese and Soviet documents to show that Stalin wanted at first to maintain cooperative relations in northeast Asia with the Americans. Stalin hoped to carry this off, Westad says, while at the same time preserving Soviet influence in Manchuria and discouraging a permanent American military presence in China. Subsequently the Soviet leader wavered in his support for Mao Zedong, and the Kremlin retained its links with the Chinese communists' Nationalist foes. Summing up, Westad sounds like Naimark on Germany: "To the historian—as to his contemporaries, Soviet and foreign—Stalin's foreign policy is not as much inexplicable in its parts as incoherent in its whole."

Stalin vacillated on his schemes for particular countries and regions because the Kremlin was hoping to pursue its overall interests based on a policy of realpolitik and cooperation with the United States and Britain but did not know if that approach would work. Vladimir Pechatnov, a diplomat trained as a historian under the Soviet regime, has uncovered three memorandums written in late 1944 and early 1945 by top Foreign Ministry officials Ivan Maisky, Maxim Litvinov, and Andrei Gromyko (who later served as foreign minister for 31 years). All three writers expected a continuation of the wartime alliance—indeed, regarded it as a prerequisite for the protection of Soviet interests in the postwar era. The United States, Britain, and the Soviet Union, they said, could divide the world into spheres of influence. According to Pechatnov, the three officials saw the Soviet sphere "largely in terms of traditional geostrategic dominance and not of Sovietization, which, as all three understood, would hardly be acceptable to the Western allies."

Pechatnov acknowledges that he has not unearthed evidence that Stalin shared these views, but he believes Stalin did. So do Vladislav Zubok and Constantine Pleshakov, as they write in their important new book *Inside the Kremlin's Cold War*. Although they claim the Kremlin pursued a "cautious expansionism in those areas that Stalin and his advisers defined as 'natural' spheres of influence," the two young Russian scholars stress that there was "no master plan in the Kremlin, and Stalin's ambitions had always been severely limited by the terrible devastation of the USSR during World War II and the existence of the American atomic monopoly."

At the end of the war, Zubok and Pleshakov emphasize, Stalin felt no great need "for an overarching ideology of confrontation." The Kremlin's foreign policy "was still based on the assumption of realpolitik," a desire to balance the power of the British and Americans and to capitalize on their anticipated rivalries.

The theme of realpolitik also reverberates through two other excellent books on Stalin's attitudes and actions. David Holloway, a British scholar who teaches at Stanford University, stresses that

> the policy Stalin pursued was one of realpolitik. Left-wing critics would later characterize it, correctly, as statist, because it treated states, rather than classes, as the primary actors in international relations, and because it put the interests of the Soviet state above those of international revolution. . . . Stalin wanted to consolidate Soviet territorial gains, establish a Soviet sphere of influence in Eastern Europe, and have a voice in the political fate of Germany and—if possible—of Japan.

Realpolitik is a motif in the fascinating work on Stalin's relations with Mao by a troika of scholars, one Russian, one American, and one Chinese. Sergei Goncharov, John Lewis, and Xue Litai write that "when it came to their face-to-face deliberations on particular external policy issues . . . the ultimate concern on both sides was not class struggle, but state interests (though the arguments were sometimes couched in revolutionary terms). In the final analysis, realpolitik governed [Mao's and Stalin's] thinking and strained their relations."

Traditionalists see the ideology of world revolution behind the Soviet policies that eventually destroyed the sovereignty of Russia's neighbors. Many of the new writings, however, suggest that the Kremlin's foreign policy was shaped by geopolitical considerations and perceptions of threat, the latter reinforced by Leninist assumptions about the behavior of capitalist nations. The Kremlin wanted to safeguard the Soviet Union against a recrudescence of German power. Like all his contemporaries, Stalin had seen Germany, largely demilitarized and partially occupied after defeat in World War I, rebuild its army and power in less than a generation under the Nazis. Then German armies again attacked, killing some 20 million Soviet soldiers and civilians and almost destroying the Soviet regime. Stalin was determined after World War II to gain control over the East European periphery so that countries like Poland could not serve as a springboard for an offensive against the Soviet Union. He was also intent, the new documents show, on preventing a revival of Japanese power. He told Chinese Nationalist diplomats in July 1945, "Japan will restore her might in 20, 30 years. [The] whole plan of our relations with China is based on this."

Stalin, the recent literature stresses, wanted to avoid military conflict with the United States. But he sought to prepare the Soviet Union to defend itself should the wartime coalition dissolve and fighting break out with the United States. This did not mean, though, that he was planning to attack the West. After scrutinizing records of Stalin's military thinking, David Holloway concludes, "There is no evidence to show that Stalin intended to invade Western Europe, except in the event of a major war." Soviet postwar military plans for 1946 and 1947 were defensive in nature, assuming a Western attack and a Soviet retreat before the launch of a major counteroffensive.

Former First Secretary and Premier Nikita Khrushchev, in reminiscences published during the glasnost years, writes, "In the days leading up to Stalin's death [in 1953] we believed that we would go to war. Stalin trembled at this prospect. How he quivered! He was afraid of war. . . . Stalin never did anything that might provoke a war with the United States. He knew his weakness." Although it is difficult to picture Stalin quivering, and although he sometimes talked more boldly to Mao Zedong, most recent writers believe that Khrushchev's characterization is basically correct: Stalin knew he was operating from a position of weakness, and wanted to avoid war with the United States.

Should a war with the West erupt, however, it was essential that the Soviet Union protect its flanks. Defense in depth reinforced the Soviet desire to retain former czarist lands lost in the Russo-Japanese War (1904–5) and World War I that had been seized during World War II. With its armies spread across most of Eastern and Central Europe as a result of the horrendously costly battle against the Nazis, and its troops ensconced in Manchuria and northern Korea as a result of the last-minute declaration of war against Japan, Moscow was well-positioned to achieve its longtime aim of control of the periphery. In his account of the rivalry between the Soviet Union and the United States in China in 1945–46, Odd Arne Westad illustrates how security concerns shaped Stalin's inconsistent actions. Kathryn Weathersby uses Russian Foreign Ministry documents to demonstrate the primarily defensive orientation of Soviet policy in the Korean Peninsula in the late 1940s. . . .

The new documents reveal an emphasis on security considerations, but ideology clearly influenced Soviet foreign policy. Stalin was a Bolshevik revolutionary, and he and his successors were imbued with the principles of Marxism-Leninism. Broadly speaking, Soviet leaders believed that economic and class imperatives shaped the policies of capitalist governments, which were assumed to be committed to socialism's destruction. Colonial lands, they also postulated, would inevitably mount wars of national liberation against their imperialist masters. Rivalries would drive the capitalist states to battle each other, and communism would eventually triumph among the people of the West. These tenets molded Soviet leaders' understanding of the world, influenced their interpretation of their adversaries' actions, and heightened their sense of threat.

But these beliefs, powerful yet vague, were subject to manipulation by a Kremlin committed to realpolitik, and in general served to legitimize or justify policy rather than determine it. Stalin used the Comintern, the association of communist parties of the world established by Lenin, and, after 1947, the Cominform, the organization charged with coordinating most European communist parties in the Soviet sphere, to enhance state interests. Stalin, write Zubok and Pleshakov, "used the common ideology of Communist parties to organize Eastern Europe into a 'security buffer' for his state."

Stalin's rift with Yugoslav leader Josip Broz Tito in 1948 stemmed in part from the former's opposition to the encouragement of revolution from below during the final stages of World War II. Moscow also refused to support the Greek left, periodically thwarted Mao's plans, and generally urged West European communists in 1944 and 1945 to participate in coalition governments, at the time when they were best positioned to win or seize power. Some of these facts have long been known, but they are even more striking in the recent literature. "Ideological declarations," write Goncharov, Lewis, and Xue Litai, "could serve power politics but not determine it. Motives found deeply rooted in national traditions far outweighed Marxism-Leninism in practice."

Traditional histories of the Cold War assume that the Soviet Union tightly controlled its clients and that their actions reflected Soviet desires. But some of the most interesting new information reveals that local communist leaders and, later, Soviet satellites and allies could exert some leverage over the Kremlin and pursue their own interests. Historians are learning that even in the immediate postwar years, relations between the Kremlin and communists in Poland, Hungary, East Germany, and elsewhere were more complicated than they had thought.

After the Nazi defeat, populist parties in Central and Eastern Europe clamored for land reform and improvements in social welfare, which often took precedence in their members' minds over the development of democracy. Although some issues played to local communists' advantage, nowhere did they have enough support to win power freely. The communists needed the assistance of Soviet officials, secret police agents, and the organs of military rule in harassing or suppressing their opponents, but their dependence on the Soviets identified them with the random brutal behavior of occupation troops and the demands of reparations teams. Soviet officials, for their part, sometimes tried to restrain their clients' revolutionary impulses, recognizing that immoderate actions might anger the British and Americans and cause a rift that the Kremlin probably did not wish to occur.

In North Asia, historians once thought Stalin ordered the North Koreans to attack South Korea in June 1950 to test American resolve. But the research in Chinese documents by historians like Shu Guang Zhang and Jian Chen, combined with the opening of Russian archives and the release of some North Korean materials, creates an altogether more complex picture of the beginning of the Korean War. North Korean leader Kim Il Sung was dependent on Moscow and needed Stalin's authorization before he could send troops south and attempt to reunite the peninsula. But it is now clear that he relentlessly pushed and prodded the reluctant Soviet leader for permission. Once the Chinese communists triumphed in their revolution in 1949, Kim benefited greatly from their support, and their success gained him additional leverage with the Kremlin. Fearing an American response, though, Stalin was loath to gamble on a North Korean attack. He gave his assent and support, Kathryn Weathersby shows, only after becoming convinced that the Americans would not intervene. Moreover, Stalin appears to have calculated that Kim's quest to unite Korea under communist rule would intensify the rift between the Chinese communists and the Americans. . . .

Although Soviet policy was primarily security-oriented and circumscribed rather than dictated by revolutionary fervor, and though clients led the Kremlin into some involvements rather than the other way around, the West still had ample reason to distrust Stalin and his successors. Stalin's letters to Molotov show a man consumed by suspicion who considered capitalism an avowed enemy. And while not a big risk-taker, Stalin would exploit adversaries' perceived weaknesses or hesitation, as in Czechoslovakia in 1948 and in Korea two years later.

But fear of American power in conjunction with ideological assumptions about the behavior of capitalist nations shaped the Soviet mindset and influenced officials' behavior. In 1946 the ambassador to the United States, Nikolai Novikov, dispatched a memorandum to Moscow that is now often compared to George Kennan's famous "Long Telegram," which characterized the Soviet Union as an implacable foe and outlined the need for containment. Novikov's analysis of American foreign policy dwelled on its expansionist impulses, focused on reactionary factions and imperialist motivations, stressed the U.S. rivalry with Britain over Middle Eastern oil, and urged Moscow to be vigilant in protecting national security. Assuming America's hostility, neither Novikov nor his successors could grasp the strategic anxieties of capitalist nations like the United States. Arriving in Washington several years later, Dobrynin admits, his mind too "was clogged by the long years of Stalinism, by our own ideological blinders, by our deep-seated beliefs and perceptions, which led to our misconstruing all American intentions as offensive."

Most writers would concur with David Holloway's opinion that the West could never have laid Stalin's suspicions to rest, yet that does not mean the West bears no responsibility for the course of the Cold War. Dobrynin, after acknowledging his ideological blinders, hastens to add, "Dogma itself was strengthened by the permanent postwar hostility of the United States and its own intransigence toward the Soviet Union." The new research clearly shows that American initiatives intensified Soviet distrust and reinforced Soviet insecurity.

After achieving victory over Germany at a terrible price and gaining a position of unprecedented strength in the middle of Europe, in August 1945 the Russians suddenly faced the reality that the Americans possessed atomic weapons and were willing to employ them. Although he had learned about the Manhattan Project through Soviet espionage, Stalin felt betrayed because Roosevelt and Truman had not leveled with him about the new weapon in their arsenal. Stalin, Holloway writes, believed "that the United States wanted to use the bomb as an instrument of political pressure." U.S. diplomatic intransigence at the Potsdam conference in July 1945, especially on the subject of reparations, seemed to confirm that belief. Gromyko recalls Stalin saying to him during the conference, rather calmly, "Washington and London are hoping we won't be able to develop the bomb ourselves for some time. And meanwhile, using America's monopoly . . . they want to force us to accept their plans on questions affecting Europe and the world. Well, that's not going to happen."

Holloway argues that the bomb did not dictate the Kremlin's adoption of a realist foreign policy; the choice for realism, rather than a revolutionary or liberal orientation, had already been made. But Stalin and Molotov believed that "the United States would use the atomic bomb to intimidate the Soviet Union, to wring concessions from it, in order to impose its own conception of the postwar order. . . . It was crucial, therefore, to show that the Soviet Union was tough, that it could not be frightened.". . .

The Marshall Plan was probably the most effective program the United States launched during the entire Cold War. But exciting new research in archives in Russia and Eastern Europe highlights the fears that the plan triggered in Moscow. Mikhail Narinsky, a Russian scholar working at the Moscow-based Institute for Universal History, and Scott Parrish, a political scientist who recently completed his doctoral dissertation at Columbia University, have shown that after initial interest, Molotov and Stalin quickly became convinced that the U.S. aid was designed to lure the Kremlin's East European neighbors out of its orbit and to rebuild German strength. They viewed the Marshall Plan and accompanying measures to revive industry in western Germany and to create the Federal Republic as fundamental threats to Soviet security. These perceptions prompted the Kremlin to form the Cominform, suppress all dissent in Poland, Romania, and Bulgaria, extinguish the opposition in Hungary, encourage a communist coup in Czechoslovakia, and blockade Berlin. These actions in turn magnified the sense of threat in Washington and London, precipitating the formation of NATO and solidifying the long-term division of Europe. "For Stalin," say Zubok and Pleshakov, "the Marshall Plan was a watershed."

It is now evident that the men in the Kremlin did not know precisely what they wanted to do. Their ideology did not chart a master plan; rather, it distorted their interpretation of other nations' behavior and heightened their perception of threat. Because of the pervasive suspicion in the apparat, officials in different agencies rarely spoke to one another, and each bureaucracy pursued its own objectives. Although the regime was brutal and centralized, policy was erratic and contingent.

One empathizes with U.S. officials who had difficulty grasping what was happening inside the Kremlin. Unsurprisingly, they chose to operate on the basis of certain assumptions: totalitarian nations seek unlimited expansion; communists have a master plan. But today the United States and Russia are in a position to inject substantially more complexity and subtlety into their understanding of the Cold War. Americans should reexamine their complacent belief in the wisdom of their country's Cold War policies. U.S. officials acted prudently in the early years of the Cold War, but their actions increased distrust, exacerbated frictions, and raised the stakes. Subsequently, their relentless pursuit of a policy of strength and counterrevolutionary warfare may have done more harm than good to Russians and the other peoples of the former Soviet Union as well as East Europeans, Koreans, and Vietnamese. Quite a few of the new books and articles suggest that American policies made it difficult for potential reformers inside the Kremlin to gain the high ground. There were times during the 1950s, 1960s, and 1970s when Stalin's successors might have liked to stabilize the relationship and curtail the competition with the West, but the perceived threat emanating from the United States held them back.

As for Stalin, he had no desire to change the totalitarian system he had established before World War II. In fact, the Cold War played into his hands, enabling him to perpetuate the system. But the evidence does not show that Stalin initially thought it would be in the Soviet Union's interest to have a cold war. Nor did the Soviet leader seek unlimited expansion. Western actions, though prudent, intensified his suspicions. Meanwhile, the presence of Soviet armies in Eastern and Central Europe created a dynamic of its own, fostering the replication of the Soviet totalitarian system in the satellites even in the absence of a grand strategy.

Americans must acknowledge that the U.S. government acted not from moral revulsion against Stalinism but out of fear of Soviet power in the international system. President Truman knew Soviet Russia was a police state, but he liked doing business with Stalin in the beginning. "I can deal with Stalin," Truman wrote in his diary. "He is honest—but smart as hell." Basically, he did not care very much what was happening behind the Iron Curtain. "You know," he jotted in his diary on another occasion, "Americans are funny birds. They are always sticking their heads into somebody's business which isn't any of theirs." Russians, he opined, "evidently like their government or they wouldn't die for it. I like ours so let's get along." Truman's views changed only when he grew to fear the prospective growth of Soviet power. Truman disliked tyrants and believed in self-government, but not enough to do anything about them unless he saw U.S. interests engaged.

Turning the Cold War into a morality play encourages the ducking of moral dilemmas present and future. What happens when virtue and self-interest do not go hand in hand? Americans and their leaders wind up beleaguered and conflicted when they come up against evil-laden situations, as in Bosnia, Rwanda, and Somalia, that do not pose a threat to vital interests. Americans' sense of rectitude, stoked by victory in the Cold War, encourages them to overlook the extent to which they have tolerated and even aligned themselves with evil regimes when their own interests were not endangered or when it served their interests to do so, thus making life worse for peoples elsewhere. The opening of their enemies' archives should hardly inspire complacency.

III

The Cold War in Asia

Nancy Bernkopf Tucker

SUBORDINATING CHINA

The Roosevelt and Truman administrations never treated China on its own terms. Rather, American policymakers, according to Nancy Bernkopf Tucker, consistently subordinated China to more pressing military and diplomatic priorities, especially European ones. Clashing political objectives, aggravated by cultural discord, thus plagued Sino-American relations throughout the 1940s—both with the Nationalist regime of Jiang Jieshi (Chiang Kai-shek) and with the communist regime that overthrew it in October 1949. Tucker argues for the controversial point that the Truman administration initially sought normalization of relations with Mao Zedong's communist government. But the administration failed to separate the China question from the distorting prism of the Cold War. Partisan Republicans turned the "loss" of Nationalist China into a hot political issue. Then, in June 1950, North Korea invaded South Korea, greatly exacerbating tensions between the United States and Communist China and, by the end of the year, bringing the two nations into open conflict. This essay demonstrates some of the important connections that obtained between the European and Asian theaters of the Cold War.

Nancy Bernkopf Tucker is a professor in Georgetown University's School of Foreign Service and History Department. She has written *Patterns in the Dust: Chinese-American Relations and the Recognition Controversy* (1983) and *Taiwan, Hong Kong, and the United States, 1945–1992* (1994).

The history of Sino-American relations in the past fifty years has been a tale of how Americans, preoccupied with the affairs of Europe, thought they could use China, subordinating its needs and interests to the realization of weightier objectives elsewhere. China played a role in defeating Japan and Germany in the 1940s, slowing Soviet industrialization in the 1950s and 1960s, and complicating Moscow's defenses in the 1970s and 1980s. The United States did not focus on China, as China, because its lack of wealth and its purely regional power did not necessitate direct attention.

Nancy Bernkopf Tucker, "China and America, 1941–1991," *Foreign Affairs*, 70 (Winter 1991–92), pp. 75–81. Reprinted by permission of *Foreign Affairs*, Copyright 1992 by the Council on Foreign Relations.

Not surprisingly, disappointment plagued this distorted relationship. Neither country seemed willing or able to fulfill the expectations of the other. Americans saw the Chinese both as allies and adversaries, as people to be helped and feared, as potential customers and competitors, as strategic partners and expansionist aggressors. Such contradictions colored the efforts of statesmen to structure policy and of the public to understand what has transpired between the two states.

Differences in political objectives were aggravated by cultural discord. Americans determined to elicit political and social reforms commensurate with their investments—financial and emotional—felt frustrated by the Chinese rejection of Western values. Both before and after the communist takeover in 1949 China sought to modernize without having to Westernize. A source of tension throughout the Third World, the clash between change and tradition has been nowhere more powerful than in China and nowhere more troublesome than in Sino-American relations.

Possibly the most striking illustration of China's peripheral status and the thwarting of both Chinese and American expectations can be found in their respective responses to the Japanese bombing of Pearl Harbor on December 7, 1941. What President Franklin D. Roosevelt called a day of infamy was a blessing to Nationalist (Kuomintang) Chinese leader Chiang Kai-shek in his fog-enshrouded wartime capital. According to an observer in Chongqing, "The military council was jubilant. Chiang was so happy he sang an old opera aria. . . . The Kuomintang government officials went around congratulating each other, as if a great victory had been won." The divergence between America's distress and China's joy underscored the differences between American and Chinese national interests. Washington, although now China's ally and a more forthright participant in the anti-Japanese struggle, put the war in Europe and the defeat of Hitler first. Roosevelt wanted to use the Chinese to bleed Japan, to thwart Tokyo's attempt to create a new order in Asia and seize European colonial holdings. To these ends the United States tried to reorganize Chiang's war effort by diverting him from China's civil conflict, training his troops and providing an American commander.

Chiang Kai-shek, in contrast, had assumed that the United States would take over the fight against Japan, freeing him to concentrate on eliminating the internal communist threat. The Nationalist leader saw no reason to send his soldiers to die opposing Tokyo when Americans could defeat Japan without them, and he had no use for the American commander and adviser in China, General Joseph Stilwell, whose efforts to replace loyal but inept Chinese officers threatened to destabilize his regime. Chiang expected Washington simply to send money, tend to the larger war and leave him to deal with China's domestic politics.

The clash in priorities escalated when Americans sought contacts with Mao Zedong's forces at Yan'an. Negotiations with the Chinese Communist Party (CCP) were vital to the rescue of downed U.S. pilots and the staging of an American assault on Japan's home islands from the Chinese coast. They would also allow the American military access to the only "allies" operating freely behind Japanese lines in north China. But the Nationalists adamantly rejected the idea of consorting with their enemy, relenting only under extreme pressure. And the Nationalists arguably had been right in their resistance, given the enthusiasm with which Americans responded to the communist Chinese. The Americans praised Mao's government and army, whose energy, integrity, efficiency and idealism so forcefully highlighted the corruption, disarray and torpor of the Nationalists. Mao Zedong and Zhou Enlai welcomed the first American observer mission by celebrating the Fourth of July in 1944 and offering to travel to Washington to meet with Roosevelt to coordinate war strategies.

Nevertheless the United States remained, if reluctantly, tied to the Kuomintang government, disappointing the communists and encouraging the Nationalist Party to maintain an unrealistic assessment of its importance to Washington. In actuality Chiang's refusal to mount an energetic effort against Japan gradually eroded U.S. support and ensured substitution of an island-hopping strategy for winning the Pacific war. But, although he despaired of making Chiang an active wartime asset, Roosevelt continued to imagine that China after the peace could become a great power and useful American partner. Thus he insisted, over the protests of British Prime Minister Winston Churchill, that the Chinese be given a seat in the Security Council of the soon to be created United Nations.

Such extravagant assertions of China's significance did not prevent Roosevelt's willing betrayal of Chinese interests at the Yalta Conference in February 1945 in pursuit of better relations with the Soviet Union and a swifter end to the war. In exchange for Moscow's agreement to fight in the Pacific and to sign a treaty with Chiang's government, Roosevelt arbitrarily sacrificed China's control over Outer Mongolia, Port Arthur and Dairen, as well as a share in the Chinese Eastern and South Manchuria railways. Although the United States could have done little to keep these territories and assets out of Soviet hands, it is also true that the president neither sought Chiang's approval nor worried much about the postwar impact of these choices on China's sovereignty.

President Roosevelt's compromises at Yalta did nothing to prevent the deterioration in Soviet-American relations that accelerated with the end of the Second World War. Americans insisted upon forward bases and open markets vulnerable to U.S. domination. The Soviets demanded security buffers and exploited unrest to spread revolutionary ideology. The resulting Cold War pitted competing blocs of antagonistic states against each other, slowly inducing the United States to see that China's strategic location and market potential could actually make it a useful partner.

America's policy in the tense days immediately following Japan's surrender consisted of creating a strong and prosperous China by avoiding renewal of civil conflict and focusing government attention on political reform and economic rehabilitation. If Harry Truman felt constrained to support anticommunist forces under Chiang Kai-shek, he nevertheless did not yet see the Cold War as the critical variable in Asia and could contemplate establishing a Nationalist-Communist coalition. But Chiang, confident of U.S. patronage, refused compromise, opting for military victory. He disregarded American advice and tried to project his forces into Manchuria beyond the capacity of his supply system. His forces squandered popular support by preying upon the newly liberated cities of east China, treating the citizenry as collaborators for having lived under Japanese rule. His interference in battlefield command threw planning into disarray, and when the People's Liberation Army trapped frontline troops Chiang bombed his own units to prevent their equipment from falling into enemy hands.

Chiang saw the key to success as unstinting American aid. In a relentless campaign to secure ever-increasing amounts of assistance, he devised inventive ways to entangle the United States directly in the war effort. But despite U.S. assistance amounting to $2 billion between 1945 and 1949, neither money nor weapons could compensate for what the Nationalists lacked in competent leadership, ideals or popular devotion. Furthermore Chiang's suspicion of foreigners and distrust of modernization projects that threatened his control reinforced Washington's inclination to focus on pressing European problems, such as the Berlin blockade and implementation of the Marshall Plan, where American help would be better utilized and more appreciated.

As a result the Truman administration searched for ways to escape Chiang's grasp and move toward diplomatic relations with a new regime in China. In August 1949 Secretary of State Dean Acheson published an exposé of Chiang's blundering, known as the China White Paper, which argued that a generous and sympathetic United States could do no more on Chiang's behalf. Acheson spoke publicly of the practical value of diplomatic relations. Despite incidents like the house arrest of Consul General Angus Ward by communist forces in Mukden and labor confrontations with businessmen in Shang-hai, American missionaries, diplomats and others remarked upon the surprising civility shown to foreigners in the midst of a civil war.

By December 1949 the Kuomintang's demise appeared imminent. Chiang had been forced to flee the mainland and had taken refuge among a hostile population on the island of Taiwan. American intelligence asserted that a communist attack would encounter little Nationalist resistance. On January 5, 1950, Truman announced that the United States would not interfere. Acheson placed Taiwan and Korea outside America's defensive perimeter in Asia. It was only a matter of time before Taiwan would collapse and the administration could accept the reality of communist control in Beijing.

For the United States, however, there could be no simple transition from Nationalist to communist control in China. Republican desperation to recapture the presidency in the late 1940s triggered a "red scare," blighting domestic affairs and undermining American foreign policy. Borrowing charges from the "China lobby" (a conglomeration of missionaries, businessmen, publishers, journalists, military figures and politicians who vigorously promoted the interests of Chiang and the Kuomintang), the GOP insisted that communist sympathizers in the State Department had "lost China." But it remained for the Korean War and Senator Joseph McCarthy (R-Wis.) to turn China's loss into political dynamite. In need of an election issue, McCarthy waged a vitriolic attack upon the Truman administration, sweeping otherwise responsible Republicans up in the frenzy. The senator knew little about China but, armed with documents from China lobby activist Alfred Kohlberg, McCarthy capitalized on the shock arising from sudden war in Asia to generate national hysteria.

North Korea's attempt to unify the Korean peninsula had a profound impact upon the course of the Cold War and Sino-American relations. Truman's resistance to huge military budgets evaporated. The administration used the Korean War to justify rearming Germany and militarizing NATO. It escalated appropriations to France for the fight against Ho Chi Minh in Indochina and dispatched its first technical advisers. Soon the United States would disregard Soviet and Chinese objections to conclude a peace treaty with Japan and would sign security pacts with Japan, Australia and New Zealand.

For Chinese-American relations the Korean War proved an unmitigated disaster. Beijing leaders had taken Truman and Acheson at their word and anticipated an unopposed effort to oust Chiang from Taiwan. But Washington now reversed itself and placed the Seventh Fleet in the Taiwan Strait to prevent expansion of the war either by a CCP attack or a Nationalist feint that would force U.S. intervention. Beijing's frustration was compounded by fear when U.S. forces, under U.N. auspices, threatened China's Yalu River border. Recently revealed documents from Beijing indicate that Mao, believing a military confrontation with the United States inevitable over either Vietnam, Taiwan or Korea, opted to fight in the arena most accessible and easiest to control. Thus Zhou Enlai cautioned the Americans not to move north, and when they dismissed his warnings because the Chinese appeared weak and preoccupied with domestic troubles—not a match in any case for American soldiers—China struck.

President Truman had hoped that a short conflict in Korea would mean but a brief reinvolvement in the Chinese civil war and a momentary distraction from European affairs. Although the president was quickly reassured that war in Korea was not simply a diversion to facilitate communist aggression in the West, he continued escalating military expenditures for Europe, revealing the administration's true priorities. But the Korean War dragged on and, despite administration antipathy, the network of economic

and military ties with the Kuomintang grew more complex and
self-perpetuating.

Robert J. McMahon

THE COLD WAR COMES TO SOUTHEAST ASIA

Areas long viewed as peripheral to core United States interests suddenly
became critical as postwar American policy makers redefined national
security imperatives in the face of what appeared to be a Soviet threat of
ominous, global proportions. Southeast Asia proved one such area. Early
in 1950, the Truman administration began providing military and economic assistance to France in its struggle against a communist-led insurgency in Indochina. That decision, as Robert J. McMahon argues in the
next selection, flowed from a complex amalgam of broad, Cold War considerations. American strategists became convinced, for example, that
the economic revival of both Japan and Western Europe necessitated a
politically stable and economically vibrant Southeast Asia. Strategic, political, and psychological factors, McMahon notes, also underscored the
importance of stability and economic recovery in Southeast Asia—and
hence the need to block any communist breakthroughs in the region.

   Robert J. McMahon is the author of *Colonialism and Cold War: The
United States and the Struggle for Indonesian Independence, 1945–49
(1981); The Cold War on the Periphery: The United States, India, and
Pakistan* (1994); and *The Limits of Empire* (1998) (on the United States
and Southeast Asia). He teaches history at the University of Florida.

Truman's decision early in 1950 to begin providing modest levels
of military and economic assistance to France in its struggle against
a communist-led indigenous insurgency in Indochina now clearly
stands as one of the most momentous of his presidency. It marked
the first milestone in what became America's longest war, a twenty-
five-year struggle to prevent communist forces from triumphing in

"Harry S. Truman and the Roots of U.S. Involvement in Indochina, 1945–1953"
by Robert J. McMahon, in David L. Anderson, ed., *Shadow on the White House:
Presidents and the Vietnam War, 1945–1975*, University Press of Kansas, 1993, pp.
19–42. Reprinted by permission of the University Press of Kansas.

Indochina. It was a struggle that ultimately claimed over 50,000 American lives, brought defeat and humiliation to the world's most powerful nation, shattered the domestic economy, divided the nation more profoundly than any event since the Civil War, and sparked an intensely emotional debate about the United States' place in the world.

The Truman administration's initial involvement in Indochina has, not surprisingly, drawn its share of historical interpreters. It has inspired a healthy amount of scholarly controversy as well. Scholars writing about this period while the war in Vietnam still raged tended either to downplay the importance of the initial U.S. commitment to the French or to ascribe that commitment to a combination of inadvertence and happenstance. They did not, for the most part, see the U.S. commitment to the French as stemming from a set of well-defined national security interests. Over the past fifteen years, a spate of articles and monographs has forced a fundamental rethinking of that view. Despite often sharp disagreements about the relative weight of the ideological, economic, strategic, political, and psychological wellsprings of the U.S. commitment, recent scholarship posits a much more conscious, deliberate, and calculated policy. It depicts the Truman administration responding to a set of clearly articulated national security objectives. Those objectives led U.S. officials to link the Franco-Vietnamese struggle to broader regional and global foreign policy goals in a deepening Cold War.

Indochina became crucial to Truman administration planners by the late 1940s because of a perceived relationship between stability in Southeast Asia and economic recovery in Western Europe and Japan. U.S. intervention in Indochina formed part of a carefully conceived, if ultimately flawed, effort to preserve the economic resources of Southeast Asia for the West while denying them to the communist powers. It grew, in short, from America's overall Cold War strategy for containing Soviet power and influence, a strategy that led to a blurring of distinctions between core and periphery and elevated Southeast Asia into a national security concern of the first order.

When Truman found the awesome joint responsibilities of president and commander in chief suddenly thrust upon him in April 1945, his understandable inclination was to continue the policies of his predecessor. Possessing neither the experience nor the self-assurance to question decisions made by a man who, even in death, overshadowed the insecure Missourian, Truman strove for continuity in the countless details of postwar planning. The new chief executive consequently leaned heavily on senior State and War Department officials for advice on national security matters, a trait that would characterize Truman's leadership style throughout his presidency. A simple and straightforward man who blended a parochial nationalist outlook with the convictions of a pragmatic internationalist, Truman gladly delegated most day-to-day diplomatic decisions to trusted advisers. During his early months in office, the new president deferred most often to Secretary of State James F. Byrnes, a former Senate colleague. Later, George C. Marshall and Dean Acheson would assume comparable roles within the administration. The policies that those advisers developed and implemented in his name—in Indochina and elsewhere—were entirely consistent with Truman's own assumptions about U.S. national security interests and global strategy. Accordingly, he gave an unusual degree of latitude to his senior diplomatic and defense appointees, confident that their policy recommendations would almost always comport with his own views of world affairs and yet spring from a much deeper reservoir of knowledge about particular issues. At the same time, Truman insisted that he remain the final decision maker.

The future of French Indochina was but one of a bewildering galaxy of problems that required an early decision by the new president. At first glance, this particular problem appeared a good deal less complex than most. During his last months in office, Franklin D. Roosevelt had assured French authorities, as he had their British and Dutch counterparts, that Washington would not oppose the reimposition of European control over colonial territories occupied by Japan during the war. Certain that he was simply following a well-established policy for the Japanese-occupied areas of Southeast Asia, Truman quickly conveyed the same message to French, British, and Dutch officials.

Truman's reassurances were entirely consistent with those given earlier by Roosevelt; they were meant to signal continuity, not change. Nonetheless, Truman's straightforward recognition of the colonial powers' claims to territorial sovereignty in Southeast Asia obscured the more complex reality surrounding the U.S. stance toward colonialism. Roosevelt's various wartime plans and pronouncements regarding European colonies in general, and French Indochina in particular, were sufficiently contradictory that Truman actually inherited a much more ambiguous legacy than he could possibly have realized. The emergence in September 1945 of an independent Vietnamese nationalist regime, demanding international recognition and framing its case in terms of American wartime statements and promises, drove home the complexities and contradictions of the Roosevelt legacy.

During the early years of World War II, Roosevelt and other top officials declared with some regularity that the United States supported the principle of self-determination for all peoples. The president, who took the lead on this issue, often prodded European officials about the need to commit themselves to a timetable for eventual colonial independence. Much to the discomfiture of America's European allies, Roosevelt and Secretary of State Cordell Hull proposed that a trusteeship system be established in the postwar period through which different developed nations, acting as trustees, would prepare local elites to assume the responsibilities of self-government. Trusteeship represented a compromise solution to Roosevelt; he believed that it would guarantee future independence while avoiding the danger of a premature transfer of power to inexperienced indigenous rulers.

Roosevelt's plans for the colonial world represented a nearly indistinguishable blend of American ideals and American interests. The president found the conditions under which so many subject peoples lived appallingly primitive. After passing through the British colony of Gambia in early 1942, for example, he railed against the poverty and disease he had witnessed everywhere, referring to the dependency as a "hellhole" and calling the experience "the most horrible thing I have ever seen in my life." Although Roosevelt never visited Indochina, the lack of personal contact did not prevent the president from berating the colony's French overlords in equally harsh terms. In fact, he considered the French the least enlightened of all the colonial powers and often singled out for particular censure their sorry record in Indochina. Despite "nearly one hundred years" of French rule in Indochina, he complained on one occasion, "the people are worse off than they were at the beginning."

Roosevelt's genuine humanitarian impulses coexisted with a more practical strain. The preservation of the colonial system stood as an impediment to the kind of world order most conducive to U.S. interests. Roosevelt was convinced that the imperial order, with its restrictive trading practices, economic exploitation, and political repression, would simply sow the seeds for future instability within the colonies and future conflicts among the great powers. The United States sought a more open world, one characterized by free trade and democratic principles. Only such a world, according to the president and his chief advisers, would ensure the peace, prosperity, stability, and security that the United States sought. Roosevelt's proselytizing on behalf of a more liberal approach to dependent areas thus bespoke an unsentimental calculation of national interests as much as it did a revulsion against imperialism's excesses.

Before his death, Roosevelt significantly modified his approach to colonial questions. Late in 1944 he jettisoned trusteeship planning for Indochina and other areas, offering instead a promise not to interfere with the reimposition of colonial rule in Southeast Asia. This policy shift reflected the president's essential pragmatism in the face of a series of complex, cross-cutting interests. From its inception, his trusteeship formula had generated heated rebukes from the colonial powers. British Prime Minister Winston Churchill, Roosevelt's most important ally, made clear on numerous occasions his unbending opposition to U.S. tampering with European colonies. Free French leader General Charles de Gaulle was no less adamant in opposing U.S. plans. The Roosevelt administration feared that an aggressive advocacy of trusteeship, in the face of such angry and unified opposition, might create intolerable strains within the wartime alliance and might jeopardize postwar cooperation in Western Europe, the most vital region of all to the United States. Defense needs also militated against persisting in an anticolonial campaign. Planners in the War and Navy Departments insisted that U.S. national security required exclusive control over the Japanese-mandated islands in the Pacific. With the president's concurrence, they intended to establish a permanent U.S. military presence throughout the Pacific in order to add depth and flexibility to the nation's air and naval capability. That high-priority goal, according to military experts, could not be compromised by trusteeship principles that could easily be applied to strategic U.S.-occupied territory as well as to

European colonies. Broader political, strategic, and military concerns, in short, necessitated a tactical retreat from earlier anticolonial pronouncements and plans.

Ho Chi Minh's declaration of an independent Vietnamese state on September 2, 1945, brought to a head many of the contradictions embedded in the Roosevelt administration's colonial policy. Quoting liberally from the American Declaration of Independence in his own independence proclamation, the veteran nationalist leader was in effect offering the opening bid in what would prove to be a concerted, if ill-fated, campaign for U.S. backing. Later that day, a Vietnamese band joined the independence-day festivities in Hanoi with a rendition of the "Star-Spangled Banner." U.S. Army officers listened from the reviewing stand as a series of Vietnamese nationalists echoed Ho with their own glowing tributes to the United States' anticolonial heritage. The previous evening Ho had invited two members of the Office of Strategic Services (OSS) for dinner. After thanking them for the valuable material assistance rendered by the United States to his guerrilla movement during the war, he appealed for "fraternal collaboration" in the future.

A shrewd tactician with the instincts of a born politician, the man previously known as Nguyen Ai Quoc was a communist, a revolutionary, but above all a Vietnamese nationalist. He sensed that the momentous events set in motion by the Japanese occupation of Indochina and the Nazi conquest of France had created a historic opportunity for the realization of his lifelong dream: independence from French rule. From the outset Ho calculated that the United States, if it remained true to its wartime statements, could become his most useful ally. That view was not born of naiveté. It grew, instead, from the mutually beneficial collaboration between U.S. military and intelligence officers and Vietminh guerrillas that had taken place in the jungles of northern Tonkin during the struggle against Japan. It was nourished by the Vietnamese leaders' belief that the United States' global interests would compel it to oppose the reestablishment of French colonialism.

Ho's assessment was not an unrealistic one. After all, Roosevelt had calculated that U.S. interests would best be served by the progressive evolution of colonial dependencies into self-governing states; the president's revulsion against French misrule in Indochina ran especially deep. Ho can hardly be faulted for failing to anticipate the shift in U.S. policy that occurred shortly before Roosevelt's death. Unaware that first Roosevelt and then Truman had reassured European allies that the United States would not block the reestablishment of the status quo antebellum, Ho appealed to Truman for recognition in a series of personal letters. "The carrying out of the Atlantic Charter and San Francisco Charter," he declared hopefully in one message, "implies the eradication of imperialism and all forms of colonial oppression."

Truman never responded to Ho's appeals. Neither he nor any of his top advisers ever seriously contemplated direct support for or diplomatic recognition of the Democratic Republic of Vietnam. To do so would have represented a sharp break with the policy Truman had inherited from Roosevelt in an area that ranked relatively low on the overall scale of U.S. priorities. Such a course must have seemed inconceivable to a president still overwhelmed by the myriad responsibilities of his new office. On August 29, during a White House meeting with de Gaulle, Truman signaled that there would be no such break. He reassured France's provisional president that the United States recognized the right of French authorities to reestablish sovereignty in Indochina. Ho's declaration of independence just three days later did not occasion a searching reexamination of that stance. Despite widespread respect for Ho's nationalist credentials and leadership abilities among U.S. intelligence and military personnel serving in Indochina, top U.S. policymakers were far more concerned with the needs and viewpoints of France. To alienate France, a country whose active support in Europe was crucial, would have undermined the overall foreign policy goals of the Truman administration. To do so on behalf of a national independence movement in remote Southeast Asia would have represented the height of diplomatic folly.

The United States instead pursued a policy of neutrality toward the colonial rebellion in Indochina, much as it did toward a contemporaneous colonial revolt in the Dutch East Indies. The Truman administration never questioned the legal right of the European sovereigns to reestablish control in Vietnam and Indonesia. At the same time, it realized that sheer pragmatism necessitated some concessions to indigenous nationalist movements. A harsh policy of political and military repression by the colonial powers would probably endanger not only the peace and order that the

United States sought in Southeast Asia but the economic recovery and political stability that it sought in Western Europe.

Throughout 1945 and 1946, U.S. diplomats consequently urged their French counterparts to negotiate in good faith with Ho and his chief lieutenants in order to avert an outright conflict that would serve the interests of neither party. Washington applauded the conclusion of a preliminary Franco-Vietnamese accord on March 6, 1946, since it seemed to open the way for an amicable political compromise. Like Roosevelt administration planners before them, Truman administration analysts believed that only a more liberal approach to colonial issues, one pointing toward eventual self-government, could establish the essential preconditions for order, stability, and prosperity in the developing world.

Those broad principles served as a general guidepost for U.S. policymakers during the four years following Vietnam's proclamation of independence. Although the principles were certainly sound, they produced little more than frustration for the Truman administration in a period punctuated by false hopes, failed negotiations, and savage fighting. The promise of the March 6 accord soon gave way to stalemated negotiations at Dalat and Paris. Although he was willing to accept less than immediate independence for all of Vietnam, Ho could not condone the retention of French supremacy in the southern province of Cochinchina. To this ardent patriot, Tonkin, Annam, and Cochinchina formed one unified country; he would rather fight than accept division. And fight he did. Following abortive talks at Fontainebleau in the summer of 1946, the imperatives of diplomacy yielded inevitably to preparations for war. In November, hostilities erupted with shattering suddenness. Following a vicious French naval bombardment of Haiphong that claimed more than 6,000 Vietnamese lives, Ho Chi Minh and his supporters fled Hanoi. The French moved quickly to establish their administrative control in the north, and the Vietminh mobilized for another guerrilla struggle. Conflict soon engulfed much of Vietnam. No one at the time could have imagined how many years would pass before peace returned to that embattled land.

U.S. analysts privately expressed dismay with France's resort to the use of force. A colonial war of reconquest represented a regrettable return to the discredited methods of the past. Even worse, the French seemed to lack the military power necessary to accomplish their goals. John Carter Vincent, director of the State Department's Office of Far Eastern Affairs, offered a pessimistic appraisal of French prospects to Under Secretary of State Dean Acheson in a memorandum of December 23. "The French themselves admit that they lack the military strength to reconquer the country," he observed. Possessing "inadequate forces, with public opinion sharply at odds, [and] with a government rendered largely ineffective through internal division," the French were embarking on a most unpromising course. "Given the present elements in the situation," Vincent predicted, "guerilla warfare may continue indefinitely."

For all of its misgivings about French policy in Indochina, the State Department carefully avoided open criticism of its European partner. On December 23, Acheson told French Ambassador Henri Bonnet of Washington's deep concern about "the unhappy situation in which the French find themselves." Calling existing conditions in Indochina "highly inflammatory," the under secretary stressed the importance of reaching a settlement as soon as possible. Only the most sensitive of diplomats could have read even an implied criticism into Acheson's mild remarks. Indeed, he made it clear that even though the United States had no wish to offer its services as a mediator, it did want the French government "to know that we are ready and willing to do anything which it might consider helpful in the circumstances."

Nineteen forty-seven brought no respite to the fighting in Indochina—and no essential change in U.S. policy toward the conflict. The Truman administration continued to view French military exertions as a misguided effort to turn back the clock. In a February 3 cable to the U.S. Embassy in Paris, Secretary of State George C. Marshall expressed "increasing concern" with the stalemate in Indochina. He deplored both the "lack [of] French understanding [for] the other side" and their "dangerously outmoded colonial outlook and methods." At the same time, Washington displayed no inclination to intervene directly in yet another nettlesome regional conflict and even less interest in exerting unwanted pressure on an invaluable ally. "We have only [the] very friendliest feelings toward France," Marshall noted, "and we are anxious in every way we can to support France in her fight to regain her economic, political and military strength and to restore herself as in fact one of [the] major powers of [the] world." The enunciation in mid-1947 of the containment strategy and the Marshall Plan just underscored France's indispensability to the broader foreign policy aims of the Truman administration. Both initiatives were conceived as part of the administration's overall strategy for containing Soviet influence and power by fostering the economic recovery and political stability of Western Europe. In the intensifying Cold War struggle between the United States and the Soviet Union, no area was more vital than Western Europe and no country more crucial than France.

In view of its transcendent importance to the United States, France's persistence in a colonial conflict that most U.S. experts believed would leave it drained and weakened posed a fundamental dilemma to Truman and his senior advisers, one that they never adequately resolved. Precisely how could the United States help France recognize that its own self-interest required a nonmilitary solution in Indochina? And what specific course of action should the United States urge France to pursue? The dilemma was posed far more easily than it could be resolved. "Frankly we have no solution of [the] problem to suggest," Marshall conceded. "It is basically [a] matter for [the] two parties to work out [for] themselves."

The communist character of the Vietnamese independence movement and the absence of viable noncommunist alternatives further clouded an already murky picture. U.S. officials were keenly aware that the movement's outstanding figure had a long record as a loyal communist. Not only had Ho Chi Minh received political training in Moscow, but he had served for decades as a dedicated Comintern agent outside Indochina. Most U.S. diplomatic and defense officials worried that if Ho prevailed over the French, it would lead to "an independent Vietnam State which would be run by orders from Moscow." A handful of junior State Department officials dissented from that analysis, advancing the argument that Ho's ardent nationalism transcended any fraternal links to the Kremlin's rulers; they speculated that he might even emerge as an Asian Tito. Such unorthodox views never permeated the upper reaches of the Truman administration, however. Most senior policymakers calculated that, regardless of Ho's undeniably powerful credentials as a Vietnamese nationalist, the establishment of a Vietminh-dominated regime would benefit the Soviet Union. Moreover, other nations would almost certainly view the emergence of such a regime as a defeat for the West.

Yet, as the State Department acknowledged in September 1948, "we are all too well aware of the unpleasant fact that Communist Ho Chi Minh is the strongest and perhaps the ablest figure in Indochina and that any suggested solution which excludes him is an expedient of uncertain outcome." Much to Washington's consternation, the French search for an alternative figure with whom to negotiate produced only the weak and vacillating former emperor Bao Dai. Charles Reed, the U.S. consul in Saigon, reminded Washington that "the reputed playboy of Hong Kong" commanded little support. Bao Dai counted among his followers only "those whose pockets will be benefited if he should return." Notwithstanding U.S. reservations and objections, the French promoted the pliant Bao Dai as their answer to Ho Chi Minh. Most U.S. analysts viewed France's "Bao Dai solution" as a transparent effort to retain colonial control; they saw it as confirmation of the bankruptcy of French policy. The restoration of Bao Dai as titular head of an "impotent puppet Gov[ernmen]t" prompted concern within the State Department that the democracies might be forced to "resort [to] monarchy as [a] weapon against Communism."

In September 1948 the State Department offered an internal assessment of U.S. policy vis-à-vis the Indochina dispute, remarkable both for its candor and for its self-critical tone. "The objectives of US policy towards Indochina have not been realized," it admitted flatly. "Three years after the termination of war a friendly ally, France, is fighting a desperate and apparently losing struggle in Indochina. The economic drain of this warfare on French recovery, while difficult to estimate, is unquestionably large. The Communist control in the nationalist movement has been increased during this period. US influence in Indochina and Asia has suffered as a result." U.S. objectives could be attained only if France satisfied "the nationalist aspirations of the peoples of Indochina." Yet a series of fundamental impediments bedeviled all U.S. efforts to nudge the French in that direction: the communist coloration of the nationalist movement; the seeming dearth of popular noncommunist alternatives; the unwillingness of the Truman administration to offer unsolicited advice to an ally on such an emotional issue; Washington's "immediate interest in maintaining in power a friendly French government, to assist in the furtherance of our aims in Europe"; and, perhaps most basic of all, the administration's "inability to suggest any practicable solution of the Indochina problem."

Over the next year and a half, the Truman administration engaged in a wide-ranging reexamination of U.S. policy toward Southeast Asia. A series of unsettling global developments, which deepened the administration's appreciation for Southeast Asia's strategic and economic salience, lent urgency to the internal debate. As a result of its reassessment, the Truman administration abandoned its quasi-neutral approach to the Indochina dispute in favor of a policy of open support for the French. On February 7, 1950, Secretary of State Acheson formally announced U.S. recognition of the Bao Dai regime, the nominally independent entity established by France the previous year, and its sister regimes in Cambodia and Laos. Emphasizing U.S. concern that neither security, democracy, nor independence could exist "in any area dominated by Soviet imperialism," he promised economic aid and military equipment for France and the Associated States of Vietnam, Cambodia, and Laos.

The decision to lend U.S. money, equipment, and prestige to France's struggle against the Vietminh cannot be understood without reference to the wider forces shaping the foreign policy of the Truman administration in late 1949 and early 1950. Those forces led both to a searching reevaluation of the world situation and to a fundamental reassessment of U.S. tactics and strategy. In the six months preceding its commitment to the French, the Truman administration came face to face with probably the gravest global crisis of the entire postwar era. In the summer of 1949 the Soviet Union exploded its first atomic device, putting an end to the United States' brief atomic monopoly and posing a host of unprecedented challenges to U.S. national security. Truman and other leading officials feared that possession of the bomb might incline the Kremlin to take greater risks in an effort to extend its global reach and power. The collapse of the U.S.-backed Kuomin-tang regime in China and the establishment of a communist government in its stead provoked additional fears in U.S. policy circles. Events in China also gave rise to a round of nasty finger-pointing at home; a swelling chorus of Republican critics blamed the president personally for China's fate. Events outside the communist bloc appeared even more ominous to America's Cold Warriors. By the end of the year it was increasingly evident that the economic recoveries of Western Europe and Japan had stalled badly. U.S. decision makers feared that continued economic stagnation in those lands would generate social unrest and political instability, conditions that might prove a fertile breeding ground for communism.

Taken together, those developments portended a potentially catastrophic threat to U.S. national security. As the communist world gained strength and self-confidence, the United States and its allies seemed poised to lose theirs. To Truman and his senior strategists, the stakes in this global struggle for power were extraordinarily high, involving nothing less than the physical safety and economic health of the United States. "The loss of Western Europe or of important parts of Asia or the Middle East," wrote Acheson, "would be a transfer of potential from West to East, which, depending on the area, might have the gravest consequences in the long run." By early 1950, top U.S. diplomatic and defense officials concentrated much of their energy on defusing this hydra-headed crisis by resuscitating the economies of Western Europe and Japan and regaining the West's political and psychological momentum in the Cold War.

U.S. policymakers recognized that a multiplicity of links tied developments in Indochina to this daunting string of global crises. In Asia, the administration's overriding objective was to orient a politically stable and economically prosperous Japan toward the West. "Were Japan added to the Communist bloc," Acheson warned, "the Soviets would acquire skilled manpower and industrial potential capable of significantly altering the balance of world power. The secretary of state and other leading officials were convinced that Japan needed the markets and raw materials of Southeast Asia in order to spark its industrial recovery. The revitalization of Asia's powerhouse economy would create the conditions necessary for stability and prosperity within both Japan and Southeast Asia. U.S. geopolitical and economic interests in this regard formed a seamless web. Truman administration planners envisioned a revitalized Japan emerging once again as the dynamic hub of commercial activity throughout Asia. Achievement of this objective would give a much-needed boost to the regional and global economic systems, thwart communism's military threat and ideological appeal, and ensure Tokyo's loyalty to the West. According to the logic subscribed to by nearly all top U.S. strategists, Japan's economic health demanded that peace and stability prevail throughout Southeast Asia. Consequently, the Vietminh insurgency in Indochina, which posed the most serious threat to regional peace and stability, had to be vanquished with the greatest possible dispatch.

For a somewhat different set of reasons, U.S. strategic and economic interests in Europe pointed in the same direction. By the end of 1949, the optimism generated by the Marshall Plan on both sides of the Atlantic had long since dissolved. The unprecedented commitment of U.S. resources to the economic rehabilitation of Western Europe had not yet brought the dramatic transformation that the Truman administration so desperately sought. Instead, the United States' most important allies found themselves facing a frightening panoply of economic and political difficulties. The increasingly costly war in Indochina stretched France's resources to the breaking point, severely hampering its contribution to the European recovery program. Although West Germany's economic performance was not quite so dismal, U.S. officials continued to fret about the fragility of Bonn's commitment to the West. Certain that the ultimate success of the Marshall Plan required the reintegration of Germany into Europe, U.S. planners agonized about how to ease France's understandable fears about a resurgent Germany.

The enormous trade and currency imbalance between the United States and its European economic partners posed an even more immediate threat to U.S. interests. This so-called dollar gap continued to grow, reaching over $3.5 billion by the middle of 1949, and posed a particularly painful problem for Great Britain. "Unless firm action is taken," British Foreign Secretary Ernest Bevin implored Acheson in July 1949, "I fear much of our work on Western Union and the Atlantic pact will be undermined and our progress in the Cold War will be halted." Experts in Washington shared Bevin's fears. Former Assistant Secretary of State William Clayton spoke for many when he conjured up the image of "the patient little man in the Kremlin [who] sits rubbing his hands and waiting for the free world to collapse in a sea of economic chaos."

By early 1950, the Truman administration's senior planners were convinced that Western Europe's troubles, like Japan's, could be aided by the stabilization and pacification of Southeast Asia. France, Great Britain, and Holland had avoided a dollar gap problem during the prewar years through the establishment of triangular trading patterns in which their colonial dependencies in Southeast Asia earned dollars through the sale of raw materials to the United States. The health of the British sterling bloc had grown unusually dependent on American purchases of rubber and tin from Malaya. The disruption of traditional trading patterns as a result of raging colonial conflicts—an insurgency erupted in Malaya in 1948, joining those that already wracked Indochina and the East Indies—thus compounded the already desperate fiscal conditions plaguing Western Europe. The Truman administration's initial commitment to Southeast Asia, then, must also be placed within this context. U.S. officials believed that financial and material assistance to the French in Indochina would abet military pacification and political stabilization in Southeast Asia. At the same time, it would permit a more active French contribution to European recovery.

Political pressures reinforced Truman's inclination to link Southeast Asian developments to larger issues. The ferocity of the partisan assaults on Truman in the wake of Chiang Kai-shek's (Jiang Jieshi's) collapse increased the political pressure on the president to show greater resolution vis-à-vis the communist challenge in Asia. Aid to the French in Indochina enabled the beleaguered Truman to answer his critics' charges by demonstrating a determination to hold the line against further communist advances *somewhere*. It is of no small significance that the initial U.S. dollar commitment of February 1950 was drawn from funds earmarked by the president's congressional critics for the containment of communism within "the general area of China."

More diffuse psychological considerations also shaped the U.S. commitment to Southeast Asia. Administration analysts were convinced that the belief in many corners of the world was that historical momentum lay with communism and not with the West. U.S. strategists feared that such a perception, whether rooted in fact or fantasy, might take on a life of its own, producing a bandwagon effect that would have an extremely pernicious impact on U.S. global interests. In the words of NSC-68, an April 1950 administration document providing a comprehensive reappraisal of U.S. national security, the Soviet Union sought "to demonstrate that force and the will to use it are on the side of the Kremlin [and] that those who lack it are decadent and doomed." Because the fighting in Indochina was widely viewed as a contest between

East and West, however erroneous that view might have been, the challenge it posed to Washington was almost as much psychological as it was geostrategic. State Department and Pentagon officials agreed that the U.S. commitment in Indochina helped meet that psychological challenge by demonstrating to adversaries and allies alike Washington's strength, resolution, and determination. The Truman administration's concern with such intangible matters as the United States' prestige, image, and reputation—in a word, its credibility—thus also entered into the complex policy calculus that made U.S. intervention in Southeast Asia seem as logical as it was unavoidable.

With the outbreak of the Korean War in June 1950, the strategic, economic, political, and psychological fears undergirding that initial commitment intensified. Convinced that Moscow and Beijing had become even more dangerously opportunistic foes, Truman and his senior advisers redoubled their efforts to contain the communist threat on every front. At the same time, they pursued with even greater vigor initiatives designed to strengthen the U.S. sphere of influence. Those vital global priorities demanded nothing less than an all-out effort to contain the communist threat to Southeast Asia, a threat manifested most immediately and most seriously by the Vietminh insurgency. Virtually all national security planners in the Truman administration agreed that Indochina was the key to Southeast Asia. If the Vietminh succeeded in routing the French, according to an analysis prepared by the Joint Strategic Survey Committee in November, "this would bring about almost immediately a dangerous condition with respect to the internal security of all of the other countries of Southeast Asia, as well as the Philippines and Indonesia, and would contribute to their probable eventual fall to communism." With uncommon unanimity, U.S. civilian and military policymakers agreed that a communist triumph in Indochina would represent a strategic nightmare for the United States. It would probably destabilize the entire region, disrupt important trading ties to Japan and Western Europe, deny to the West and make available to the communist powers important raw materials, endanger vital transportation and communication routes between the Pacific Ocean and the Middle East, and render vulnerable the United States' chain of off-shore military bases in the Pacific. "In addition, this loss would have widespread political and psychological repercussions upon other non-communist states throughout the world."

If the intersection of geostrategic, economic, political, and psychological imperatives helped crystallize U.S. policy objectives in Indochina, they did little to clarify the means necessary for the attainment of those objectives. . . .

The Truman administration, which had done so much to elevate Southeast Asia to a diplomatic prize of the greatest importance, failed to develop the means necessary to secure that prize. It never reconciled strategy with tactics. Nor did the administration ever decide on an appropriate U.S. response should the French position suddenly collapse. Truman simply passed those daunting issues, along with an increasingly perilous U.S. commitment to Southeast Asia, on to his successor. It was a legacy fully as problematic and as wracked with contradictory currents as the one he had inherited from Roosevelt.

Sergei Goncharev, John W. Lewis, and Xue Litai

THE CONFLICTED AND TROUBLED ORIGINS OF THE SINO-SOVIET ALLIANCE

The conclusion in February 1950 of a formal alliance between Stalin's Soviet Union and Mao's newly established People's Republic of China constituted one of the Cold War's seminal events. In the following selection from their collaborative book, *Uncertain Partners* (1993), Sergei Goncharev, John W. Lewis, and Xue Litai trace the origins and highlight the limitations of the Sino-Soviet alliance. They see it as a product of hard negotiating, complicated calculations, and reluctant compromises.

Excerpted from *Uncertain Partners: Stalin, Mao, and the Korean War* by Sergei Goncharev, John W. Lewis, Xue Litai, with permission of the publishers, Stanford University Press. © 1993 by the Board of Trustees of the Leland Stanford Junior Universtiy.

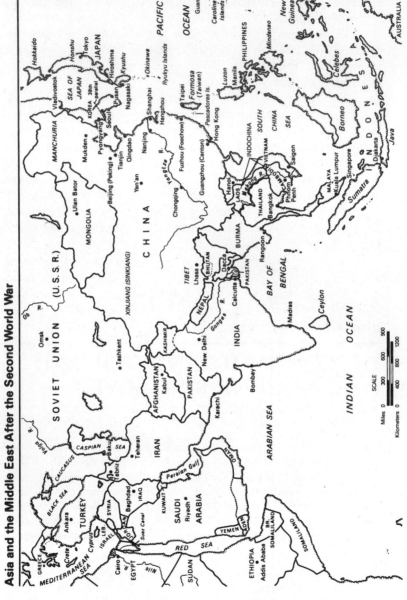

Asia and the Middle East After the Second World War

From the first, the authors suggest, the Sino-Soviet partnership was built on mutual distrust and competing national ambitions, thus containing the seeds of its ultimate destruction. Goncharev, Lewis, and Xue Litai also emphasize that security considerations largely determined both Soviet and Chinese actions, with ideology serving as a reinforcing, but secondary, factor.

Sergei Goncharev is a member of the Russian Ministry of Foreign Affairs. John W. Lewis, who teaches Chinese politics at Stanford University, has also written *Leadership in Communist China* (1963); *Communist China: Crisis and Change* (1966), and, with Xue Litai, *China Builds the Bomb* (1988) and *China's Strategic Seapower* (1994). Xue Litai is a research associate at Stanford University.

Like the imperial Russian rulers before him, Joseph Stalin after the Second World War strove to dominate the periphery of the Soviet Union and to recover lost lands and influence in Asia, as well as in Europe and the Middle East. The postwar antecedents of the Sino-Soviet alliance of 1950 can be traced as much to traditional Russian objectives as to Stalin's policies in 1945. His ambition to annihilate rivals built on an imperial urge to seize buffer zones and thereby fortify the Soviet Union's geopolitical position. Although history might have suggested to him that hatred most often greeted countries pursuing hegemony over neighboring lands, Stalin insisted on the legitimacy and the mutual benefit of that pursuit. Since the Soviet Union had emerged from the war as a world power, the argument ran, ensuring its security would inevitably yield a safer world. Now that Russia's "historic borders" had been restored, southern Sakhalin and the Kurils no longer served as a base for Japanese aggression, and a "free and independent" Poland denied Germany a future springboard for attacking the Soviet Union.

Chairman Mao Zedong, leader of the Chinese Communist Party (CCP), long shared with the Soviet Union the preference for buffer zones beyond his nation's border. This outlook was, after all, in accord with the traditional Chinese view of the just ordering of foreign relations: a stable hierarchy leading from the emperor's rule of the Middle Kingdom to suzerainty over Inner Asia and the outer barbarians, a dominion acknowledged and ritualized in the tribute paid to the emperor. Mao's nationalistic outlook coincided in many ways with Stalin's basic orientation but, of course, with reverse import for Chinese territory.

So it was that the two Communist leaders appraised the implications of external glacis for their own national security. Locked in a mental world of warring armies and aircraft, neither squarely faced the coming of the nuclear age or contemplated the possibilities for peaceful accommodation with the West. They regarded a third world war as probable, for Stalin even inevitable, and likely to replay the gruesome features of the monstrous conflict then just ending. For them, the goal went beyond mere survival; each anticipated in his own way his regime's eventual triumph over hostile forces and daunting odds. The pathway to the future would be paved with the stepping-stones of the past, and the events of 1945 constituted the gateway to the certain confrontations just ahead.

The fundamentals coupling Moscow and the revolutionary Chinese government, established in Beijing on October 1, 1949, thus did not originate at the time of Mao's trip to the Soviet Union that December. As so many scholars and officials have noted, their relationship lay rooted in actions and outcomes years before, and many of the issues the two addressed in Moscow reflected their long history of painful, wrenching encounters. Competing security interests, ideological prejudices, and personality quirks had bounded those issues and their approaches to them. . . .

The Chinese Communists' preoccupation with war and its instruments did not blot out the history of their prewar contacts with Russia or expunge the bitter personal memories among those who had been betrayed by Stalin. It did dominate Mao's policy agenda and make security questions paramount. Both the previous history and its legacies are the subject of a vast literature in the West, which explains and confirms the importance of earlier wounds to contemporary politics. Within the Communist world, however, the Chinese civil war and the emerging Cold War temporarily stifled the most painful memories. As both the Soviet Union and the warring Chinese factions contemplated their optimal tactics, virtually all matters of importance became encrusted in the security dilemma.

During the postwar revolutionary years in China, 1946–49, the supreme goal of Mao and his comrades was total victory. That goal could not be attained without adjusting the Chinese Communist Party's policies to the international situation and counterbalancing the competing interests of the major powers present in the country. The comparative weakness of the CCP at the onset of the renewed civil war and the combined might of Mao's domestic enemies and their foreign friends forced him to accept compromise and to adjust his tactics, even while not losing sight of his ultimate objectives.

Mao had to accommodate Soviet designs for China. During the first months after Japan's capitulation in the fall of 1945, he had to bow to Stalin's insistence on Chinese Communist participation in peace talks with the Nationalists. Later, while the fighting proceeded, the Chinese Communists had to maneuver between the Soviet leader's meddling and his implied threats to abandon them. They only faintly understood that his repeated attempts to mediate a truce in the civil war were intended to exclude any possibility of a Soviet clash with the United States in Asia.

Nevertheless, Mao kept his sights firmly fixed on his ultimate goal: to build a unified and powerful Chinese state that could cast off the legacy of past wrongs and, freed from inherited agonies, achieve equal status in a world system of hostile powers. The resolve to attain total victory at home not only sharpened the confrontation with the Nationalists; it also forced the United States to commit to Chiang Kai-shek, or so it seemed to Mao. The appearance of a growing bond between the Nationalists and Washington in turn strained and eventually ruptured the relations between Stalin and Chiang. Although the Truman administration's support of Chiang was often tentative and always the subject of controversy among policymakers, it did deepen the animosity of China's future Communist rulers toward the United States. These changes, coupled with the PLA's [People's Liberation Army] military successes, led inexorably to closer contacts between Moscow and Mao and helped infuse Cold War politics into Asian developments.

By mid-1948, it was becoming ever more obvious how power and future conflicts would be configured in East Asia after the defeat of the Nationalists on the Chinese mainland. Overly conditional and halfhearted as Stalin's military and economic backing may have seemed to Mao, in the Northeast it proved enough to tip the balance toward their closer ties. As the sides were being formed, no one could accurately predict the exact shape of the future political-military system in East Asia or how the interests within it would crystalize.

In 1949, the United States began detaching itself from Chiang as his government neared collapse and his fate was plain for all to see. It made a few faltering attempts to probe potential openings to Mao, but these were either misperceived or bungled. Stalin, too, began to prepare to deal officially with a Communist regime in China, but he delayed giving any unequivocal commitment that would reveal his hand or check his bargaining position. The Kremlin leader, moreover, wanted to maintain the fiction of his noninvolvement in the civil war as long as possible and to extract the last ounce of flesh from the perishing Nationalist government. Mao earnestly sought maximum Soviet support in these final days of the war but resisted making irreversible concessions. He obliquely attempted to use a conceivable rapprochement with the United States as a bargaining chip with Stalin.

By the summer of 1949, events had narrowed Mao's strategic options even further. He faced America's intransigence in reaching a modus vivendi and simultaneously feared Stalin's wrath if the Chinese Communist Party appeared eager to work with Washington. This was the moment the Chairman chose to proclaim his leaning-to-one-side policy and to prepare for the alliance with Moscow. He reluctantly concluded that only the Soviet Union could assure his fledgling government protection from external threats and sufficient help to facilitate its economic rebirth.

Mao did not intend to allow China to become Moscow's satellite. In line with his grand design, he exploited China's strategic value to Stalin in order to build toward a position of equality and to substantiate the case for revoking the worst features of the treaty between Stalin and Chiang. From Mao's point of view, his alliance with the Soviet Union would only be a first step toward establishing China's rightful position in the world.

On Stalin's side, what mattered most was the coming confrontation between communism and capitalism, the inevitable Third World War that would deliver the death blow to world imperialism. He wanted to enter this war with maximum military readiness and reliable allies. His central priority was to create the conditions under which only Moscow could determine the time and place of the showdown. As a result, during the immediate postwar years, he did everything possible to avert a direct clash with the United States over China. For him, the time and place were wrong. While paying close attention to China, Stalin regarded Europe as the main battleground.

Perpetuating the tradition of Tsarist diplomacy, Stalin held that a necessary condition for his control of the timing and outcome of a future global conflict was the creation of a security belt along his borders. The concessions that he had extracted from the Nationalists in the treaty of 1945 satisfied this prerequisite in the East, and Stalin's dilemma during the next years was how to keep these gains if the Communists won the civil war. The CCP victories, coupled with the sharpening of the Cold War in Europe, gradually caused Stalin to rethink his Asian policies. Although the Soviet leader was still loath to cancel the most offensive terms of the 1945 accords as he moved closer to Mao, he came to view China under communism as a force for countering the U.S. "encirclement" of the Soviet empire. He redefined those terms to fit his concept of partnership.

In order to turn China into a true knight in his counter-encirclement game, Stalin considered two conditions absolutely essential. First of all, he needed to control Mao's relations with the Americans; only then could Mao's power be employed against the United States and coordinated with Soviet actions. In addition, he needed to ensure that the Soviet buffer zone in China would be preserved. Despite his appraisal of China's role as a strategic asset, Stalin was well aware that this role carried hidden perils and could present future obstacles to his policies.

[Chinese Prime Minister] Liu Shaoqi's visit to Moscow in July August 1949 highlighted the myriad complexities in correlating Soviet and Chinese interests on the eve of the Communist victory in China. The visit served as a rehearsal for the coming Stalin-Mao summit and in large measure shaped its general content and direction. Moreover, it bore directly on the overall Communist approach to East Asia and the idea of dividing the world into spheres of strategic responsibility.

After the formation of NATO in April 1949, Stalin was faced with stalemate in Europe in the immediate future and possible permanent military inferiority over the long term. This new environment suddenly gave the Asian theater added significance. By stressing that the center of the world struggle against the United States had shifted to East Asia and by assigning the Chinese a major leadership role in the competition, Stalin unveiled a shift in strategy. The Chinese could open up a new anti-American front to the East, where the United States and its allies were dramatically retreating and where they could not fight, let alone win, without weakening their stronghold in Europe. China offered the Soviet leader a way to recapture the strategic initiative.

Stalin understood that a Chinese endorsement of Moscow's strategic outlook would require his acknowledgment of the global significance of Mao and his revolution. The Soviet leader would have to accept the need for mutual concessions in dealing with the Chinese and would be forced to provide them extensive economic and military assistance. He found a way to make these adjustments in a manner that would not sacrifice his most cherished objectives, or so he appears to have believed. During his talks with Liu Shaoqi, he unambiguously implied that China's actions in East Asia must be in harmony with Soviet interests (through the creation of a union of Asian Communist parties with Soviet participation), and that Mao would have to abandon any thought of normalizing his relations with Washington. Stalin stated quite bluntly that he would never risk a conflict with the United States over Taiwan and pressed the Chinese to put off their planned "liberation" of the island.

Stalin's views on Taiwan during the summer of 1949 can be traced to his anxieties about nuclear war. The talks with Liu Shaoqi were conducted on the eve of the first Soviet atomic blast. Though politically and psychologically the test was an important event for Moscow, enabling it to unleash a propaganda campaign about "the end of the American atomic monopoly," the possession of the bomb raised serious issues for Soviet defense. Stalin had to keep in mind the possibility of an American preemptive strike before the Soviet Union acquired the means to retaliate against the U.S. homeland. Although the Soviet leader did not consider the U.S. nuclear edge fatal for his plans, he had to be especially cautious until he could complete his preparations for the decisive engagement some decades down the road.

The Chinese leaders undoubtedly relished Stalin's high appraisal of their revolution. They were pleased that the Soviet dictator had at last admitted his many mistakes in dealing with them. Having long striven to become the Soviet Union's strategic partner and to have a sphere of responsibility of their own, they welcomed Stalin's granting them their dream and his recognition that East Asia was no less critical for Soviet security than Europe was. The Kremlin pledge to provide military and economic support for the conquest of Xinjiang demonstrated that Sino-Soviet interests were converging. The time had come to negotiate the terms of the alliance.

Stalin's actions convinced the Chinese that to a limited extent they could resist and channel Moscow's demands. Yet they would have to temporarily accept the Soviet presence and influence and to recognize the fact that the elimination of Soviet special rights in China would take time and great political finesse. They were not in danger of becoming the Kremlin's puppet, but neither were they truly independent. Because of that and adhering to Stalin's advice, they quickly formulated a revolutionary line for Asia in which they would play a leading role. At the same time, they ignored Stalin's other recommendations on establishing a union of Asian Communist parties with Soviet participation and postponing the invasion of Taiwan.

They would use Stalin as much as he used them. The Chinese high command had immense respect for the Soviet experience but no more than it had for its own revolutionary history. Mao never hesitated to underscore the uniqueness of his nation and its needs or to point out the deficiencies of the Soviet blueprint for East Asia as a whole.

The cables and other exchanges between the Chinese and Soviet leaders throughout 1949 alerted both to the complexities and potential difficulties in forming a legal partnership. These impediments governed the subject matter and the limits for their talks in December and January and shaped alternative negotiating strategies. Beyond this, both sides entered the talks much clearer about their bottom-line positions and how hard they would fight for them. Stalin in particular had done his best to demonstrate to the Chinese the value of the cards that he was holding.

As a result, Soviet influence in Xinjiang and in the Northeast weighed on Mao's mind. Stalin had demonstrated his willingness to cooperate with the Chinese Communists in strengthening their control in these crucial territories, but he could easily reverse his policies should Mao prove unwilling to comply with his basic demands. Each was the uncertain partner of the other.

The PLA's failure at Quemoy in late October 1949 came at a particularly bad moment for the Chinese, engaged as they were in the planning for the summit. The debacle served as a powerful proof of the PRC's need for Soviet military and economic assistance. Aid did begin to pour into China, but it provided Moscow greater leverage just as the talks began. Moscow could reduce or even withdraw that aid at any point, a sword that Beijing knew hung over its head.

Moreover, Stalin was ready to extend what we would now call assured deterrence to China only in the framework of his global strategy. He added the condition that the Chinese not draw him into any conflicts with the United States, but he promoted those confrontations that would divide Washington from Beijing. The Soviet leader was worried by reports from his representatives in Beijing that the PRC leaders were attempting to improve relations with the West, were bent on achieving a hegemonic role in East Asia, and were determined to proceed with the "liberation" of Taiwan. If the Chinese were unwilling to act within the boundaries set by Moscow on any of these key strategic policies, Soviet security guarantees were sure to be drastically compromised.

Thus on the very eve of the Moscow summit between Stalin and Mao, cooperative interests became mixed with basic differences in the perceived need for and approaches to common action. Moreover, when the two leaders met in December, they had sharply contrasting mind-sets. Stalin, the leader of an emerging superpower, was trying to preserve what he had already won through conquest and to use China for making further advances. China, by contrast, had yet to be accepted as a legitimate state, let alone a leading player in world politics. For Beijing, the relationship with Moscow involved a paradox: the need to accept inequality in order to achieve equality. Only clever tactics on Mao's part could prevent a temporary contradiction from becoming permanent subservience.

In our discussion of the negotiations between Stalin and Mao, we discerned two distinct stages. During the first of them, lasting from Mao's arrival in the Soviet capital on December 16, 1949, until January 2–3, 1950, the two leaders strove unsuccessfully to define and agree on the basic principles of their relations. Stalin did his best to preserve key aspects of the treaty of 1945 in order to safeguard the Soviet Union's security belt, and Mao spared no effort in restricting them in order to restore China's self-esteem and sovereignty.

During this phase of the talks, Stalin and Mao waged a war of nerves. It was a contest that exposed the unparalleled ruthlessness and arrogance of both, especially so of Stalin. The senior Russian translator recalls, "The very room where the talks were held was like a stage where a demonic show was being acted out. When Stalin walked in, everyone seemed to stop breathing, to freeze. He brought danger. An atmosphere of fear arose." Mao struck the translator as a "loyal follower," whose words delivered in coarse Hunan dialect seemed "somehow crumbly." Time and again, high politics gave way to a test of wills between two pugnacious egos.

With basic interests at stake, they played out a classic zero-sum game, in which common interests and diplomatic niceties fell by the wayside. Neither leader was used to giving way, and both bargained as if there could be no accord at all. Within this surrealistic drama, however, the two central actors had no doubt about the absolute requirement for a treaty. Even as they tested each other's will, they knew that they could not cast the game board aside. The breakthrough in the early days of January was as foreordained as it was essential.

That breakthrough ushered in the next stage of the negotiations. Stalin was profoundly disturbed by Britain's recognition of China and considered it the forerunner of a Sino-American normalization that would ruin all his strategic calculations. Truman and Acheson's announced hands-off policy toward Taiwan provided additional grounds for Stalin's suspicions. Suddenly the tables were turned. The Americans' seeming willingness to tolerate a PLA seizure of the island might well lay the basis for a Beijing-Washington rapprochement. Since the Soviet dictator could not openly oppose the invasion of Taiwan, he had only one recourse: to take stronger measures to separate China from the West. At this point, Mao did not have to do anything more than stand on Stalin's side of the dividing line.

The Chinese Chairman was of two minds. He could be gratified by the fact that, in exchange for submitting to Stalin's demands, he had extracted important pledges from the Kremlin to assist China in its military buildup for the Taiwan invasion. On the other hand, all the subsequent agreements—secret and public, formal and informal—resulted from compromises from which Stalin emerged the clear winner.

There were many examples of this imbalance. Stalin did accept the withdrawal of Soviet forces from the Northeast sooner than stipulated in the 1945 treaty, but the price was the secret Additional Agreement barring "the citizens of third countries" from living or working in Manchuria and Xinjiang and the accord on the movement of Soviet troops via the Chinese Changchun Railroad. The two protocols consolidated Moscow's security zone in China's far west and Northeast. Stalin further manipulated Mao into exerting pressure on the Japanese Communist Party and taking a more hostile stand toward the West, though, at Mao's insistence, he recognized the revolutionary regime of Ho Chi Minh. Most significantly, Stalin promised to defend China against aggression by the United States "by all means" at his disposal but hedged his bets by conditioning the Soviet obligation on the declaration of "a state of war."

Both leaders, of course, had cause for satisfaction as a result of their meeting. The alliance was a reality. Nonetheless, each left the talks more suspicious and more uncertain than when they began. The treaty and accompanying agreements, as we remarked, had many more pluses for Stalin than for Mao, and some of the provisions reminded the Chinese of the unequal treaties of the past. The Additional Agreement was the most vivid manifestation of this fact, and Mao returned to Beijing dedicated to overturning it at the earliest possible moment. He was more determined than ever to revitalize China and restore its sovereignty.

Stalin's judgments on the talks ran in the opposite direction to Mao's. He appears to have understood quite clearly the Chinese abhorrence of the Additional Agreement. The Soviet leader realized that Mao would demand more equality in the relationship as soon as he could overcome China's most acute domestic problems and would try to establish relations with the West from a position of strength. A successful takeover of Taiwan could remove the most serious obstacle in the relations between Beijing and Washington and thus would create the circumstances for the acceleration of this process. Thus, Stalin had to worry that his military aid for the assault against the island would in fact bolster China's power and weaken its hostility toward the United States. Should this train of events come to pass, Mao Zedong would undoubtedly call for a renegotiation of the bilateral arrangements of February 1950.

How fundamental these concerns would be only time would tell. Moreover, the concerns were lessened by the understandings reached at the summit on the outlines of the global power struggle. The talks had touched on the problems of war and peace and elaborated a rationale for a serious reevaluation of the confrontation with the West. After the conclusion of the treaty, the Soviet and Chinese leadership and press consciously filled in the general outlines and reiterated common themes derived from the summit. They jointly boasted about the basic shift in the "correlation of forces" in favor of socialism. The alliance, they emphasized, had put the United States on the defensive and reduced its ability to check the development of revolutions in Asia. The "forces of socialism" had now gone on the march worldwide.

After late 1949, Stalin became more assertive in his strategic planning. The period from the inauguration of NATO to the completion of the West's buildup in Europe provided a window of time to fortify his country and to get ready to fight. Truman's rush to reverse the course of reform and democratization in Japan and his announcement in January 1950 of his decision to build the H-bomb added to the urgency of Moscow's planning.

We now know that this was the period in which the Soviet Union halted its military cutbacks and initiated a massive arms buildup. Circumstantial evidence suggests that Stalin's agreements with Mao on the assignment of spheres of responsibility gave the Soviet leader new confidence in his ability to thwart U.S. power. Stalin had begun to believe that the Third World War would erupt not in 20 or 30 years but by the middle of the 1950s. He would have to be ready either to break an early American assault or to wage a preemptive blitzkrieg before the Americans were ready.

Mao could help. His task would be to promote revolutionary struggle in Vietnam and Southeast Asia, threaten to attack Taiwan, and assist [North Korean leader] Kim Il Sung in his takeover of South Korea. Korea was important for Stalin not only because it was part of the security belt on his eastern flank but also because it provided him with a springboard for an invasion of Japan in case of war. A more aggressive China would cause the United States to split its forces and to face combat on two global fronts.

The toughening of the Soviet-Chinese partnership was closely watched by Washington. From February to March 1950, the debates in the Truman administration explored the grounds for reevaluating its cautious policy toward Taiwan and Korea and for a more resolute global military posture to counter the Communist offensive. NSC 68 of April 14, 1950, was a landmark document in this process and helped draw East Asia into the Cold War.

What part the Stalin-Mao talks played in the outbreak of the Korean War a half year later is hard to pin down, for whether by design or not, the two leaders did not go into the issue of Kim Il Sung's charted invasion of the South. Although both Stalin and Mao endorsed Kim's concept of a "revolutionary war against the lackeys of American imperialism," they had not yet refined their stand on how, beyond military and economic aid, they would support it. We have described the complicated intercourse among the three leaders that led to the final decision to attack and the Soviet part in devising the plan of operations.

On the other hand, the facts now available do clearly call into question the arguments that Kim was driven to war by the South's recurring provocations or that his decision was taken solely on his own initiative. Kim began lobbying for a Soviet-backed invasion of the South as early as March 1949. He proposed it, fought for it, and with a Soviet army battle plan to guide him, executed it. The invasion of June 25, 1950, was pre-planned, blessed, and directly assisted by Stalin and his generals, and reluctantly backed by Mao at Stalin's insistence. Mao knew that preparations for the invasion were under way and, in general, upheld the idea of Korean unification under Kim's rule. But he also expressed reservations about Kim's assumptions and was deliberately kept in the dark on the details of the North's preparations, including the timing of the attack. He acted to reduce his armies and proceed with the invasion of Taiwan even after Kim launched the attack, and the PLA command could only watch in dismay and obey.

In our view, the decision to go to war cannot be laid alone to Stalin's pressure, or to Kim's adventurism, or to a Soviet–North Korean (let alone Sino–North Korean) conspiracy. In fact, the decision came in bits and pieces and was never coordinated or even thoroughly scrutinized by the three states. It was reckless war-making of the worst kind. Each of three Communist leaders was operating on premises that were largely concealed and facts that were fabricated or at best half true. The process was partially driven by Soviet and Chinese policies and perceptions that had nothing to do with Korean reunification as such. The alliance had not provided any mechanisms for joint analysis and joint decision-making, and in any case had not included North Korea.

Kim Il Sung had decided on the need for an invasion by conventional forces because his guerrilla tactics, approved by Stalin in March 1949, had miscarried. Kim presented his case for the invasion on the grounds that these tactics would somehow succeed in the wake of a full-scale attack, but he never fully apprised Stalin of the reasons behind the earlier failures. To win Stalin's backing, he relied on his position of faithful supporter and the basic Soviet interest in a bolder Asian challenge to the West. During his secret visit to Moscow, Kim Il Sung did his best to persuade Stalin that a popular uprising in the South would be triggered by the invasion, that victory would come quickly, and that the Americans would remain on the sidelines until it was too late.

Stalin had no incentive to question Kim's arguments, but he gave the go-ahead on the basis of Soviet interests and on the condition that Mao agree. We have examined his general beliefs that Kim's victory would enlarge the Soviet security zone, provide a vital springboard against Japan, and force a diversion of U.S. forces from Europe to Asia. These were all positive factors for the Soviet dictator. On the other hand, Stalin was willing to support Kim only if the possibility of a Soviet-American clash in Korea would be excluded. He determined that the way to do this was to implicate Mao in the decision and thereby make him bear the full burden for ensuring Kim's survival if the Americans intervened. A Sino-American war, should it erupt in Korea, would have the added benefit of widening the break between Beijing and the West.

Mao could not deny his Korean comrades the very opportunity for unifying their country that the Chinese had demanded for themselves. At the same time, he explicitly worried that Kim's action would provoke a U.S. response, threaten China's security, and preclude the seizure of Taiwan. But he had to minimize the likelihood of American intervention in the Korean conflict when Stalin asked about this possibility in January. He could not claim the opposite for Korea without calling his own assurances into question. Mao was being hoisted by his own petard. All he could do was to accelerate the preparations for the Taiwan operation and hope that the battle for Korea would not spoil his own plans.

In May 1950, Stalin finally gave Kim the signal to proceed. We argue that this decision must be understood against the background of general Soviet calculations about American policy. Although the United States was still avowedly committed to Truman's hands-off approach, signs of a hardening of the U.S. stance toward Asia had surfaced and suggested to Stalin that Washington might reverse course. Appreciating that there would be a window of opportunity as the United States translated its new policy into a substantial military buildup on the ground, Stalin presumably judged that for Kim it was now or never. A more belligerent American attitude toward Asian communism enlarged the chances of U.S. interference in Korea after Kim's assault, to be sure. But Stalin was satisfied that he could maintain the appearance of neutrality if Mao carried the burden of direct military involvement.

Given the sloppy decision-making, misperceptions, and perverted objectives, it is small wonder that the invasion was a disaster. The outbreak of the war was a fatal blow to Mao's plans for Taiwan. Although he proclaimed that Truman had betrayed his word to keep U.S. hands off, the Chinese leader simply misjudged the nature of American decision-making and the mood in Washington. When he learned that the American Seventh Fleet had moved into the Taiwan Strait, Mao pronounced the action tantamount to a declaration of war. He knew, nonetheless, that his government could not declare war without antagonizing Stalin and jeopardizing its alliance with the Soviet Union.

After the war began, Mao postponed his plans for the Taiwan invasion and turned his attention to the defense of the Northeast and possible intervention in Korea. Stalin, on the other hand, took steps to exclude Soviet participation in the war. By preventing the Soviet representative from returning to the Security Council meeting that put the Korean "police action" under UN command, he effectively precluded any formal declaration of war by either the Chinese or the American side and so avoided activating the Sino-Soviet treaty.

The period from the [American] landing at Inchon on September 15 to mid-October, when the first [Chinese] "volunteer" detachments crossed the Yalu, provides an unparalleled opportunity to assess Chinese decision-making in action. Immediately after Inchon, Stalin urged Mao to come to Kim's rescue, promising air cover for the Chinese troops and direct Soviet involvement in case the Chinese were defeated. Mao understood quite well that the danger to China's security had now grown immensely, and he accelerated the deployment of his best armies along the Yalu frontier.

At the same time, both Mao and his comrades were uneasy about Stalin's promise to dispatch Soviet troops in the event of a Chinese defeat. Moreover, many Politburo and military leaders resisted going to war before their own rule had been consolidated. The Chinese economy lay in shambles, and the task of national reunification was far from complete. Mao had to deal with dissent at home, as well as the high probability of war with the United States. As his military commanders hastily set about upgrading the Northeast Frontier Force, his chief foreign policy lieutenant, Zhou Enlai, twice warned the Americans not to cross the 38th parallel and strike north.

By October 8, when the Chinese warnings were ignored and American units had punched across the parallel, the Chairman, not without hesitation and recurrent debate with his colleagues, made up his mind to send in the Chinese People's Volunteers. The threshold between war and peace had been crossed. The motives behind the decision were mixed: the menace that would result from an American presence on the border with the Northeast, the rising unrest throughout the country as the enemy advanced toward the Yalu, and Mao's obviously increasing dependence on an ally that was bent on China's entering the war. In the mountains of Korea, the numerical superiority of the Chinese People's Volunteers could offset American firepower, particularly if reinforced by Soviet arms, and it was Mao's conclusion that American nuclear weapons would not be used there. Korea was the place to take a stand.

When Stalin reneged on his promise to provide air cover for their forces, the Chinese momentarily flinched. The price of war had suddenly gone up. The Soviet dictator, relying on reports of his representatives in Beijing, as well as on his own perception of Mao's intentions, saw the Chinese delay in answering his call for military action as a deliberate ploy to force his hand on Soviet assistance and participation. Stalin held firm, and thereby demonstrated his determination not to face the United States in Korea. The Pyongyang regime could be destroyed, but he would not go to war to rescue it.

For Mao, the die had been cast. He had to proceed even without Soviet air cover in order to save, not North Korea, but

China. That bold decision in turn persuaded Stalin to modify his position somewhat and to provide the PLA Soviet weapons and equipment. On the night of October 18–19, after Zhou had briefed the Politburo on the results of his talks in Moscow, the final orders were issued to cross the Yalu. Only after Stalin was certain that the Chinese were fully engaged in the fighting did he secretly introduce fighter planes and send his troops to China. For a time, the uncertainty of the alliance evaporated.

Mao knew that the decision to go to war immeasurably strengthened Stalin's trust in him and dispelled his suspicions. After the Chinese armies struck, Stalin became much more willing to provide assistance to China and to end the most notorious manifestations of inequality in his relations with it. This willingness and, after Stalin's death in 1953, Khrushchev's downgrading of buffer zones and satellite regimes created the conditions for the "golden age" in Sino-Soviet relations that lasted until about 1958.

A close examination of Sino-Soviet relations from September 1945 through October 1950 strips away much of the simplicity that one sometimes finds in analyses of these relations. We have found no evidence that suggests the absolute domination of Stalin or the unlimited servility of Mao Zedong. All of the outcomes of their ties resulted from complicated calculations and compromises, with bilateral considerations often held hostage to domestic or unilaterally defined global requirements.

Although Stalin usually (but not always) got more from the relationship than Mao did, it was at the cost of certain concessions that worked fundamentally to China's benefit over the next decade. Stalin realized that if the Chinese could extract commitments when they were weak and vulnerable, they could become very tough partners indeed as their power grew.

Although we have focused on the history of bilateral Sino-Soviet relations, the United States was always an invisible third partner. Its "presence" at the negotiating table during the talks between Stalin and Mao added to the complexity and uncertainties of the alliance. In fact, both leaders made repeated estimates of how Washington might respond to their actions and statements, and the American factor was a constant in alliance decision-making. The "great strategic triangle" shaped the conduct of Soviet-Chinese relations perhaps no less (but less visibly) in the 1950s than it did in the 1970s. The triangular relationship, in different forms, repeatedly infiltrated the political agendas in Moscow and Beijing over the coming decades.

There is no evidence that in the period of our study the Chinese and Soviets ever attempted to analyze in any serious detail how each perceived the American threat or proposed to cope with it. Indeed, with so many aspects of the alliance unspoken and ambiguous, it is not difficult to see why the unresolved misinterpretations and fundamental disagreements would later lead to a deepening rift.

Their superficial discursion into topics touching the United States should have alerted them to the risks of silence. Even tangential issues that related to perceptions of U.S. power or minor tactics toward it fueled miniconfrontations between Stalin and Mao, and a full-blown quest for common approaches to that power might have brought the talks to a halt. Without raising and addressing major unanswered questions about policies toward the United States, the two Communist leaders could never come to a meaningful accord about the nature of the alliance itself.

The two allies did not discuss whether their relationship could or should be one of political equality. Given the power imbalance favoring the Soviet Union, perhaps China should have accepted a political (and ideological) status consistent with its lesser military and economic power. It did not. Although the Kremlin gave lip service to the need for equality, its attitude throughout the early period of cooperation was that Beijing's real political status was an inferior one. Moscow never accepted the idea that Mao's ideological pretensions were anything more than that.

We see here a lack of any clear, mutually understood, and accepted "basic principles of relations" that could guide cooperation and resolve disputes. Among the questions that should have been posed by the two parties, but were not, several come immediately to mind: What were the political (as opposed to technical) issues that could be legitimately raised and genuinely aired? How should policy differences and real grievances be handled procedurally? What were the external threats facing the alliance itself (as opposed to either nation) and how should they be met? Under what conditions would one side go to war (rather than not go to war) on behalf of the other, and how would the terms of assistance be worked out? What weight should be given to reciprocity, and how would the value of each quid pro quo be determined? Who had the final say? If neither (because of their equality), how would a meeting of minds be reached? Without explicit answers to these questions, the only recourse in a crisis would be the adoption of ad hoc and probably self-serving principles and procedures that each side would try to impose on the other.

Neither leader appears to have fully understood or appreciated the inherent hazards and folly of leaving so much unexplored. In their pursuit of untarnished unity, they perpetuated their differences on security—which were to become so central to the eventual rupturing of the alliance—as well as on other critical issues of perceived common interest.

Built on distrust and forced concessions, the alliance contained the seeds of its own destruction. Its creation had an important impact on the West, but herein lay the fundamental contradiction. The terms of the partnership were inequitable, but in operation the alliance, when facing West, required Moscow to treat China as an equal and to assist its quest for global standing. Stalin needed a dependent ally but promised to help create a powerful and independent one. For Stalin, a more robust China would erase the line between itself and the West and the buffer zone created by the Additional Agreement. Building a stronger China, one objective of the alliance, would also lessen the external security threats that justified the treaty's very existence. From opposing perspectives, neither Stalin nor Mao expected—or in Mao's case wanted—the partnership to last.

In analyzing the foreign policies of Stalin and Mao, we have raised indirectly another question that should now be answered. What mattered most to them when they formulated their grand strategies and tactics, ideology or realpolitik? We shall long debate the possible approaches to this question, and it seems clear that an unqualified choice of one or the other would be wrong. On balance, a striking feature of Mao and Stalin *in camera* is that neither was motivated by the ideology that so characterized their public declarations of the period.

Their private communications mostly carried a message of naked military-political interests and a priority for national security. The concept of security, of course, combines and oversimplifies a host of complex and interrelated realities. National culture, historical experience, leadership ambition and style, military potential and attitudes toward power, and recent memories of war and upheaval all can and did enter into the concept's definition in both nations. In practice, the two leaders typically avoided making precise distinctions when reaching and promulgating their most important decisions and often, for political purposes, couched their security policies in deceptive language. More commonly in Communist societies than others, perhaps, ideology provides the framework for projecting a broad internationalist vision based on pure nationalism and naked power.

Ideology, we find, played a secondary role, despite the apparent similarities between their socioeconomic systems, bureaucratic doctrines, Kafkaesque institutions, and avowed adherence to Marxism-Leninism. On the surface, ideology served as an important link during the creation of the alliance and on some later occasions, but again the documents deflate ideology's significance. This is not to discount the influence of ideology on the foreign policies of the two nations altogether but simply to suggest that it carried far less weight than other facets of the essential dynamics shaping their foreign policy decisions.

True enough, both Mao and Stalin gave ideology pride of place in their foreign policy statements and public pronouncements on domestic questions. It is also true that Marxist-Leninist quotations provided a reliable conceptual framework for discussions within their inner circles. Nevertheless, the two leaders' actions were almost always guided by far more mundane considerations. Ideological declarations could serve power politics but not determine it. Motives found deeply rooted in national traditions far outweighed Marxism-Leninism in practice.

Ideology was extremely important for them on the most general level, to be sure, especially in the selection and treatment of enemies. In their thinking, imperialism was essentially evil, communism good; the final aim of all their political activities was the annihilation of the "imperialist" states. Ideology also had a clear impact on another sphere of foreign policy: the analysis of the domestic situations in other countries, where class concepts often proved crucial. When it came to their face-to-face deliberations on particular external policy issues, however, the ultimate concern on both sides was not class struggle, but state interests (though the arguments were sometimes couched in revolutionary terms). In the final analysis, realpolitik governed their thinking and strained their relations. Time and again, issues of security—general assessments of the American threat, peaceful coexistence, nuclear war, national liberation struggles, and, above all, military cooperation—were the triggers that brought Stalin and Mao into verbal combat and, in the early years, temporary agreement. They were bound to come to grief on these issues in the end, given the profound differences in their strategic outlook and perceptions of their own vital security interests. . . .

That the fate of a historic alliance should turn so much on personality and outdated perceptions is one of the great ironies of the Cold War and of communism in practice. Beyond the theories of politics and conflict, we discover emperors disrobed and men both heroic and petty. Their uncertain alliance failed and caused so much suffering not because of its systemic flaws—and there were many—but because of their inability to curb their nationalistic aims and to turn with the same passion to their nations' needs.

Within a decade, the alliance fashioned and tested in 1950 had collapsed. Its heritage of power corrupted survived.

SUGGESTIONS FOR FURTHER READING

For an extensive annotated bibliography, including articles and books on all aspects of Soviet-American relations, see Richard Dean Burns, ed., *Guide to American Foreign Relations since 1700* (1983). Handy references, with essays on major events, concepts, and leaders, are Richard S. Kirkendall, ed., *The Harry S. Truman Encyclopedia* (1989) and Bruce Jentleson and Thomas G. Paterson, eds., *Encyclopedia of U.S. Foreign Relations* (1997). For a thorough review of the secondary literature, see Michael J. Hogan, ed., *America in the World: The Historiography of American Foreign Relations Since 1941* (1995).

General works on the Soviet-American relationship include John Lewis Gaddis, *Russia, the Soviet Union, and the United States* (1990) and N. V. Sivachev and N. N. Yakovlev, *Russia and the United States* (1979), a pre-*glasnost* Soviet account. For America's response to the Bolshevik Revolution, including military intervention, see Betty Miller Unterberger, *The United States, Revolutionary Russia, and the Rise of Czechoslovakia* (1989); Lloyd C. Gardner, *Safe for Democracy* (1984); N. Gordon Levin, *Woodrow Wilson and World Politics* (1968); George F. Kennan, *Russia Leaves the War* (1956) and *The Decision to Intervene* (1958); David Foglesong, *America's Secret War Against Bolshevism* (1996); and Georg Schild, *Between Ideology and Realpolitik: Woodrow Wilson and the Russian Revolution* (1995). Books on early relations include Joan Hoff Wilson, *Ideology and Foreign Policy: U.S. Relations with the Soviet Union, 1918–1933* (1974); Peter Filene, *Americans and the Soviet Experiment, 1917–1933* (1967); George F. Kennan, *Russia and the West under Lenin and Stalin* (1969); David W. McFadden, *Alternative Paths: Soviet-American Relations, 1917–1920* (1993); and B. Ponomaryov et. al., eds., *History of Soviet Foreign Policy, 1917–1945* (1974). An important topic is discussed in Anthony Sutton, *Western Technology and Soviet Economic Development, 1917–1930* (1977).

For the 1933 United States decision to open diplomatic relations, see Edward Bennett, *Recognition of Russia* (1970), and

Donald G. Bishop, *The Roosevelt-Litvinov Agreements* (1965). The 1930s are treated in Edward Bennett, *Franklin D. Roosevelt and the Search for Security* (1985); Beatrice Farnsworth, *William C. Bullitt and the Soviet Union* (1967); Thomas R. Maddux, *Years of Estrangement* (1980); and Keith D. Eagles, *Ambassador Joseph E. Davies and American-Soviet Relations, 1937–1941* (1985).

For the Second World War, see Herbert Feis, *Churchill, Roosevelt, and Stalin* (1957) and *Between War and Peace: The Potsdam Conference* (1960); James MacGregor Burns, *Roosevelt: The Soldier of Freedom* (1970); Gabriel Kolko, *The Politics of War* (1968); Lloyd C. Gardner, *Spheres of Influence* (1993); Gary Hess, *The United States at War, 1941–1945* (1986); William H. McNeill, *America, Britain, and Russia* (1953); Steven M. Miner, *Between Churchill and Stalin* (1988); Gaddis Smith, *American Diplomacy During the Second World War* (1985); Robert Dallek, *Franklin D. Roosevelt and American Foreign Policy, 1933–1945* (1979); Robert A. Divine, *Roosevelt and World War II* (1969); Ralph B. Levering, *American Opinion and the Russian Alliance* (1976); George C. Herring, *Aid to Russia, 1941–1945* (1973); Vojtech Mastny, *Russia's Road to the Cold War* (1979); and Mark A. Stoler, *The Politics of the Second Front* (1977). A key wartime conference that produced Cold War consequences is the subject of Diane Clemens, *Yalta* (1970), a sympathetic account, whereas Russell D. Buhite, in *Decision at Yalta* (1986), is critical of Roosevelt's diplomacy.

For studies of the Cold War that include the origins period, see Stephen Ambrose and Douglas Brinkley, *Rise to Globalism* (1998); S. J. Ball, *The Cold War* (1998); H. W. Brands, *The Devil We Knew* (1993); Warren I. Cohen, *America in the Age of Soviet Power* (1993); Gordon A. Craig and Francis L. Loewenheim, *The Diplomats* (1994); Richard Crockatt, *The Fifty Year War* (1994); Robert H. Johnson, *Improbable Dangers: Conception of Threat in the Cold War and After* (1994); Walter LaFeber, *America, Russia, and the Cold War* (1993); Deborah Larson, *Anatomy of Mistrust* (1997); Ralph Levering, *The Cold War* (1994); Ronald E. Powaski, *The Cold War* (1998); and Martin Walker, *The Cold War* (1994).

General analyses of the origins of the Cold War that for the most part reflect the traditionalist perspective include John Lewis Gaddis, *The United States and the Origins of the Cold War, 1941–1947* (1972), *The Long Peace* (1987), *Strategies of Containment*

(1982), and *We Now Know* (1997); Herbert Feis, *From Trust to Terror* (1970); Paul Y. Hammond, *Cold War and Detente* (1975); Vojtech Mastny, *The Cold War and Soviet Insecurity* (1996); Walt Rostow, *The Diffusion of Power* (1971); John Spanier, *American Foreign Policy Since World War II* (1988); William Taubman, *Stalin's American Policy* (1982); Hugh Thomas, *Armed Truce* (1987); Kenneth W. Thompson, *Cold War Theories* (1981); Adam Ulam, *The Rivals* (1971) and *Expansion and Coexistence: The History of Soviet Foreign Policy, 1917–1973* (1974); and Randall B. Woods and Howard Jones, *Dawning of the Cold War* (1991).

For works largely revisionist in perspective, see Thomas G. Paterson, *On Every Front: The Making and Unmaking of the Cold War* (1992), *Meeting the Communist Threat* (1988), and *Soviet-American Confrontation* (1973); Richard J. Barnet, *The Giants* (1977); Barton J. Bernstein, ed., *Politics and Policies of the Truman Administration* (1970); Lloyd C. Gardner, *Architects of Illusion* (1970); Gabriel Kolko and Joyce Kolko, *The Limits of Power* (1972); Athan Theoharis, *The Yalta Myths* (1970); Thomas J. McCormick, *America's Half-Century* (1989); Daniel Yergin, *Shattered Peace* (1977); and Melvyn P. Leffler, *A Preponderance of Power* (1992) and *The Specter of Communism* (1994).

Other works that discuss early Cold War questions, with a variety of perspectives, are James L. Gormly, *The Collapse of the Grand Alliance, 1945–1948* (1987); Linda Killen, *The Soviet Union and the United States* (1989); Hugh DeSantis, *The Diplomacy of Silence* (1980); Mark R. Elliot, *Pawns of Yalta: Soviet Refugees and America's Role in Their Repatriation* (1982); Charles Gati, ed., *Caging the Bear: Containment and the Cold War* (1974); Michael Sherry, *Preparing for the Next War* (1977); Deborah Larson, *The Origins of Containment: A Psychological Explanation* (1985); Philip J. Funigello, *American-Soviet Trade in the Cold War* (1988); Robert L. Messer, *The End of an Alliance* (1982); Frank Ninkovich, *The Diplomacy of Ideas* (1981); William O. McCagg, *Stalin Embattled, 1943–1948* (1978); Ronald Radosh, *American Labor and U.S. Foreign Policy* (1969); David Reynolds, ed., *The Origins of the Cold War in Europe* (1994); Göran Rystad, *Prisoners of the Past: The Munich Syndrome and Makers of American Foreign Policy in the Cold War Era* (1982); Hannes Adomeit, *Soviet Risk-Taking and Crisis Behavior* (1982); Marshall D. Shulman, *Stalin's Foreign*

Policy Reappraised (1963); Vladislav Zubok and Constantine Pleshakov, *Inside the Kremlin's Cold War* (1996); Wesley T. Wooley, *Alternatives to Anarchy: American Supranationalism Since World War II* (1988); and Patricia Dawson Ward, *The Threat of Peace* (1979).

Analyses of scholars' interpretive differences, especially the traditionalist-revisionist debate, can be found in Robert W. Tucker, *The Radical Left and American Foreign Policy* (1971); Richard Kirkendall, ed., *The Truman Period as a Research Field* (1974); Warren F. Kimball, "The Cold War Warmed Over," *American Historical Review*, LXXIX (October 1974), 1119–1136; J. Samuel Walker, "Historians and Cold War Origins," in Gerald K. Haines and J. Samuel Walker, eds., *American Foreign Relations: A Historiographical Review* (1981); Edward Crapol, "Some Reflections on the Historiography of the Cold War," *The History Teacher*, XX (1986/87), 251–262; William Welch, *American Images of Soviet Foreign Policy* (1970); Peter Novick, *That Noble Dream: The "Objectivity Question" and the American Historical Profession* (1988); John Lewis Gaddis, "The Emerging Post-Revisionist Synthesis on the Origins of the Cold War," *Diplomatic History*, VII (Summer 1983), 171–190; Richard A. Melanson, *Writing History and Making Policy* (1983); and Geir Lundestad, "Moralism, Presentism, Exceptionalism, Provincialism, and Other Extravagances in American Writings on the Early Cold War Years," *Diplomatic History*, XIII (Fall 1989), 527–545.

Two works which place the early Cold War period and the two major adversaries in broad, comparative perspective are Paul Kennedy, *The Rise and Fall of the Great Powers: Economic Change and Military Conflict from 1500 to 2000* (1987), and Michael Mandelbaum, *The Fate of Nations: The Search for National Security in the Nineteenth and Twentieth Centuries* (1988).

General studies of Harry S. Truman and his presidency abound. They include Donald R. McCoy, *The Presidency of Harry S. Truman* (1984); William E. Pemberton, *Harry S. Truman (1989);* Robert J. Donovan, *Conflict and Crisis* (1977) and *Tumultuous Years* (1982); David McCullough, *Truman* (1992); Robert H. Ferrell, *Harry S. Truman* (1994); Alonzo L. Hamby, *Man of the People* (1995); and Michael J. Lacey, ed., *The Truman Presidency* (1989). The election of 1948 is discussed in Robert A. Divine, *Foreign Policy and U.S. Presidential Elections, 1940–1960* (1974).

Other American political and diplomatic leaders in the early Cold War era can be found in Michael T. Ruddy, *The Cautious Diplomat: Charles E. Bohlen and the Soviet Union* (1986); Ronald Pruessen, *John Foster Dulles* (1982); Gaddis Smith, *Dean Acheson* (1972); Douglas Brinkley, ed., *Dean Acheson and the Making of U.S. Foreign Policy* (1993); Stephen E. Ambrose, *Nixon* (1987); David McLellan, *Dean Acheson* (1976); H. W. Brands, *Inside the Cold War: Loy Henderson and the Rise of the American Empire* (1991); Forrest C. Pogue, *George C. Marshall: Statesman, 1945–1950* (1987); Mark A. Stoler, *George C. Marshall: Soldier-Statesman of the American Century* (1989); Townsend Hoopes and Douglas Brinkley, *Driven Patriot: The Life and Times of James Forrestal* (1992); Frank Merli and Theodore Wilson, eds., *Makers of American Diplomacy* (1974); Kendrick A. Clements, ed., *James F. Byrnes and the Origins of the Cold War* (1982); and Walter Isaacson and Evan Thomas, *The Wise Men* (1986). George F. Kennan has received intensive analysis in Barton Gellmann, *Contending with Kennan* (1984); Walter L. Hixson, *George F. Kennan: Cold War Iconoclast* (1990); David Mayers, *George Kennan and the Dilemma of U.S. Foreign Policy* (1988); Wilson D. Miscamble, *George F. Kennan and the Making of American Foreign Policy* (1992); and Anders Stephenson, *Kennan and the Art of Foreign Policy* (1989).

American dissenters from Truman policies can be explored in J. Samuel Walker, *Henry A. Wallace and American Foreign Policy* (1976); Lawrence S. Wittner, *Rebels Against War: The American Peace Movement, 1941–1960* (1974); Justus Doenecke, *Not to the Swift: The Old Isolationists in the Cold War Era* (1979); Graham White and John Maze, *Henry A. Wallace* (1995); and Thomas G. Paterson, ed., *Cold War Critics* (1971).

For anti-communism at home, including Truman's role in fostering McCarthyism, see Michael R. Belknap, *Cold War Political Justice* (1977); David Caute, *The Great Fear* (1978); Richard M. Fried, *Men Against McCarthy* (1976) and *Nightmare in Red* (1990); Robert Griffith, *The Politics of Fear* (1970); Robert Griffith and Athan Theoharis, eds., *The Specter* (1974); William W. Keller, *The Liberals and J. Edgar Hoover* (1989); Harvey Klehr and Ronald Radosh, *The Amerasia Spy Case* (1996); Stanley I. Kutler, *The American Inquisition* (1982); Mary S. McAuliffe, *Crisis on the Left: Cold War Politics and American Liberals, 1947–1954* (1978); William L. O'Neill, *A Better World: Stalinism and the American*

Intellectuals (1983); Brenda Plummer, *Rising Wind: Black Americans and U.S. Foreign Affairs, 1935–1960* (1996); Richard G. Powers, *Secrecy and Power: The Life of J. Edgar Hoover* (1987); Ronald Radosh and Joyce Milton, *The Rosenberg File* (1983); Thomas C. Reeves, *The Life and Times of Joe McCarthy* (1982); Ellen W. Schrecker, *No Ivory Tower: McCarthyism in the Universities* (1986); Athan Theoharis, *Seeds of Repression: Harry S. Truman and the Origins of McCarthyism* (1971); Athan Theoharis and John S. Cox, *The Boss: J. Edgar Hoover and the Great American Inquisition* (1988); Edward Pessen, *Losing Our Souls: The American Experience in the Cold War* (1993); Allen Weinstein, *Perjury: The Hiss-Chambers Case* (1978); and Stephen J. Whitfield, *The Culture of the Cold War* (1991).

The impact of the atomic bomb on American thinking, Soviet-American relations, and international relations is the topic of several works: Gar Alperovitz, *Atomic Diplomacy* (1985) and *The Decision to Use the Bomb* (1995); Paul Boyer, *By the Bomb's Early Light* (1986); Herbert Feis, *The Atomic Bomb and the End of World War II* (1966); Gregg Herken, *The Winning Weapon* (1981); Richard Hewlett and Oscar Anderson, *The New World* (1962); Michael Mandelbaum, *The Nuclear Question* (1979); Steven L. Rearden, *The Origins of U.S. Nuclear Strategy* (1993); Daniel Holloway, *The Soviet Union and the Arms Race* (1984) and *Stalin and the Bomb* (1994); Ronald E. Powaski, *March to Armageddon* (1987); Richard Rhodes, *The Making of the Atomic Bomb* (1987); Martin Sherwin, *A World Destroyed* (1975); John Newhouse, *War and Peace in the Nuclear Age* (1989); McGeorge Bundy, *Danger and Survival* (1990); Michael J. Hogan, ed., *Hiroshima in History and Memory* (1996); J. Samuel Walker, *Prompt and Utter Destruction* (1997); Alan Winkler, *Life Under a Cloud* (1993); and Lawrence Wittner, *One World or None* (1993). Barton J. Bernstein, ed., *The Atomic Bomb* (1975), provides surveys of the literature and issues.

The creation of the United Nations and disputes over and in it are explored in James Barros, *Trygvie Lie and the Cold War: The UN Secretary-General Pursues Peace, 1946–1953* (1989); Thomas Campbell, *Masquerade Peace: America's UN Policy* (1973); Robert A. Divine, *Second Chance: The Triumph of Internationalism in American Foreign Policy During World War II* (1967); Max Harrelson, *Fires All Around the Horizon* (1989); Robert C. Hilderbrand, *Dumbarton Oaks* (1990); Townsend Hoopes and Douglas Brinkley, *FDR and the Creation of the U.N.* (1997); Evan Luard, *A History of the United Nations* (1982); and George T. Mazuzan, *Warren T. Austin at the U.N., 1946–1953* (1977).

For events in Eastern Europe, over which the Soviets and Americans frequently clashed, see Phyliss Auty, *Tito* (1970); Michael M. Boll, *Cold War in the Balkans* (1984); Richard Lukas, *Bitter Legacy: Polish-American Relations in the Wake of World War II* (1982); Thomas Hammond, ed., *Witnesses to the Origins of the Cold War* (1987); Geir Lundestad, *The American Non-Policy Towards Eastern Europe, 1943–1947* (1975); Stanley M. Max, *The United States, Great Britain, and the Sovietization of Hungary, 1945–1948* (1985); Charles Gati, *Hungary and the Soviet Bloc* (1983); Walter Ullmann, *The United States and Prague, 1945–1948* (1978), and Pjotr Wandycz, *The United States and Poland* (1980).

Anglo-American relations in the early Cold War and the growing partnership on many issues and competition over others have received active attention as British records have been opened to scholars. Among the many studies are Terry H. Anderson, *The United States, Great Britain, and the Cold War, 1944–1947* (1981); Elisabeth Barker, *The British Between the Superpowers, 1945–1950* (1983); Richard A. Best, Jr., *Co-operation with Like-Minded Peoples* (1986); Timothy J. Botti, *The Long Wait: The Forging of the Anglo-American Nuclear Alliance, 1945–1958* (1987); Allan Bullock, *Ernest Bevin* (1984); Robin Edmonds, *Setting the Mould* (1987); Fraser J. Harbutt, *The Iron Curtain* (1986); Robert M. Hathaway, *Ambiguous Partnership* (1981) and *Great Britain and the United States* (1990); W. Roger Louis and Hedley Bull, eds., *The Special Relationship* (1986); Richard Ovendale, *The English-Speaking Alliance* (1985); Henry B. Ryan, *The Vision of Anglo-America* (1988); Kenneth W. Thompson, *Winston Churchill's World View* (1983); and Randall B. Woods, *A Changing of the Guard* (1990).

For Canada's relationship with the emerging Cold War, see Denis Smith, *Diplomacy of Fear* (1988); Joseph T. Jockel, *No Boundaries Upstairs: Canada, the United States and the Origins of the North American Air Defence, 1945–1958* (1989); Robert Bothwell, *Canada and the United States* (1992); John H. Thompson and Stephen J. Randall, *Canada and the United States* (1998); and

Lawrence Aronsen and Martin Kitchen, *The Origins of the Cold War in Comparative Perspective* (1988).

Postwar wrangling over the status of Germany, including the Berlin Blockade, is explained in John H. Backer, *Winds of History: The German Years of Lucius DuBignon Clay* (1984); Avi Shlaim, *The United States and the Berlin Blockade, 1948–1949* (1983); Daniel F. Harrington, "The Berlin Blockade Revisited," *International History Review*, VI (February 1984), 88–112; Carolyn Eisenberg, *Drawing the Line* (1996); Thomas A. Schwartz, *America's Germany* (1991); Frank Ninkovich, *Germany and the United States* (1988); John Gimbel, *The American Occupation of Germany* (1968), *The Origins of the Marshall Plan* (1976), and *Science, Technology, and Reparations: Exploitation and the Plunder in Postwar Germany* (1990); Robert Wolfe, ed., *Americans as Proconsuls* (1984); Bruce Kuklick, *American Reparations Policy and the Division of Germany* (1972); Edward N. Peterson, *The American Occupation of Germany* (1976); and Norman Naimark, *The Russians in Germany* (1995).

For the American response to developments in Greece and Turkey, including the Truman Doctrine and its aftermath, consult Bruce R. Kuniholm, *The Origins of the Cold War in the Near East* (1980); Christopher M. Woodhouse, *The Struggle for Greece, 1941–1949* (1976); John Oneal, *Foreign Policy Making in Times of Crisis* (1982); John O. Iatrides, *Revolt in Athens* (1972); John O. Iatrides, ed., *Greece in the 1940s* (1981); Lawrence S. Wittner, *American Intervention in Greece, 1943–1949* (1982); Howard Jones, *A New Kind of War: America's Global Strategy and the Truman Doctrine in Greece (1989);* David J. Alvarez, *Bureaucracy and Cold War Ideology* (1980) (on Turkey); Harry N. Howard, *Turkey, the Straits, and U.S. Policy* (1974); Melvyn P. Leffler, "Strategy, Diplomacy, and the Cold War: The United States, Turkey, and NATO, 1945–1952," *Journal of American History*, LXXI (March 1985), 807–825; Richard Barnet, *Intervention and Revolution* (1972); Richard Freeland, *The Truman Doctrine and the Origins of McCarthyism* (1971); and Jon V. Kofas, *Intervention and Underdevelopment: Greece During the Cold War* (1989).

Relations with various European nations and European issues can be studied in Josef Becker and Franz Knipping, *Power in Europe: Great Britain, France, Italy and Germany in a Postwar World, 1945–1950* (1986); A. W. DePorte, *De Gaulle's Foreign Policy,*

1944–1946 (1968); Jussi M. Hanhmäki, *Containing Coexistence: America, Russia, and "Finnish Solution"* (1997); Geir Lundestad, *America, Scandinavia, and the Cold War* (1980); James Edward Miller, *The United States and Italy, 1940–1950* (1986); John L. Harper, *The United States and the Reconstruction of Italy* (1986); Audrey K. Cronin, *Great Power Politics and the Struggle over Austria, 1945–1955* (1986); Donald Whiting and Edgar L. Erickson, *The American Occupation of Austria* (1985); Reinhold Wagnleiter, *Coca-Colonization and the Cold War* (1994) (on Austria); John W. Young, *Britain, France, and the Unity of Europe, 1945–1951* (1984); Roberto G. Rabel, *Between East and West* (1986) (on Trieste); Frank Costigliola, *The Cold Alliance* (1990) (on France); and Irwin M. Wall, *The United States and the Making of Postwar France* (1991).

For the Marshall Plan, European reconstruction, and economic issues, see Harry Price, *The Marshall Plan and Its Meaning* (1955); Richard Gardner, *Sterling-Dollar Diplomacy* (1969); Fred L. Block, *The Origins of International Economic Disorder* (1977); Alfred E. Eckes, Jr., *A Search for Solvency* (1975); Richard Mayne, *Recovery of Europe* (1973); George C. Herring, *Aid to Russia, 1941–1946* (1973); Thomas G. Paterson, *Soviet-American Confrontation* (1973); Robert A. Pollard, *Economic Security and the Origins of the Cold War* (1985); John Gimbel, *The Origins of the Marshall Plan* (1976); Diane Kunz, *Butter and Guns: America's Cold War Economic Policy* (1997); Fred L. Block, *The Origins of International Economic Disorder* (1977); Hadley Arkes, *Bureaucracy, the Marshall Plan, and the National Interest* (1972); Immanuel Wexler, *The Marshall Plan Revisited* (1983); Alan S. Milward, *The Reconstruction of Western Europe, 1945–51* (1984); Armand Clesse and Archie C. Epps, eds., *Present at the Creation: The Fortieth Anniversay of the Marshall Plan* (1990); and Michael J. Hogan, *The Marshall Plan* (1987).

Joseph Stalin is the subject of Isaac Deutscher, *Stalin* (1967); Adam Ulam, *Stalin* (1973); Ian Grey, *Stalin, Man of History* (1979); Robert H. McNeal, *Stalin: Man and Ruler* (1988); Edvard Radzinskii, *Stalin* (1996); and Dmitri Volkogonov, *Stalin* (1991).

The origins of the North Atlantic Treaty Organization are explored in Lawrence Kaplan, *NATO and The United States* (1988) and *The United States and NATO: The Formative Years*

(1984); Olav Riste, ed., *Western Security* (1985); and Timothy P. Ireland, *Creating the Entangling Alliance* (1981). Two articles that discuss postwar Soviet military capabilities and American assumptions about the Soviet threat are Matthew A. Evangelista, "Stalin's Postwar Army Reappraised," *International Security*, VII (Winter 1982/1983), 110–138, and Samuel F. Wells, Jr., "Sounding the Tocsin: NSC 68 and the Soviet Threat," *International Security*, IV (Fall 1979), 116–158.

General works on Asian-American relations include Akira Iriye, *The Cold War in Asia* (1974); Yōnosuke Nagai and Akira Iriye, eds., *The Origins of the Cold War in Asia* (1977); Russell Buhite, *Soviet-American Relations in Asia, 1945–1954* (1982); Edward Friedman and Mark Selden, eds., *America's Asia* (1971); Mark Selden, ed., *Remaking Asia* (1974); Mark S. Gallicchio, *The Cold War Begins in Asia* (1988); William W. Stueck, Jr., *The Road to Confrontation* (1981); and Robert Blum, *Drawing the Line* (1982).

For relations with China, see Herbert Feis, *China Tangle* (1953); Tang Tsou, *America's Failure in China* (1963); John Paton Davies, Jr., *Dragon By the Tail* (1972); Ross Koen, *The China Lobby in American Politics* (1974); Russell Buhite, *Patrick J. Hurley and American Foreign Policy* (1973); Louis M. Purifoy, *Harry Truman's China Policy* (1979); Warren I. Cohen, *America's Response to China* (1989); Dorothy Borg and Waldo Heinrichs, eds., *Uncertain Years: Chinese-American Relations, 1947–1950* (1980); Harry Harding and Yuan Ming, eds., *Sino-American Relations, 1945–1955* (1989); Michael Schaller, *The U.S. Crusade in China* (1979) and *The United States and China in the Twentieth Century* (1989); Nancy B. Tucker, *Patterns in the Dust* (1983); Odd Arne Westad, *Cold War and Revolution* (1993); T. Christopher Jesperson, *American Images of China, 1931–1949* (1996); Gary May, *China Scapegoat: The Diplomatic Ordeal of John Carter Vincent* (1979); Ronald C. Keith, *The Diplomacy of Zhou Enlai* (1989); James Reardon-Anderson, *Yenan and the Great Powers* (1980); William W. Stueck, *The Wedemeyer Mission* (1984); Edward W. Martin, *Divided Counsel: The Anglo-American Response to Communist Victory in China* (1986); David Allan Mayers, *Cracking the Monolith: U.S. Policy Against the Sino-Soviet Alliance* (1986); Gordon H. Chang, *Friends and Enemies: The United States, China, and the Soviet Union* (1990); David McLean, "American Nationalism, the China Myth, and the Truman Doctrine," *Diplomatic History*, X (Winter 1986), 25–42; Shu Guang Zhang, *Deterrence and Strategic Culture* (1992); Chen Jian, *China's Road to the Korean War* (1994); and Nancy Bernkopf Tucker, *Taiwan, Hong Kong, and the United States* (1994).

For the American occupation of Japan and Japanese-American relations, see William Neumann, *America Encounters Japan* (1963); William S. Borden, *The Pacific Alliance* (1984); Roger Buckley, *Occupation Diplomacy* (1982); Lawrence H. Redford, ed., *The Occupation of Japan* (1984); Michael Schaller, *The American Occupation of Japan* (1985), *Douglas MacArthur: The Far Eastern General* (1989), and *Altered States* (1997); Michael M. Yoshitsu, *Japan and the San Francisco Peace Settlement* (1983); D. Clayton James, *The Years of MacArthur*, vol. 3 (1985); Howard B. Schonberger, *Aftermath of War: Americans and the Remaking of Japan, 1945–1952* (1989); John W. Dower, *Empire and Aftermath* (1979); Toshio Nishi, *Unconditional Democracy* (1982); and Walter LaFeber, *The Clash* (1997).

For United States policy toward Southeast Asia, see Russell H. Fifield, *Americans in Southeast Asia* (1973); Evelyn Colbert, *International Politics in Southeast Asia, 1941–1956* (1977); Gary R. Hess, *The United States' Emergence as a Southeast Asian Power* (1987); Stephen R. Shalom, *The United States and the Philippines* (1981); Nick Cullather, *Illusions of Influence: The Political Economy of United States–Philippines Relations* (1994); Robert J. McMahon, *Colonialism and Cold War: The United States and the Struggle for Indonesian Independence* (1981) and *The Limits of Empire* (1998).

The historical literature on United States policy toward Indochina during the early Cold War is voluminous. See especially Andrew J. Rotter, *The Path to Vietnam* (1987); Lloyd C. Gardner, *Approaching Vietnam* (1988); George C. Herring, *America's Longest War* (1996); Gary R. Hess, *Vietnam and the United States* (1990); Gabriel Kolko, *Anatomy of a War* (1985); Ronald H. Spector, *Advice and Support: The Early Years of the U.S. Army in Vietnam* (1983); Stanley Karnow, *Vietnam* (1983); Anthony Short, *The Origins of the Vietnam War* (1989); George McT. Kahin, *Intervention* (1986); Marilyn B. Young, *The Vietnam Wars* (1991); and Robert D. Schulzinger, *A Time for War* (1997).

For developments in the Middle East, see Robert W. Stookey, *America and the Arab States* (1975); William R. Polk, *The United States and the Arab World* (1975); Nadav Safran, *Israel: Embattled*

Ally (1978); Gail E. Meyer, *Egypt and the United States* (1980); Kenneth R. Bain, *The March to Zion* (1979); George Lenczowski, *American Presidents and the Middle East* (1989); Michael J. Cohen, *Palestine and the Great Powers, 1945–1948* (1979); Evan M. Wilson, *Decision on Palestine* (1979); John Snetsinger, *Truman, the Jewish Vote and the Creation of Israel* (1974); Leonard Dinnerstein, *America and the Survivors of the Holocaust* (1982); Michael Cohen, *Truman and Israel* (1990); W. Roger Louis, *The British Empire in the Middle East, 1945–1951* (1984); W. Roger Louis and Robert W. Stookey, eds., *The End of the Palestine Mandate* (1986); Burton I. Kaufman, *The Arab Middle East and the United States* (1996); Barry Rubin, *Paved with Good Intentions: The American Experience and Iran* (1980); Mark H. Lytle, *The Origins of the Iranian-American Alliance, 1941–1953* (1987); James A. Bill, *The Eagle and the Lion: The Tragedy of American-Iranian Relations* (1988); Steven L. Speigel, *The Other Arab-Israeli Conflict* (1985); Michael B. Stoff, *Oil, War, and American Security* (1980); Aaron D. Miller, *Search for Security* (1980); David S. Painter, *Oil and the American Century* (1986); Peter L. Hahn, *The United States, Great Britain, and Egypt, 1945–1956* (1991); and David Schoenman, *The United States and the State of Israel* (1993).

United States relations with Latin America during the Truman years can be followed in Samuel Baily, *The United States and the Development of South America, 1945–1975* (1976); Leslie Bethell and Ian Roxborough, *Latin America Between the Second World War and the Cold War* (1993); John Child, *Unequal Alliance: The Inter-American Military System* (1980); Cole Blasier, *The Hovering Giant* (1976); Gordon Connell-Smith, *The United States and Latin America* (1975); Frederick B. Pike, *The United States and Latin America* (1992); Gaddis Smith, *The Last Years of the Monroe Doctrine* (1994); Chester J. Pach, Jr., "The Containment of U.S. Military Aid to Latin America, 1944–1949," *Diplomatic History*, VI (Summer 1982), 225–243; Stephen G. Rabe, "The Elusive Conference: United States Economic Relations with Latin America, 1945–1952, *Diplomatic History*, II (Summer 1978), 279–294; Gerald K. Haines, *The Americanization of Brazil* (1990); David Green, "The Cold War Comes to Latin America," in Barton J. Bernstein, ed., *Politics and Policies of the Truman Ad-*

ministration (1970); Richard H. Immerman, *The CIA in Guatemala* (1982); Michael L. Krenn, *The Chains of Interdependence* (1996) (on Central America); Walter LaFeber, *Inevitable Revolutions* (1983); W. Michael Weis, *Cold Warriors and Coups D'État: Brazilian-American Relations, 1945–1964* (1993); and Elizabeth A. Cobbs, *The Rich Neighbor: Rockefeller and Kaiser in Brazil* (1992).